Burning Books and
Leveling Libraries

Burning Books and Leveling Libraries

EXTREMIST VIOLENCE AND CULTURAL DESTRUCTION

Rebecca Knuth

PRAEGER

Westport, Connecticut
London

Library of Congress Cataloging-in-Publication Data

Knuth, Rebecca, 1949–
    Burning books and leveling libraries : extremist violence and cultural destruction / Rebecca Knuth.
        p.   cm.
    Includes index.
    ISBN 0–275–99007–9
    1. Libraries—Destruction and pillage—History—20th century. 2. Libraries—Destruction and pillage—History—21st century. 3. Book burning—History—20th century. 4. Book burning—History—21st century. 5. Radicalism—History—20th century. 6. Radicalism—History—21st century. 7. Cultural property. I. Title.
    Z659.K57   2006
    025.8'2—dc22   2006002747

British Library Cataloguing in Publication Data is available.

Library of Congress Catalog Card Number: 2006002747
ISBN: 0–275–99007–9

First published in 2006

Praeger Publishers, 88 Post Road West, Westport, CT 06881
An imprint of Greenwood Publishing Group, Inc.
www.praeger.com

Printed in the United States of America

The paper used in this book complies with the
Permanent Paper Standard issued by the National
Information Standards Organization (Z39.48–1984).

10 9 8 7 6 5 4 3 2 1

Copyright Acknowledgments

The author and publisher gratefully acknowledge permission to reprint material from the following sources:

Excerpts from Sivaramani, "A War-Torn Night." In *Lutesong and Lament: Tamil Writing from Sri Lanka*, ed. Chelva Kanaganayakam. Toronto: TSAR Publications, 2001. Reprinted with the permission of TSAR Publications.

Excerpts from F. R. Scott, "Degeneration." In *F. R. Scott: Selected Poems*. Toronto: Oxford University Press, 1966. Reprinted with the permission of William Toye, literary executor for the estate of F. R. Scott.

Every reasonable effort has been made to trace the owners of copyrighted materials in this book, but in some instances this has proven impossible. The author and publisher will be glad to receive information leading to more complete acknowledgments in subsequent printings of the book and in the meantime extend their apologies for any omissions.

This book is dedicated to **_Charlene Gilmore_**, my treasured writing mentor. Her insight, editing, and comments have vastly improved the quality of the book. She has been tenacious, demanding, and totally dedicated to excellence in expression and the use of language to unlock meaning.

Contents

Preface

After the manuscript for my previous book, *Libricide: The Regime-Sponsored Destruction of Books and Libraries in the Twentieth Century*, was packed off to the publisher, I forestalled postpartum writing arrest and prepublication jitters by beginning another book. There was much work to be done on the topic of library destruction, and I was struggling to see the forest for the trees. Regime-sponsored, ideologically driven destruction seemed clearly to be just one facet of global patterns that were threatening books and libraries. Idiosyncratic incidents cried out for analysis, as did the loss of books in the familiar conditions of war and civil unrest, as well as in extraordinary circumstances like strategic bombing. But the path forward was unclear.

The libricide model had emerged rather quickly and was fleshed out in discrete case studies, but the structure and scope of what would become *Burning Books and Leveling Libraries: Extremist Violence and Cultural Destruction* emerged over time. Instead of a relatively straightforward process of searching for information, performing analysis, formulating and substantiating a model, and posing explanations and conclusions, I was faced with intimations—seemingly disparate pieces to a puzzle whose contours were unclear. I would move from a case to background materials to theory and interdisciplinary perspectives, and then back to cases. Each chapter was rewritten at least five times in the process, and the order and structure of the chapters, the scaffolding of the entire book, underwent many revisions. From the disparate cases and gross ambiguity there finally emerged clarity and a unifying thread behind book and library destruction.

I began with the cultural losses that resulted from the Allies' strategic bombing in World War II because this was the biggest conceptual hurdle

I had faced in the first book. Having chosen not to label this behavior as libricide, mainly on the premise that the bombers did not intentionally target libraries, I needed to resolve my qualms about exempting the Allies from direct culpability. I wanted to understand the Allied mindset and how those who acted in the name of democracy and civilization could have committed destruction on the scale of what occurred in Germany and Japan. I soon came to see that modern global wars are fought over ideas and ways of life, and that ideology lends a desperate ferocity to the proceedings. Modernism, with its open-ended use of ideas to mold society and guide the state, provides many different venues by which extremism, including the mindsets of total war, flourishes. The tactics and theory of total war are, for example, an outcome of the extreme application of logic to a social problem. Unbridled militarism vests all parties in violence.

In *Libricide* my focus was on intentional, systematic, and large-scale destruction that was driven by ideological mandates. But for the book that would follow, I had an intuition that a more complex set of motivations would subsume my explanations of libricide, and that this framework would also embrace local and contained incidents. When I began probing the impulses behind high-profile bonfires of Harry Potter books, staged in 2001 and 2003 by church groups in Pennsylvania, Maine, New Mexico, and Michigan, I stumbled upon a pattern of extremism, renunciation, and affirmation that quickly gained significance. In these relatively isolated, localized cases of destruction, fundamentalist congregations burned books, videos, and other pop-cultural items in protests against offensive values that, they said, had increasingly pushed their Christian faith and influence to the margins of American life. Pastors declared that burning Harry Potter books was a means for Christians to build community, affirm their allegiance to God, and separate themselves from a pop culture they believed to be detrimental to society. Although this chapter was eventually dropped because the ceremonies did not match in scale and seriousness the other cases under study, my observations about the fundamentalists' motivation and mindsets became key to identifying dynamics of book destruction that, I believe, play out worldwide.

My next exposure to this pattern came with an investigation into the Suffragettes' firebombing of a public library in Birmingham, England, in 1914. Achieving the vote for British women was a cause pursued with a zeal that transmuted into militancy. The Suffragettes were radicals who endured public abuse and incarcerations; their hunger strikes were broken by brutal forced feedings. Vandalism and iconoclasm (though never physical violence against people) became justifiable tactics in their war against a corrupt social order that degraded women. Firebombing the library was an act of desperation, a protest against public and official indifference to their cause. Again, most of the material I collected on the Suffragette incident would be left on the cutting-room floor, but this case reinforced my sense of a strong connection between vandalism, iconoclasm, and book destruction. Those who destroy libraries were emerging from the forest, and the profile of a beleaguered lot, desperate for voice and vulnerable to the influence of ideas that demanded action, came into sharper focus still.

And soon after, library destruction began to materialize as an attention-garnering tactic of political protest, an emblematic way for extremists to carry totalistic logic to a natural and apparently constructive endpoint. The case of the anti-apartheid protestors who destroyed Amsterdam's South African Institute in 1984 was key to unlocking the phenomenon of biblioclasm and establishing such behavior as a function of extremism. The attack unleashed a storm of derision that battered the walls of ethical immunity the perpetrators had erected, and the sociological perspectives that provided a theoretical ballast for this chapter ultimately served to ground the whole book in notions of conflict, social protest, and vandalism.

As the book unfolded, extremism emerged again and again as a key element in book and library destruction. The pattern of righteous protest I had identified in the American religious fundamentalist incidents held explanatory power in my examination of the annihilation of texts during ethnic conflicts in India, Kashmir, and Sri Lanka, where cultural violence was a means of simultaneously striking out at corrupting influences and antithetical values and affirming identification with a "superior" religious or ethnic group. The Nazis burned books to extinguish the intellectual freedom and alternate lifestyles that had been allowed free reign during the Weimar Republic. They pledged themselves, instead, to a racially and ideologically pure Third Reich. As Taliban Afghanistan and Pol Pot's Cambodia became increasingly totalitarian, destruction of culture escalated and renunciation and affirmation processes spun out of control. Both regimes used extreme violence to fend off external influences and put in place an orthodoxy enforced by punishment of death.

When books and libraries are destroyed, it is inevitably in the context of a struggle over beliefs and resources. Local incidents, framed as political or religious protests, may, with onset of war, escalate into ethnic cleansing and colonization initiatives that include the destruction of libraries. In war, destroying an enemy's cultural infrastructure is key to domination and surrender. There are many subtexts to war that affect the fate of books. Libraries, as well as other public institutions, are lost during the anarchy and chaos that result from conditions in which no distinction is made between combat zones and civilian areas. Violent regime change may result in collateral damage from combat, iconoclastic destruction of the fallen regime's books and cultural institutions, or nihilistic mob responses to power vacuum and the fall of a regime that had oppressed and failed them. Military theorist Carl von Clausewitz labeled war as the continuation of policy [politics] by other means. In most cases, wartime biblioclasm is a continuation, though escalation, of existing power struggles and patterns of destruction.

The ethnic cleansing that occurred in Bosnia in the 1990s was followed closely by the pillage of Iraq's museums and libraries in 2003. Both led to an international outcry over cultural destruction. As global discussion reached critical mass, diverse communities united around the issue. Journalists, who had been sounding the alarm for years, were now joined by scholars who interacted online with heritage managers, curators, and other interested parties to protest the ongoing loss of what was characterized as the common cultural heritage of the world. UNESCO promoted multinational initiatives to protect culture, and coalitions of international organizations issued statements warning of what could happen in Iraq and, then, condemnations of what did happen. The number of conference presentations on cultural destruction doubled and tripled in the last decade. The American Library Association's Library History Seminar XI, held every five years and scheduled for October 2005, was entirely devoted to the fate of libraries in war, revolution, and social change. Concern over cultural destruction, however, was completely eclipsed by public panic, even hysteria, over terrorism.

Burning Books and Leveling Libraries analyzes the influence of extreme mindsets on the destruction of books and libraries. Chapters 1 and 2 introduce biblioclasm, subject it to a sociological lens, and argue that the roots of this form of vandalism lie in the Enlightenment. Subsequent chapters document and explain the extremist-inspired book and library destruction that characterized the twentieth century and persists today. The chapters are grouped in three parts, on the basis of type of conflict and the perpetrators' issues concerning power. Part 1 (Chapters 3 and 4) is devoted to local struggles by extremists over voice and influence in which biblioclasm was a tactic of political or ethnic protest. Part 2 (Chapters 5, 6, and 7) deals with the aftermath of power struggles in Germany, Afghanistan, and Cambodia, where the winners were utopians who destroyed libraries in efforts to purify their societies and maintain hegemony. Part 3 (Chapters 8, 9, and 10) examines the fate of libraries during war, revolution, and power vacuum. It begins with a chapter on cultural destruction during World War II, when rogue regimes triggered total war and entangled both sides in extremism and cultural destruction. Chapter 9 documents the fate of libraries during civil war and regime collapse, with special attention to the looting of Iraq's cultural institutions in 2003.

The book concludes with discussion of extremism and cultural destruction and the responsibility of American war strategists in the widespread pillage that ensued after the toppling of Saddam Hussein's regime. Assessing accountability for these losses involved a conceptual hurdle similar to that faced in determining the Allies' culpability in World War II cultural destruction. The invasion of Iraq demonstrated the futility of using military might to enforce ideals (in this case, democracy and freedom) when insufficient consideration is given to humanitarian, security, and cultural factors.

Burning Books and Leveling Libraries is an interdisciplinary book. Its general orientation and style place it in the realm of international studies and comparative sociology, particularly the scholarship of genocide. The book focuses on modern book and library destruction, offers a detailed analysis of motivation, and provides substantive case studies. I do not identify myself as a historian, political scientist, or sociologist. Reviewers will look in vain for strict adherence to the methodological and stylistic constraints of these disciplines. The book's content and arguments are informed by sociological perspectives, but the focus is not on sociological theory per se.

I will readily disclose the fact that I am a liberal humanist with a deep respect for intellectual freedom and individual rights. When books and libraries are destroyed, I feel a profound sense of loss. Emotion was the starting point for writing my first book, *Libricide: The Regime-Sponsored Destruction of Books and Libraries in the Twentieth Century*, and the book was a repudiation of the intense relativity that characterizes modern society. R. J. Rummel (1991, xii), a statistician who focuses on political violence, curbs his tendency toward emotionality while forging a style that is perhaps more "assertive" and less "balanced" than some specialists and historians might desire. "If this be so," he wrote, "then I can only say that it is to others I must leave writing with dispassion about the murder of millions of human beings." I feel similarly about the subject of the loss of texts because they are finite and, in many cases, irreplaceable. The loss of a library bears historical and social ramifications of a scale that cries for thoughtful and heartfelt objectivity.

The burden of recent history and the complicity of the United States in the destruction of Iraqi cultural institutions weigh heavily on me as I bring this project to a close. Chapters 8 and 10 reflect my concerns that there can be a slide toward extremism even in those whose motives are not as fanatical as ideologues such as Hitler and Pol Pot. Extremists who participate in the destruction of libraries are driven by self-serving agendas and prone to glib rationalizations. The Bush administration has a lock on moral rectitude, resists criticism, and suppresses dissent and reflection. These things, along with its inability to admit mistakes, the militarism of its national security advisors, and its tendency to rationalize aggression in the name of universal values, are disturbing because, as this book will show, this is the typical profile of an extremist regime. Do I equate George Bush and his officials with the Nazis or Taliban? Of course not. However, I see the influence of ideological extremism on his military decisions, and I am deeply concerned about questions of responsibility and the cultural consequences of American actions in Iraq. Arriving at the conclusion that even those who value books and libraries, and even the leaders of my country (a democracy), can become complicit by action or omission in the destruction of these cultural pillars was a painful outcome of my inquiries, and one that I carry with me reluctantly.

I wish to acknowledge my professional home, the University of Hawaii's Library and Information Science Program, Information and Computer Sciences Department. I am very appreciative of the welcome extended by the University of Edinburgh's Institute for Advanced Studies in the Humanities, which hosted my sabbatical in 2002. Special thanks to Anthea Taylor, the institute's administrator.

Professors look to their students for enthusiasm and feedback. My students have been wonderfully supportive, especially the enthusiastic Spring 2004 Intellectual Freedom class: Sheri Britsch, Christine Bryan, Tom Coleman, Junie Hayashi, Jan Kamiya, Vicky Lee, Lillian Nicolich, Jennifer Ogg, Mahate Osborne, Trent Reynolds, Diane Todd, Suzanne Urutani, and Laura Welsh. My family was, of course, a major source of encouragement: aloha to Barbara Parker, Edwin Knuth, William Beck, and Eve Beck. The interest of friends and colleagues, especially Donna Bair-Mundy, Christian DeLay, Gail Morimoto, Mary Lu Chee, David Bruner, Martha Crosby, Diane Nahl, Helen Nakano, Sunyeen Pai, Luz Quiroga, Miriam Reed, Zoe Shinno, Edith and Art Wartburg, and Andrew Wertheimer, meant a lot. Jeffrey Kastner's (2003) phone interview was very encouraging, and I appreciate the thoughtful and positive reviews written about *Libricide*.

Key people provided direct and indirect assistance in improving the *Burning Books* manuscript, and they deserve a heartfelt thank you. Praeger acquisitions editor Hilary Claggett made some crucial suggestions regarding the sequence of chapters and proposed an excellent new title, and I really appreciate her efforts. Joyce Apsel, past president of the International Association of Genocide Scholars, read and provided feedback on several chapters. Joyce Apsel exemplifies for me a sterling commitment to academic ethics and service. Many thanks to Berlin librarian Manfred Herzer, who kindly critiqued the chapter on the Institute for Sexual Knowledge. Charming Claire Van Wengen translated all the Dutch materials and proofed the Dutch citations in Chapter 3. Corine de Maijer at the South African Institute provided materials on the destruction of the South African Institute and graciously answered follow-up questions. Ellen Chapman sent a constant stream of news articles and relevant e-mails and is responsible for the excellent index.

REFERENCES

Kastner, Jeffrey. 2003. "The Past Is in Flames: An Interview with Rebecca Knuth." *Cabinet: A Quarterly of Art and Culture* 12:78–79.

Rummel, R. J. 1991. *China's Bloody Century: Genocide and Mass Murder since 1900.* New Brunswick, N.J.: Transaction Publishers.

CHAPTER 1

Understanding Modern Biblioclasm

Each decision we make, each action we take, is born out of an intention.
—Sharon Salzberg, "The Power of Intention"

In 1795, at the height of the French Revolution, moderate revolutionary François-Antoine Boissy d'Anglas pronounced, "France is bathed in blood, both at the hand of the enemy and of its executioners . . . [It is] devastated by anarchy, suffocated by acts of vandalism, prey to the ravages of greed and a victim of the excesses of ignorance and savagery" (Poulet 1995, 196). His observation describes much more than the event of his times, unparalleled though it was in modern history. In many modern social conflicts, deep-seated strife has led both sides to commit extreme acts of violence, and just as often, the bloodletting has been accompanied by the destruction of books. D'Anglas's sentiment in expressing the reaches of the tragedy resonates with Western civilization's collective memories of sixth-century Vandals sacking Rome, Saracens burning the Alexandrian Library, Vikings attacking the Christian monasteries that had sustained learning through the Dark Ages, and the burning of heretics and their texts during the Spanish Inquisition. We carry a distinct sense of loss at these events, despite their historical distance, and we share the view that the destruction of culture is senseless and perilous to society.

More recent events have also been formative to our condemnation of cultural destruction, especially those involving the destruction of books and libraries. The Nazis' book fires of 1933 (among the regime's other atrocities) exposed the vulnerability of the very foundations of modern civilizations. The Nazi regime shook the world with the reality of how effective unchecked vandalism and unbounded racial pride could be in reversing our progress toward a modernity based on pluralism and tolerance. Though Germany's book fires were by far the most well-known incidents of cultural destruction from the last century, the phenomenon recurred in many forms across the globe, and by century's end a litany of pejorative terms had been cemented into our vocabulary. "Vandals!" "Fanatics!" "Fascists!" we have cried repeatedly in horror and denunciation. But by our judgments we have admitted an inability or reluctance to probe the behavior for a cause.

Condemnations imply that the destruction has no meaning other than to signify the presence of irrational forces. They effectively dismiss the destroyers of books as barbaric, ignorant, evil—as outside the bounds of morality, reason, even understanding. If instead we acknowledge the perpetrators as human beings with concerns and a goal—albeit misguided—of effecting social change, a number of questions emerge that usher us into the subject with clearer meaning and purpose. What is it about texts and libraries that puts them in the line of fire during social conflict? What compels a group to enact its alienation through violence aimed at print materials and the institutions and buildings that house them? What do various incidents of book destruction have in common, and what makes them unique? And, is there an identifiable pattern to such acts?

Modern conflicts involving books have ranged from sporadic local incidents of protest and isolated programs of censorship to systemic crusades aimed at totalitarian implementation of a new orthodoxy. Hindu nationalists destroyed the Bhandarkar Oriental Research Institute in Pune, India, because it provided documentation for historical works that challenged their myths. The National Socialist Party in Germany dismantled Berlin's Institute for Sexual Knowledge to purge the nation of "un-German" elements: homosexuality, cosmopolitanism, independent inquiry, and humanism in general. Afghanistan's Taliban regime purified the nation's print collections in the name of the Koran, and Pol Pot's Communist regime purged Cambodia of its texts and intellectual community for the cause of socialist transformation. Cultural destruction has become an almost familiar gesture of defiance that signals the immediate threat of censorship and cultural homogenization. The destruction of books and libraries is at once a public assertion of choice and a radical repudiation of intellectual freedom, individualism, pluralism, and tolerance. In the name of the common man, an ethnic group, or a belief system, modern radicals have sought to reestablish pre-Enlightenment prerogatives of absolutism, threatening to bring 300 years of history full circle.

This book argues that modern biblioclasm occurs when books and libraries are perceived by a social group as undermining ideological goals, threatening the orthodoxy of revered doctrine, or representing a despised establishment. Although it seems a precursor to more extensive violence (as so famously put forth by Heinrich Heine: "When they burn books, they will also, in the end, burn human beings"), biblioclasm is actually a signal that social discord has progressed to a critical point and that the foundations of modern civilization are at risk. Our attention to the circumstances in which the violence occurs is imperative if we seek to revise our response to social outcasts, acknowledge and respond to protests of marginalized groups before they progress to violence, and strengthen the humanist foundations upon which international peace and the modern democratic state depend.

Book and library destruction shares many elements with iconoclasm, the destruction of images that a perpetrator associates with corrupt establishments ("Iconoclasm" 1989, 609). I have chosen to use the term *biblioclasm* in this book because of its linguistic relation to iconoclasm and because, by association, it suggests that there is a moral judgment, on the part of the perpetrator, concerning what the target represents. In the *Oxford English Dictionary*, *biblioclasm* is defined as "the breaking of books" and cited as first appearing in print in 1864 in a text on religious theory. Twenty years later, a passionate scholar used the term to denounce the Catholic priests who had burned Maya and Aztec manuscripts after the Spanish conquest: "May these bishops expiate their crimes in the purgatory of biblioclasts!" ("Biblioclasm" 1989, 169). In this book the term is used not to levy judgment, but to denote purposeful action that is rooted in moral repugnance or judgment.

The history of biblioclasm is entwined with the history of vandalism and political violence in general. In ancient times, libraries were routinely destroyed in wars over territory. Texts were lost in combat, and, because the leveling of cities was a prominent feature of conquest, through fire, exposure to the elements, and burial in the rubble. Neglect destroyed many of the texts that had survived the initial violence. As scrolls gained in commercial value, the looting of libraries eventually (especially during the Roman Empire) became a prerogative of victors, who sold the enemy's patrimony for personal profit or co-opted its symbols and institutions for the glory and use of their own empire. As generals carried off entire libraries as trophies of war, deposed elites came to associate the loss of written works with both political and spiritual subjugation. From very early on, the wholesale annihilation of texts had much to do with the perception that they carried heretical beliefs. Although seizing the enemy's texts enforced a victor's dominance and lent some legitimacy to the central power structure of the expanding empire, many texts were intentionally destroyed because they were seen as repositories of antithetical religious beliefs and identity. The powerful association between texts, group identity, and preservation of a society's belief system is evidenced in apocryphal stories recounting the destruction of many cultures' texts by paranoid or fanatical rulers who sought to extinguish opposing beliefs and cultures. The Chinese cite Emperor Ch'in Shih-huang as the embodiment of political tyranny for his decimation of books and scholars, and Iraqis remain traumatized by the thirteenth-century destruction of Baghdad's books by the Moguls. The destruction of the Library of Alexandria by Omar the Caliph (though largely apocryphal) haunts Western civilization to this day. By the same token, resistance to cultural extinction has, throughout history, triggered heroic efforts to preserve books. Over centuries of persecution and diaspora, the cultural survival of the Jewish people was related in large part to their tenacious guarding of sacred works. The past provides a powerful incentive for groups concerned with preventing cultural decline and extinction: preserving texts is a necessary condition for cultural autonomy and survival.

When the Vandals plundered Rome in 455 A.D., they carried away all of the city's portable treasure. Although contemporary historians disagree as to whether the Vandals were quite as savage as portrayed in the historical record (Jones 1999, 890), the Roman people were united in the devastation they felt at the ignorance of their attackers and, with time, came to see all Germanic tribes as a singular danger to civilization itself. During the Dark Ages that followed the fall of Rome, the original losses were compounded by Viking raids on monasteries in Ireland and northern Europe. Here, recorded knowledge survived only tenuously as handwritten manuscripts were looted, burned, or ripped apart for their decorative elements. Viking depredations served as an intermediate step in etching the trauma of cultural violence into the collective consciousness of Western civilization. The Vandals, characterized by historical sources as the "great destroyers of Roman art, civilization and literature," ultimately became a term for any people demonstrating "a general barbaric ignorance" (Cohen 1973, 34). The *Oxford English Dictionary* cites the first written use of the general term *vandal* as occurring in 1663, in reference to a "willful or ignorant destroyer of anything beautiful, venerable or worthy of preservation" ("Vandal" 1989, 425).

The term *vandal* accrued further nuance during the French Revolution (1789–1799), when the people revolted and destroyed monuments, paintings, books, and documents in public ceremonies that celebrated their freedom from despotism. Abbé Grégoire, an influential deputy in the Constituent Assembly and a member of the National Convention (the ruling bodies during the revolution), cemented the association of cultural destruction with barbarism and ignorance when he used the term *vandalisme* (vandalism) to condemn the revolutionaries' actions. In his *Mémoires*, Grégoire wrote: "I invented the word to abolish the act" (Poulet 1995, 195). Attacks on symbols of the monarchy and the Ancien Régime were especially rampant during the Reign of Terror, a radical and bloody period, 1793–1794. In calling for an end to the destruction, Grégoire recalled the invasion of Rome and judged his contemporaries as indistinguishable from the Vandals, whom he viewed as the epitome of tyranny and ignorance (Baczko 1989). In a series of reports to the convention, Grégoire listed examples of damage, singling out books in particular, and advocated preservation efforts to curtail a "destructive fury" that, at its fiercest, called for burning the Bibliothéque Nationale and all libraries (Baczko 1989, 860). His followers would eventually publicly decry the ethos of revolutionary terrorists, "riff-raff disguised as patriots" who "debased all public life" by acting out their hatred of culture (Baczko 1989, 862). They legislated protection for books and records, redefining them as the common property of the nation.

Grégoire's response to biblioclasm was based on a strand of Enlightenment thinking that recognized the importance of intellectual freedom and books as crucial pillars of reason and cultural progress—and their destruction, consequently, as regression of tragic proportions. He used the Enlightenment's recognition of human agency to construct a view of books as an integral part of a group's heritage, a source of intellectual stimulation, and the foundation of civilized living—much more than mere fetishes of the elite. In France and the rest of Europe, the term *vandalism* soon became commonplace, as did *vandalistes* (vandals)—those who commit violent acts against the symbols of the establishment or those who profit from such violence. In later centuries, many educated and respectable people adopted Grégoire's premises along with the term, and the upper classes tended to reject vandalism as hysterical violence committed by the lowest sort of people (Gamboni 1997, 15, 22). This is a departure from the spirit of his ideas, though, polarizing the classes yet again. In the nineteenth and early twentieth centuries, with mass literacy fostered by public education, the importance of preserving books became a relatively stable and widespread sentiment, a collective attitude or value-based "unit of thought-feeling" embraced by society as a whole (Leighton 1959, 415). A case can now be made that when biblioclasm occurs, it is because books (as well as art) stand at "the center of interest of all civilized people . . . [they are] a guarantee for the modern spirit and thus, at the same time, its Achilles heel, the point at which the cultivated may most easily be touched" (as quoted in Gamboni, 1997, 105–106).

In the mid-twentieth century, as sociology came into its own as a discipline, the term *vandalism* acquired still another nuance, beyond its association with cultural destruction: it came to signify the seemingly random destruction of public property that had become prevalent in industrialized urban settings. Sociologists used the term in this narrowed sense and developed the view that vandalism, like all forms of violence, was a rational expression of frustration. Summarily rejecting the common interpretation of modern vandalism as merely random and ignorant, sociologists argued that acts such as disfiguring telephone booths, breaking windows, and scribbling graffiti are complicated, purposeful behaviors that send an important message to society of underlying social malaise and unfulfilled needs (Lumsden 1983, 4). To interpret the message, we must consider not only the target itself, but also the society in which this target is embedded (Sperandio 1984, 106). By destroying a telephone booth, a person may be reacting not only to a malfunctioning phone or a negative call, but to a system in which the perpetrator cannot find work, for example, or meaningful identity. Interpreting the message can be difficult because it is being conveyed through action and symbol. Modern vandals often attack public property because it is the accessible, material aspect of a society that they perceive as having marginalized them. By understanding the motivation of vandals, the sociologist argues, society can better respond to the needs of these alienated members. It has been an ongoing battle to avoid simplistic conflation of vandalism with deviance, but sociologists have generated a knowledge base about the subject and advanced theories and models that have beneficially affected social policy. I believe their work may profitably be applied to book destruction because, as Grégoire so presciently established, biblioclasm can be seen as a form of vandalism.

Of particular interest in this application are explanations of vandalism that acknowledge the presence of diverse emotional influences at the individual perpetrator's level. Acts of vandalism can express feelings of fear, hate, and frustration. Some perpetrators find satisfaction in the physical act of destruction and the state of mind that emerges from seizing the opportunity for destruction. A major affective motivation of vandalism has been identified by Vernon L. Allen (1984, 80), who determined that the act of destruction can be intrinsically enjoyable in itself—"an aesthetic experience" that links creation and destruction. Smashing a window can be experienced as an imaginative and original act. Scrawling graffiti on public surfaces superimposes a personal statement on an otherwise static environment. With his colleague David Greenberger, Allen (1980b) has also identified cognitive impulses behind violent acts: the increase in an individual's perception of personal control or efficacy that destruction can effect. If vandalism is, as Allen and Greenberger (1980b, 85) claim, influenced by self-identity and subjective states, including alienation and frustration, a lowered level of "perceived control" (efficacy or competence) will, under certain conditions, stimulate attempts to change the environment through acts of destruction.

A third motivation—social identity—provides "theoretical unification of aesthetic factors and perceived control" and suggests "a link between internal psychological processes and units in the social environment such as role, group, and social structure" (Allen and Greenberger 1980a, 194). Destruction, which is cathartic and empowering (affective and cognitive motivations), can also feel noble to the perpetrator when he or she perceives it as serving a higher purpose (social identity). In the case of the Nazis, who exuberantly participated in book-burning ceremonies, the ideas of National Socialism appealed to those who were humiliated by the World War I defeat, alienated by values of the Weimar Republic, and victimized by economic depression. Participants in the book fires were persuaded by propagandists and orators of a fundamental connection between creation and destruction: out of the ashes of the un-German element would rise the new reich. It was exhilarating for participants to repudiate all that had held them back, to unleash their power in a public spectacle. In standing with their comrades and pledging allegiance to National Socialism, they were united in a transformative and affirmative act, their social identity fused by an intensely satisfying emotional experience.

The usefulness of Allen and Greenberger's tripartite approach to vandalism is apparent when we look at the most commonly cited typology of vandalism, which directly categorizes incidents according to the perpetrator's motivation. Stanley Cohen's (1973) seminal work on vandalism in the 1970s distinguished six categories of vandalism, while acknowledging that a mixture of motivations is common. These are Cohen's terms and his definitions, which are based on motivation; for comparative purposes, Allen and Greenberger's motives have been placed in italics and parentheses after each definition.

PLAY: Heedless damage that results from play or self-entertainment (*Affective*)

MALICIOUS: Destruction motivated by hatred or pleasure in destroying but is relatively non-specific in target (*Affective and Cognitive*)

VINDICTIVE: Damage carried out as a form of revenge (*Affective and Cognitive*)

ACQUISITIVE: Destructive actions aimed at acquiring money or property (*Cognitive*)

TACTICAL: Damage that results from a considered, planned initiative to reach a goal beyond money (*Social*)

IDEOLOGICAL: Damage calculated to support a specific social or political cause, similar to tactical (*Social*)

As we juxtapose Cohen's categories of vandalism against Allen and Greenberger's schemata of motivations, we see that as one progresses down the list, the emotional aspect is overshadowed by more deliberate elements. *Play* and *malicious* forms of vandalism display a strong affective component. Malicious vandalism, which is non-specific in target, expresses both affective (impotence, hatred, hostility, and rage) and cognitive motivations (the desire for control and efficacy); it resonates in emotive quality with the *vindictive* category, in which damage is carried out as a form of revenge. Although often perceived as senseless, malicious vandalism is akin to the vindictive category in that both are responding to a perceived violation or irritant (which may or may not be evident to an observer). The grievance that triggers a destructive response may be real or imagined, and the eventual target only indirectly or symbolically related to the original cause of hostility. In incidents of *acquisitive* vandalism, cognitive motivations are prominent, and the motive is laced with opportunism, although the perpetrators justify their actions as a response to deprivation and lack.

The social aspect of motivation identifies other, ostensibly higher roads that may be taken in pursuit of psychological satisfaction: *tactical* vandalism, the pursuit of a goal beyond money, and *ideological* vandalism, similar behavior committed in the name of a cause. Individuals aggrieved by debilitating or alienating social circumstances may embrace extreme ideas and identities and, in their thrall, engage in acts of violence that they believe will achieve desirable goals beyond benefit only to themselves. Cohen (1973) suggests that most *ideological* vandalism is tactically motivated, committed in the interest of drawing attention to a certain cause. In both tactical and ideological acts of vandalism, the choice of target is deliberate, and an attempt is made to anticipate the possible consequences of the action before it is carried out. Together, Allen and Greenberger's focus on internal states leading to destruction and Cohen's typology of vandalism according to motivation effectively dismantle explanations that attribute pleasure in destruction to a simple frustration-aggression reflex.

Sociologists in the 1980s built on Cohen's idea that motivations might overlap and continued the process of investigating their relative influence. Some viewed perception of power as a key construct and perceived control over one's circumstances as both an "antecedent and consequence of destruction" (Allen and Greenberger 1980b, 85). Social psychologist David Canter (1984, 346–347) surveyed research on the vandals' locus of control and concluded that the vandal might be both motivated from within and challenged from without to respond to a threatening physical and sociopolitical environment. In other words, both internal and external circumstances were catalysts to action. Reuben Baron and Jeffrey Fisher's (1984, 65) examination of the influence of external factors on internal states led them to describe the contemporary vandal as driven by a sense of injustice. They posited that people's perceived control over influences in their personal lives exerts a proportional influence on their ability to cope with inequity; a low sense of control leaves an individual little with which to combat frustration and can lead to vandalism. Claude Lèvy-Leboyer (1984) has argued that vandals' perception of injustice may be a reaction to a social or political system that rejects them. For marginalized people who feel thwarted by mainstream society and unable to control their circumstances, defacing or destroying public property can increase feelings of power and control. Allen and Greenberger's (1980b) studies show that destroying something, and the feeling of control this engenders, lessens the individual's sense of helplessness. This work confirmed the observations of earlier researchers that vandalism often attracts those with little attachment to others, who lack any sense of control over the future, and who live in milieus in which there is a stress on toughness and tests of masculinity (Baron and Fisher 1984).

Identification with a group assuages feelings of powerlessness and fosters a "herd mentality" that vastly expands the scope of the vandalism that results. When there is a progression from individual and anonymous acts to group and public acts of vandalism, it is usually because the perpetrators' sense of control and perception that their actions are legitimate have been strengthened by identification with like-minded others and a system of values. And although individual destructive impulses are often reactive and spontaneous, group consensus may channel such impulses into broader protests against larger and more symbolic targets: motivations shift from affective and cognitive to social as the perpetrators find company and identity. In this process the destruction takes on a more decidedly tactical and ideological orientation. Taking action, with the security of a group, comes to be seen as a way of changing entire systems, and is no longer merely an outlet for personal frustration and a question of the affective domain. Physical objects and structures (institutions, businesses) lend themselves to being viewed in a symbolic way, which gives special meaning to acts of destruction targeting them. The target of destruction is selected on an instrumental basis, based on its appropriateness in terms of reaching the goal of change.

Group dynamics strongly influence the development of consensual values and the translation of the values into action. During social conflict, values that are not altogether discontinuous with more accepted ones may become radicalized. In the 1980s, recourse to violence seemed a logical step for Dutch anti-apartheid protestors whose movement began as one dedicated to peace and nonviolence. As apartheid remained in place and frustration mounted, their thinking became more rigid and doctrinaire: destroying Amsterdam's South African Institute became a "reasonable" and honorable act of protest. The Buddhists in Sri Lanka embraced ethnic nationalism and racial supremacy to such a degree that their nonviolent creed became a fundamentalist platform that rationalized the murder of Hindu Tamils and the destruction of their beloved Jaffna Library. In both cases, group identity drove the translation of values into action.

Regardless of their motivation, vandals show little remorse for their destructive acts. Indeed, vandals driven primarily by affective and cognitive influences rarely are able to reflect on their actions. Either they are nihilistic and random, hedonistic, or they view themselves as chronic victims entitled to a period of dominance—however brief. Perpetrators who are socially motivated and who commit ideological or tactical vandalism generally give their actions a political context or religious justification. Insulated by the knowledge that they derive no direct benefit from destruction, they evade any awareness of wrongdoing and even see their actions as laudatory. Their beliefs about themselves and their actions, reinforced by their group, run counter to the general public's view, which associates vandalism with hostility rather than political purposefulness and routinely condemns all vandals for violating the social contract. Vandals are dismissed as brutal, immature, and degenerate and or diagnosed as sick or evil—labels that have become psychiatric metaphors for deviance. Vandals construct their social identity in opposition to dominant mores. Criticism of their actions merely reinforces their distance from the mainstream and may, in fact, encourage extreme reactions against systems that they, in turn, see as socially deviant.

By interpreting rule-breaking activities as meaningful action, sociologists have suggested that a rule-breaker is trying to engage society in a conversation or transaction (Cohen 1971, 14), or that the rule-breaker is attempting to respond to something about which dialogue is not welcome. Of course, the sociologist is inferring the perpetrator's motive from his or her action and circumstance, and this inference can differ markedly from the perpetrator's own belief about the reason for his or her actions. The "vocabularies of motive" that vandals use to justify or normalize their actions was a prominent feature of Stanley Cohen's *Images of Deviance*, which came out in 1971, just prior to his typology (Ward 1973, 19). Perhaps the most cited sociologist of vandalism, Cohen (1984, 55) suggested that judgments about vandalism almost always involve struggles between perpetrators and their audience over respective interpretations of a particular act.

This is particularly true when biblioclasm is committed by extremists who are labeled by society as terrorists. Terrorism is the systematic use or threat of violence to communicate a political message. Its perpetrators often employ symbolic targets. A defining characteristic of terrorism is that "its users expect rewards that are out of proportion to both the resources they possess and the risks they assume" (Crenshaw 2001, 15604). Here are two examples of messages gone astray. In the early part of the twentieth century, the British feminist movement split and one faction turned militant, targeting public property to draw attention to its cause. In 1914, Suffragettes firebombed a public library in an act designed to arouse a complacent public to put pressure on the government to grant women the vote. Arson seemed one of the few options left to their beleaguered movement, and the horrors of female disenfranchisement to them far outweighed the costs of property loss. But an outraged public branded them terrorists and summarily rejected their message. Another example of biblioclasm as terrorism, possibly coincidental, is the loss of historic documents and texts in the 1993 bombing of Florence's renowned Uffizi Gallery. The phrase "cultural terrorism" was employed for the first time after this disaster, expressing public dismay at the damage to the gallery, its contents, and the historic documents that were housed in a nearby archive. Whether or not the archive was the intended target, the perpetrators were clearly attacking "symbolic places, tokens of the very culture and identity of the state and the nation" and thus its authority and legitimacy (Gamboni 1997, 105). When the cause is construed as a moral one, the exercise of force against an opponent is, to the perpetrator, a legitimate and even exalted activity. Like other extremists, terrorists find it easy to slip into totalistic thinking, and they acknowledge no limitations to their actions. The violence of terrorism is provocative, and it is typically committed by small numbers of people who otherwise lack the capacity to challenge those in power. Labeling vandals as terrorists is, however, an attempt to silence them. Terrorists demand attention, yet their actions set up a reaction that closes the public mind and guarantees that the intended message will not be heard.

If the destruction of books is an attempt to communicate, then the targeting of an entire library—its physical structure, furnishings, and books—must have a meaning that is unique and distinct from the destruction of books alone. Destroying a library may bring the usual affective pleasure from destructiveness as well as cognitive rewards—a heightened release from powerlessness that comes with targeting an institution associated with the establishment and given status by the elite. When a library's contents offend a group's beliefs or ideology, destroying the entire structure can be a way of weakening the group to whom the collection belongs (the tactical element). By attacking libraries that are public institutions, vandals may be facing off against the state, a specific social group, or authority in general. In such cases, there is often a strong iconoclastic force at play. The iconic status accorded texts by those in power is offensive to groups who feel undervalued and misunderstood by global and local social systems that do not recognize the superiority of their moral framework.

During conditions of civil unrest, rebellion, and war, various motivations for biblioclasm operate simultaneously as violence is fed by the polarization and dehumanization that accompany militant mindsets. In these circumstances, the full range of biblioclasm can occur. The enemy and its possessions are considered to be outside the bounds of moral obligation, and under the cover of general chaos, brutalized troops and civilians turn to destroying books for reasons of cathartic play, malice, or vindictiveness. Sometimes economic or practical advantage is the goal of the destruction. Books may be torn apart and used for practical purposes in a mixture of disdain and pragmatism, or they may be stolen to be resold or kept as trophies (acquisitive). Books are easy targets because of their symbolic nature and relative vulnerability. They are fragile and easily destroyed by fire, pulping, and exposure to the elements. A library may be damaged in the generalized shelling and door-to-door fighting that is a prelude to the taking of a city. The collateral damage that is usually written off by the military as an unfortunate byproduct of direct combat is associated, nevertheless, with tactical and ideological goals. The destruction of the enemies' texts eliminates antithetical beliefs and documentation that support claims to contested lands and identities. The loss of libraries signals to the population that they are vulnerable to the enemy and a superior army. Invading troops may set fire to a library to reinforce their victory over the deposed government, or to exact revenge for civil resistance, or as a preliminary step to colonizing occupied territory—all of which comprise tactical and/or ideological motives.

Cohen's (1973, 53) observation that urban vandalism is the ideal form of rule-breaking "both in *expressive* (expressing certain values) and *instrumental* terms (solving certain structural problems)" can be extrapolated to wartime vandalism against libraries. Armed conflict sets an open stage for biblioclasm by setting up conditions in which affective, cognitive, and social motivations find the outlet of action. These same conditions can make it hard to discern primary forces behind an incident of biblioclasm. In a paper on the Russian Revolution, historian Richard Stites (1981, 6–7) recounted the story of an insurgent army of Ukrainian peasants entering the city of Ekaterinoslav in 1918 and firing point-blank into the "tallest and most beautiful buildings." They set fire to the prisons, libraries, and archives. Stites posed several questions: "Was this playfulness—the warrior ebullience and military macho which takes joy from ejaculating shells into a passive target . . . a mere act of drunkenness . . . deep hatred of the city . . . [or] a crude example of military tactics? Was it class war and political vengeance against the bourgeoisie?" His final question approaches an answer: "Or was it all of these things?"

Full-scale war is the most frequent host to biblioclastic events, but it is not the only arena. Civil conflicts can intensify to the point of mimicking war in their destructive potential. Because vandalism and bibloclasm are inextricably entwined with conflict in its many forms, throughout this book we will return to the perspective of sociology to ask about each case: What conflicts existed and gave rise to extremism and violence? What motivated the perpetrators, and what did they hope to achieve? How can we interpret their acts? What does this case tell us about the nature of biblioclasm and social conditions that open the door to cultural destruction? These questions, plus those posed earlier about what it is about books and libraries that causes them to be targeted, will surface repeatedly throughout this book.

Often (though not always) the impulse behind biblioclasm is religious or quasireligious dedication to an ideology. Religious texts (and sometime political texts, like Mao's *Red Book*) play a symbolic role as the material representations of a community of belief. It is common for members of a group that defines itself by its beliefs to showcase and celebrate their hallowed texts and dedicate themselves to preserving the volumes. These texts contain the basic articles of faith and, in the eyes of followers, the "truth." The influence of sacred texts is so powerful that devout followers tend to fear the texts of other religious groups as Trojan horses, vessels of alternate perspectives with the potential to undermine their belief system. For much of history, in the interest of spreading their faith and achieving homogeneous societies, competing religious groups have destroyed the books of their rivals, and sometimes the rivals themselves. Orthodoxy has been enforced by government and by mob alike. The familiar tale of the destruction of the Alexandrian Library (circa 640 A.D.) had Caliph Omar rationalizing it thus: "If these writings of the Greeks agree with the book of God [the Koran], they are useless and need not be preserved: if they disagree, they are pernicious and ought to be destroyed" (Gibbon 1994, 284–285). Though Omar's forces may not have been solely responsible for the library's loss (evidence now points to several hundred years of purging by competing groups—pagans, Christians, and Muslims alike), all versions attribute the destruction of the famous library to religious conflict (Thiem 1979). Like their predecessors, twentieth-century fundamentalists and zealots practiced little restraint in ordering the obliteration of libraries, and they were highly effective in mobilizing their followers to destroy the texts of those with beliefs differing from their own.

Throughout history, books have been destroyed by extremists because they offended the religion, morals, or politics of the day (Farrer 1977, 4). Religious motives, however, have often exacted the highest price. The Greeks and Romans burned books, but it was the Christians who burned the books *and* their authors, and the fifteenth, sixteenth, and seventeenth centuries were particularly dangerous times for heretics and their texts. Biblioclasm was standard policy for powerful Western religious-based governments throughout this time. In both France and England, the official hangman was also charged with burning offensive books in public ceremonies. In sixteenth-century France, book-burning served as a popular form of "street theater": "In one instance a Catholic mob hanged a Protestant printer and burned his 'seditious' volumes as part of the same public ceremony" (O'Toole 1993, 254). In sixteenth-century England, the fury of biblioclasts was terrible during conflicts over religion. Tens, possibly hundreds, of thousands of texts were lost in attempts by Henry VII and, later, by Protestant reformers, to purge England's monasteries of manuscripts, religious images, and icons of the Roman Catholic Church. But, by the eighteenth century, the decoupling of church and state had caused a decrease in imposed orthodoxy and put government-sponsored book burning out of fashion in Europe (Gillett 1964). In many parts of the world, however, biblioclasm for religious reasons remains a prevalent feature of ethnic conflict, especially when secular governments are overtaken by groups with messianic religious missions. In Bosnia, for example, the destruction of Muslim books and libraries by the Serbs in the 1990s, while an expedient function of rampant nationalism, was linked also to religious extremism.

During the twentieth century, book destruction increasingly became the prerogative of groups whose ideals served as the basis for attacks on rival ethnic and political groups. During times of social and political discord, mainstream values radicalized into immoderate principles that rationalized intemperate, often violent actions. Deteriorating conditions within a country led groups to polarize over possession of resources or opposing beliefs. In the scramble for power, books and libraries sometimes fell victim to communal demonstrations, as in India, where right-wing Hindu groups regularly attacked Muslims and their institutions, or in Kashmir, where the Muslims purged the region of Hindu Pandits and their books. The group that managed to assert control in situations of ethnic polarization, where the central government was weak, was often the one that most effectively mobilized followers behind a compelling program, based on charismatic ideas, that promised to solve immediate social and economic problems. The solution to socioeconomic issues under these circumstances inevitably involves taking back from an enemy that which is due to their own people. Leaders took advantage of chaotic conditions to seize and expand their power. With assumption of absolute power came the ability to transform beliefs into dogma, legislate orthodoxy, and put into effect systemic library destruction.

In a previous book, I have made a case that the ideologically driven, systemic destruction of books and libraries emerged, in the twentieth century, as patterned behavior (Knuth 2003). And I introduced the term *libricide* for this kind of campaign. Its etymology and dynamics implicitly link it to genocide and ethnocide. Libricide is an organized form of biblioclasm that stems from an extremist regime's pursuit, at all costs, of millennial ambitions and territorial claims that are held as the solution to social chaos (Knuth 2003). Ideals alone determine for extremists what institutions and groups must be swept out of the way. If the regime is racist, it will destroy the books of groups deemed inferior; if nationalistic, the books of competing nations and cultures; if religious, all texts that contradict sacred doctrines and teachings. Libricide often occurs during struggles over territory, when ideas imposed within a nation's borders are used to justify the colonization of neighboring states. Ideologues in possession of absolute power follow the template of history; their decisions mirror in fanaticism those of Ch'in Shih-huang or Omar the Caliph. Contemporary extremist regimes have repeatedly elevated nationalism into an ideology, channeling nationalistic sentiments into reinforcing the primary belief system. As modern secular societies have used texts to bolster national identity and built national libraries and archives that stand as monuments to the nation's strength, libraries have become increasingly attractive targets. And with increasing frequency, extremist regimes have attacked libraries during war precisely because they understand the role of these institutions in sustaining cultural vitality, national identity and pride, and the will to resist outside aggression.

Extreme forms of nationalism (often laced with racism, militarism, and imperialism) have also joined forces with modern technology to give new impetus to historic patterns of library destruction during war. All types of governments have used the doctrine of total war to justify extreme acts of violence—including strategic urban bombing in World War II, which resulted in horrific losses of life and property. The extreme tactics of total warfare are adopted by both those who initiate aggression and those who merely respond to incursions. War is, by nature, a situation of extremities in which ordinary norms and civic order break down, inviting physical violence and cultural vandalism and opening the door to the rationalized ethnic and political cleansing favored by extremists. For twentieth-century totalitarian regimes, war was a way to achieve righteous ideological mandates and impose orthodoxy on a chaotic world. As biblioclasts, they were soldiers fighting for a "better" world. Their opponents summoned a like intensity to withstand such offensives because they realized that they were fighting for cultural survival. Imposition of the enemy's ideology would mean the end of life as they knew it. Such was the virulence and countervirulence that ideological duels were often fought to the point of national collapse and unconditional surrender. Attackers and defenders alike were vested in extremism and cultural destruction.

Outside of war and revolution, book and library destruction has occurred when the social and political environment is conflict-ridden, and when social groups become polarized, reactive, and prone to extreme gestures. Biblioclasm is a public protest that releases tension and often takes tactical form. Books, of course, are part record, part artifact, and part symbol of forces or ideas that are taken by extremists to be dangerous or oppressive; when they are destroyed, they are symbolically standing in for something that cannot be so readily touched (O'Toole 1993, 238, 254). Books can serve as surrogate targets for a competing religious and ethnic group, caste, or political and ideological enemy; a public building like a library may stand for "the State, Law and Order, Repression, Money or a particular social class" (Sperandio 1984, 106). The protest may be sponsored by a regime but staged to look spontaneous (like the book fires of the Nazis and Maoists), or it may be carried out by a maverick group in service to a particular cause.

Twentieth-century biblioclasts were extremists of a new breed. They were moderns, sophisticated about using the enemy's own symbols against them and garnering maximum attention. Many mastered the technique of using ideas to tap into popular discontent, muster support, and rationalize their seizure of power. Theirs was a deliberate choice to operate outside of and against prevailing norms. The essence of extremism is dissatisfaction with the status quo and a desire for its replacement with "better" circumstances—albeit through the imposition of a homogeneous worldview. This brings in its wake a compulsion to challenge prevailing values and reject the pluralism associated with cosmopolitan, secular, and modern attitudes. Like vandalism and others forms of violence, book destruction enacts a struggle for power. At stake is the form society should take: Is a healthy society a homogeneous autocracy, where orthodoxy prevails and decisions are made by the few in the collective interest of all? Or is it a liberal democracy, where, in the end, individual human rights, pluralism, and intellectual freedom truly matter?

REFERENCES

Allen, V. L. 1984. "Toward an Understanding of the Hedonic Component of Vandalism." In *Vandalism: Behaviour and Motivations*, ed. Claude Lèvy-Leboyer. Amsterdam: Elsevier Science, 77–89.

Allen, Vernon L., and David B. Greenberger. 1980a. "Aesthetic Theory, Perceived Control, and Social Identity: Toward an Understanding of Vandalism." In *Violence and Crime in the Schools*, eds. Keith Baker and Robert J. Rubel. Lexington, Mass.: Lexington Books, 193–207.

Allen, Vernon L., and David B. Greenberger. 1980b. "Destruction and Perceived Control." In *Advances in Environmental Psychology*, Vol. 2, eds. Andrew Baum and Jerome E. Singer. Hillsdale, N.J.: Lawrence Erlbaum, 85–109.

Baczko, Bronislaw. 1989. "Vandalism." In *A Critical Dictionary of the French Revolution*, eds. François Furet and Mona Ozouf, trans. Arthur Goldhammer. Cambridge, Mass.: Belknap Press, 860–868.

Baron, Reuben M., and Jeffrey D. Fisher. 1984. "The Equity-Control Model of Vandalism: A Refinement." In *Vandalism: Behaviour and Motivations*, ed. Claude Lèvy-Leboyer. Amsterdam: Elsevier Science, 63–75.

"Biblioclasm." 1989. In *Oxford English Dictionary*, Second Edition, Vol. 2, prepared by J. A. Simpson and E.S.C. Weiner. Oxford: Clarendon Press, 169.

Canter, David. 1984. "Vandalism: Overview and Prospect." In *Vandalism: Behaviour and Motivations*, ed. Claude Lèvy-Leboyer. Amsterdam: Elsevier Science, 345–356.

Cohen, Stanley. 1971. "Introduction." In *Images of Deviance*, ed. Stanley Cohen. Harmondsworth, England: Penguin, 9–24.

Cohen, Stanley. 1973. "Property Destruction: Motives and Meanings." In *Vandalism*, ed. Colin Ward. London: Architectural Press, 23–53.

Cohen, Stanley. 1984. "Sociological Approaches to Vandalism." In *Vandalism: Behaviour and Motivations*, ed. Claude Lèvy-Leboyer. Amsterdam: Elsevier Science, 51–61.

Crenshaw, M. 2001. "Terrorism." In *International Encyclopedia of the Social and Behavioral Sciences*, Vol. 23, eds. Neil J. Smelser and Paul. B. Baltes. Amsterdam: Elsevier Science, 15604–15606.

Farrer, James Anson. 1977. *Books Condemned to Be Burnt.* Reissue of 1892 Edition (London: Elliot Stock). Norwood, Penn.: Norwood Editions.

Gamboni, Dario. 1997. *The Destruction of Art: Iconoclasm and Vandalism since the French Revolution*. New Haven, Conn.: Yale University Press.

Gibbon, Edward. 1994. *The History of the Decline and Fall of the Roman Empire*. Vols. 5 and 6. Ed. David Womersley. London: Allen Lane.

Gillett, Charles Ripley. 1964. *Burned Books: Neglected Chapters in British History and Literature*. Port Washington, N.Y.: Kennikat Press.

"Iconoclasm." 1989. In *Oxford English Dictionary*, Second Edition, Vol. 7, prepared by J. A. Simpson and E.S.C. Weiner. Oxford: Clarendon Press, 609.

Jones, Tom B. 1999. "Vandals." In *Encyclopedia Americana International Edition*. Danbury, Conn.: Grolier, 890.

Knuth, Rebecca. 2003. *Libricide: The Regime-Sponsored Destruction of Books and Libraries in the Twentieth Century*. Westport, Conn.: Praeger.

Leighton, Alexander H. 1959. *My Name Is Legion: Foundations for a Theory of Man in Relation to Culture*. New York: Basic Books.

Lèvy-Leboyer, Claude. 1984. "Vandalism and the Social Sciences." In *Vandalism: Behaviour and Motivations*, ed. Claude Lèvy-Leboyer. Amsterdam: Elsevier Science, 1–11.

Lumsden, Malvern. 1983. "Sources of Violence in the International System." In *International Violence*, eds. Tunde Adeniran and Yonah Alexander. Westport, Conn.: Praeger, 3–19.

O'Toole, James. 1993. "The Symbolic Significance of Archives." *American Archivist* 56 (2):234–255.

Poulet, Dominique. 1995. "Revolutionary 'Vandalism' and the Birth of the Museum: The Effects of a Representation of Modern Cultural Terror." In *Art in Museums*, ed. Susan Pearce. London: Athlone, 192–213.

Salzberg, Sharon. 2004. "The Power of Intention." *O Magazine* (January 2004): 83–84.

Sperandio, J.C.L. 1984. "Vandalism as a Fact of Life in Society." In *Vandalism: Behaviour and Motivations*, ed. Claude Lèvy-Leboyer. Amsterdam: Elsevier Science, 105–107.

Stites, Richard. 1981. "Iconoclasm in the Russian Revolution: Destroying and Preserving the Past." Kennan Institute for Advanced Russian Studies, Occasional Paper Number 147. Conference on the Origins of Soviet Culture. May 18–19, 1981. Washington, D.C.: The Wilson Center.

Thiem, Jon. 1979. "The Great Library of Alexandria Burnt: Towards the History of a Symbol." *Journal of the History of Ideas* 40 (4):507–526.

"Vandal." 1989. In *Oxford English Dictionary*, Second Edition, Vol. 19, prepared by J. A. Simpson and E.S.C. Weiner. Oxford: Clarendon Press, 425.

Ward, Colin. 1973. "Introduction." In *Vandalism*, ed. Colin Ward. London: Architectural Press, 13–22.

CHAPTER 2

Tracing the Path of Extremism from Robespierre to Milosevic

> [Let us] amputate all the gangrenous members from the bibliographic body. Let us remove from our libraries the swelling which presages death; let us leave only the plumpness which is a sign of health.
> —Urbain Domergue, French revolutionary

The Enlightenment was the European philosophical movement of the seventeenth and eighteenth centuries that advocated the application of critical intelligence to social problems in the belief that mankind and society are perfectible (Gay 1969). The notion that cultural heritage is public property, and the corresponding belief that violence against it is a public concern, began to take shape during this period. These ideas emerged full force during the French Revolution when prominent revolutionaries asserted the public's right to demand social change and to use ideas to fashion a rational society. As highly educated students of the Enlightenment, the leaders of the French Revolution juggled two contradictory ideas from that movement: the belief that forging a new future required questioning authority and "regenerating and purifying a past tainted by centuries of tyranny and prejudice," and a belief that learning and the use of accumulated knowledge were essential to progress (Baczko 1989, 866). Although most of the leaders actively encouraged cultural destruction as a means of maintaining revolutionary momentum, an undercurrent of appreciation for books and learning served at times as a counterforce to revolutionary iconoclasm. Of course, those who would preserve libraries had to tread carefully, mindful that their reservations might be perceived as counterrevolutionary. "The boundary between preservation and destruction, the two sides of 'regeneration,' was elusive if not impossible to grasp" (Baczko 1989, 866).

In unstable twentieth-century societies, discontented populations revisited notions of revolution and social engineering. When modern values and economies threatened existing ways of life but proved inadequate in following through on promises of social security, alienated groups turned to charismatic ideas as their solution to social and psychological distress. Then orthodoxy was the order of the day, and libraries fell under close scrutiny because of the diversity of the ideas they contained. Modern extremists (like their predecessors, the French radicals) embraced the notion that books and libraries are idols of the status quo. The very premise of a lending collection encouraged individual autonomy, and autonomy was highly suspect to leaders who ruled in the name of the collective. For ideologues of all persuasions, the choice to destroy books was easily rationalized. Armed with the certainty of their right to impose ideas and values, militant dissenters embraced book and library destruction as an effective tool of social protest and reform. This choice placed them on a collision path with liberals and an international community that believed libraries support the tolerance and pluralism that is conducive to global peace and must be preserved.

From our perspective in the twenty-first century, we can see the powerful effect of the Enlightenment. Because of this movement, humans were no longer the passive pawn of kings and religious hierarchies: people came to view themselves as autonomous beings vested with the ability to use reason to fashion a better life and reform society. Ideas were the tools of change. With an evolved understanding of reason, human agency, and choice, the mind became the ultimate battlefield. The French Revolution provided occasion for transforming these ideals into action and gave impetus to two influential movements, which in turn spawned radically divergent views of books and libraries that persist to this day. One group sees them as cultural bulwarks and actively promotes access and preservation; another group despises them as props of the elite and corrupt systems, a view that is a powerful incentive for destruction.

In eighteenth-century France, the libraries were often splendid. The *Bibliothèque du Roi* (the king's library) was the largest in Europe, with 300,000 printed volumes and 30,000 Greek, Latin, French, and Oriental manuscripts (Martin 1993, 177). Books and libraries were generally the property of the monarchy, a small group of aristocrats, and the religious establishment. As the century progressed, the hegemony of this triad of elites was undermined by increased public access to books whose authors argued the Enlightenment idea that human reason could be used to fashion an ideal world. Literate Frenchmen were imbibing the notion that progress required thinking for oneself and breaking with "obligatory thought patterns inherited from the past" (Chartier 1991, 23). They began to think that all institutions and spheres (social, ethical, political, and intellectual) should be subject to critical examination. For example, progress in one area, such as education—the teaching of truth and exposure of error—would generate progress in others (Gay, 1969).

In a country in which literacy provided impetus toward revolution, the onset of revolt ironically jeopardized the fate of recorded knowledge, because the general public fixed on books and libraries as symbols of the feudal system that had enforced class hierarchy and illiteracy for centuries.

During the course of the revolution (1789–1799), angry crowds destroyed private and religious libraries, vast quantities of historical documents, and the monuments of the Ancien Régime (Posner 1940, 162). France's books and records were often at the whim of mobs, for whom destruction held practical purpose as well as symbolic and affective features. The inflamed populace destroyed local charters and seigneurial archives because these documents were the primary legal basis for the claims of the monarchy and the nobility to feudal legitimacy. People participated enthusiastically in the destruction as if it were a ritual of purification, and they were empowered by their active involvement in the dismantling of the old Bourbon regime and the religious establishment. Archivist Judith Panitch (1996, 35) has concluded that "destroying the symbols of the old regime demonstrated the extent of one's hatred of that government and, conversely, one's devotion to the Republic." There was a tremendous desire to "escape from history" and to substitute a vision of emptiness from which a new order could emerge. The revolutionary government even revised French calendars to pose recorded time as beginning again with the first day of Year I—September 22, 1792, the day the republic was proclaimed. According to Panitch's (1996, 44) interpretation of revolutionary vandalism during the French Revolution,

On the one hand, the desire to destroy the records of the Ancien Régime appears to be, first and foremost, an intuitive, cathartic, and eminently understandable expression of rage, directed at one of the most prominent symbols of a hated and villified class. Viewed with a bit more distance and dispassion, however, the impulse for destruction appears not merely as an act of negation and denial, but also the necessary prelude and counterpart to more constructive institutions, as though the past had to be put definitively to rest if it were not to endanger the emergent Republican future.

Revolutionary leaders, especially in the first years, did little to counter the damage. In fact, they often participated in public ceremonies of destruction, which were viewed as a legitimate response to social injustice. Revolution, in their minds, required rupture, the demolishing of existing structures, and the elimination of a shameful past. Violence would effect quick and dramatic social transformation. The revolutionary regime (the General Assembly) explicitly sanctioned the destruction of symbols of feudal rule, and directives aimed at "purifying" France escalated in 1792 and 1793 (Panitch 1996, 34). To destroy "the last vestiges of privilege," it ordered the burning of genealogical papers in all public repositories (Lokke 1968, 27). On a single day in 1792, 600 volumes of noble genealogies went up in flames at the foot of the statue of Louis XIV. The Marquis de Condorcet, a scholar, ex-noble, and fervent revolutionary, praised the bonfire in a speech before the assembly, saying "Reason" itself was the agent responsible for burning volumes that witnessed the claims of a vain aristocracy (Panitch 1996, 34).

The destruction intensified even further during a period of radicalization and extreme social violence aptly called the Reign of Terror (1793–1794). In a little more than a year, the guillotine claimed 16,000 lives as Maximilien Robespierre and his cohort of radicals, the Jacobins, engineered the execution of aristocrats and political adversaries. One radical, Urbain Domergue, viewed the dismantling of library contents as akin to executing counterrevolutionaries. He advocated taking "a scalpel to our huge depositories of books and amputat[ing] all the gangrenous members from the bibliographic body. Let us remove from our libraries the swelling which presages death" (as quoted in Martin 1993, 188). During the Reign of Terror, massive amounts of books and records were burned. Clerical and émigré collections that had been confiscated at the start of the revolution lay rotting in warehouses and were subjected to damage, theft, and sale by speculators. Some materials (liturgical books in particular) were sold to munitions firms for manufacturing cartridges and charges for cannons (Martin 1993, 182). As centralized authority broke down and revolutionary fury overtook the country, there were wild proposals, part resolution and part fantasy, to burn the *Bibliothéque Nationale* in Paris. In Marseilles, there was talk of burning *all* libraries (Baczko 1989, 860). Decades later, in 1856, Director of the Imperial Archives Marquis Léon de Laborde calculated that more than 10,000 archives had been affected by revolutionary activities, some to a devastating extent. Of one billion documents, two-thirds were destroyed and the rest left in upheaval in warehouses and public buildings (Panitch 1996, 37).

The tide turned toward preservation when Abbé Henri Grégoire coined the term *vandalism* and inspired a critical change of consciousness about what he called the "killing of things": the destruction of cultural artifacts such as monuments, paintings, and books that symbolized the past (Baczko 1989, 860). His reports to the National Convention in 1794 and 1795 included extensive lists of lost or endangered artifacts and collections. The wide dissemination of his reports through public and private correspondence resulted in acceptance of *vandalistes* as the name for those who either committed destructive acts or profited from them (Baczko 1989, 861). Grégoire and his allies saw Jacobin radicalism as a tyranny not unlike that from which they had so recently freed themselves. They openly denounced the Jacobins for their fanaticism and ignorant destruction of cultural objects, as well as for their brutal executions. It became cliché to call Robespierre a vandal and a barbarian; the revolutionary Louis Marie Stanislas Fréron referred to him as "the New Omar who wanted to burn the libraries" (Baczko 1989, 861). By linking vandalism to a specific faction and posing that faction as having fostered the *encanaillement* (degradation) of France and the Revolution, the moderates also reinforced in the public mind a link between tyranny and ignorance (Baczko 1989, 861).

Ultimately, the moderates were able to carve out a new role for government in the civilized protection and support of culture. They retained cultural and historical artifacts—previously the exclusive possessions of the elite—and claimed them as possessions of the state to be used for education and the founding of a new egalitarian republic (Gamboni 1997, 36). In accordance with their newly conceived policies, the assembly made ambitious plans to centralize the country's texts and create a 10-million-volume national library—plans that came to naught because of the sheer scale of the project. But collections that had survived the mob, revolutionary radicals, neglect, and cupidity were salvaged and placed in municipal libraries after the Reign of Terror. The country's archival records, now reconceived as public documents, were eventually gathered together and reorganized into the National Archives, an institution charged by the government with maintaining the documentary basis of national identity and testifying to the legality of the revolutionary state (Panitch 1996, 41).

From François-Marie Arouet Voltaire, Alexander Pope, Denis Diderot, and other Enlightenment thinkers who revered books and learning, and from those, like Jean Jacques Rousseau, who were ambivalent about preserving knowledge, came the belief that reason, science, and intellect could influence the course of history and advance social justice. Their ideas left a mixed legacy. On one hand, the primacy of reason, joined by emerging ideals of individualism, provided the basis for precedents set by the moderates of the French Revolution who officially assigned libraries and archives a public-service role. Certainly, reason and individualism helped shape modern ideas that have made the preservation of libraries a public concern and their protection an essential response to those whose logic rationalized destruction. These two ideas also provided the basis for movements that would advance liberal democracy and universal human rights over the next two centuries. The emphasis on ideals of democracy, individualism, and pluralism that was adopted in the twentieth century by the United Nations came after autocratic extremists had launched World War II. Liberals and internationalists successfully argued for a global consensus (at least on a rhetorical level), identifying these values as conducive to social progress and peace. From the Enlightenment onward, as liberal democratic values gained credence, libraries acquired status as pillars of informed and civilized societies—societies that value education, a print culture, and the accumulation of knowledge upon which to base decision making.

The other arm to the Enlightenment's legacy also had to do with the primacy of reason, which led ideologues to rationalize the imposition of orthodoxy. Effectively curtailing individualism and intellectual freedom, this arm swung back at the notion of the supremacy of reason that had freed it from the constraints of the historical period prior. The French Revolution was the first major instance in modern history of conscious, systemic iconoclasm, with mobs and radicals committing violence against cultural items in the name of an idea: equality. A case can be made that twentieth-century extremists were direct heirs to the French revolutionaries' notion that ideas could rationalize biblioclasm, that "the destruction of the learning of the past, or its radical revision and reduction, represents the cessation of historical process and constitutes a basic precondition for happiness and justice" (Thiem 1979, 519). French biblioclasts were responding to a variety of traditions that viewed the destruction of books as productive. Influential figures included the sixteenth-century humanist Louis LeRoy, who felt that the cumulative weight of the past burdened the present and smothered originality; and Jean Jacques Rousseau (1712–1778), a leading figure in the "vanity of learning" movement, who feared that "the decadent influence of learning, however truthful," would impede the progress of the reading public (Thiem 1979, 518). French radicals put into action the line of reasoning that books and library destruction could be purposeful, rational, and productive behavior, and these notions were built upon by numerous thinkers and theorists in subsequent centuries, including Edward Gibbon, Miguel de Cervantes, George Bernard Shaw, and Friedrich Nietzsche. We can see their influence in the works of Karl Marx (1818–1883), who believed that "[t]he tradition of all the dead generations weighs like a nightmare on the brain of the living" (Marx 1963, 15), and in the nineteenth-century anarchist Mikhail Bakunin's conception of the destructive impulse as the creative source of all life. Utopians of the twentieth century drew inspiration from these radical predecessors and even boasted of their association with historic biblioclasts. In a closed meeting of Communist Party cadres in 1958, Mao Tse-tung gleefully responded to comparisons of the Communist Party to Ch'in Shih-huang (259–210 B.C.), who famously ordered the destruction of China's literary heritage and the massacre of its scholars. The party, he said, should be given credit for having surpassed the tyrant's record a hundred times (Leys 1977, 145).

Mao's anti-intellectualism mirrored that of radicals during the Reign of Terror, when there was an organized assault on scientists, artists, and literary figures as well as cultural artifacts. A story, later proven apocryphal, circulated among the French moderates that the brilliant scientist Antoine-Laurent Lavoisier, when condemned to the guillotine, asked first to finish his experiments. A Tribunal spokesman replied: "The Revolution has no need of scientists." The story encapsulates the Jacobins' utter disdain for learning and scholars, a view common among extremists in later centuries. Adolf Hitler responded similarly to protests about the effect on German science of the removal of Jews: Germany had no need, he said, of a science tainted by Judaism. During the Russian Revolution, books and libraries were gravely endangered by a revolutionary radicalism heavily laced with anti-intellectualism. In January 1918, the Petrograd publication *Burevestnik* warned against the "tawdry" hypnotic and deceptive brilliance of professors and scientists, and then called for the destruction of universities, "that nest of bourgeois lies" (Avrich 1973, 48). Russian Communist Party members harbored, thereafter, a mindset that intellectuals were hampered by an overabundance of scruples. Effective Communists knew that it was better to "cut down human trees blindly than to wonder which among them are really rotten" (Milosz

1990, 77). Likewise, it was considered better to overshoot in purging book collections. From the French Revolution onward, vandalism, iconoclasm, nihilism, antiliberalism, and anti-intellectualism were frequently overlapping phenomena (Stites 1981, 3). Often extremists have viewed intellectuals and books as troublesome parts of despised establishments and institutions, leading them to pinpoint libraries as a key barrier to substantive reform.

Under Hitler's influence, the Nazis achieved an iconic climax to the "vanity of learning" movement and brought book burning and fascist ideals of violent rebirth sharply into the public consciousness. When fascism, a potent package of nationalistic and often racist doctrines, surfaced as a mass movement after World War I, it became a vehicle for the acquisition of power by charismatic autocrats and eager followers. In Italy and Germany, where fascism emerged full force, the populations had been traumatized by losses in World War I and alienated by a modern society that rejected many of their most cherished values. Outsiders were repelled by its mysticism and brutality as "echoes from a dark past" (Taylor 1993, 36), but fascism garnered favor among those who felt betrayed by modernity. The promise of shelter, food, social stability, jobs, and an effective political system was compelling to those desperate for such assurances (Einaudi 1968). Fascism rapidly achieved strong group identification by engendering mass hatred of enemies. To rally the masses behind their programs, leaders used propaganda, parades, demonstrations, symbols, uniforms, and an emphasis on action and violence as "an elevating and creative experience" (Curtis 1979, 93). In 1933, the Nazi Party heralded a triumphant new era by staging bonfires of books deemed contaminating by virtue of their authors (Jews, in particular) or their content (which bore witness to opposing beliefs such as pacifism, humanism, and democracy). The party's orators drove home notions of regeneration from destruction. The fires deeply shocked observers around the world, renewing a revulsion toward book destruction and also reviving the historic fear that civilization is ever vulnerable to barbarism.

The history of modern book and library destruction is one of collision between liberal humanists and extremists. Liberal humanists view the multiplicity of viewpoints found in books as necessary to individual development (which leads incrementally to a strong civil society), healthy dissent, and the critical analysis that drives ongoing societal reform. To them, social progress is a gradual and inclusive process, and libraries are seen as essential to a free society. What matters, for extremists, is the ideology and its mandates. For extremists who gain control of the government and follow their logic to totalistic ends, "there is a sole and exclusive truth in politics [which] postulates a preordained, harmonious, perfect plan of society . . . and recognizes only one, all-inclusive sphere of human action, which is the political" (Cobban 1960, 183). They target autonomy and intellectual freedom because, from an ideological mindset, the greatest hurdle to the achievement of social transformation is the individual's pursuit of his or her own aims without regard for communal goals (Van Velzen, Thoden, and Van Beek 1988, 7). The possession of superior ideas imposes a moral mandate on believers to act upon these ideas and purge alternate ideas and influences from society in general—and libraries in particular. Repression and violence are easily rationalized. Indeed, twentieth-century extremists seized freedom as their prerogative, claiming violence as one of their liberties.

Leaders of extremist groups acquire political power by taking advantage of conditions of social disintegration and posing idealistic alternatives to prevailing sociopolitical systems. Millennial visions can offer security to those who feel disillusioned, enraged, or impotent by specifying a fixed belief system, enforcing a stable social order, and promising a perfect world. They lure many into willing participation. Discontented and beleaguered individuals may be willing to cede moral authority to the collective, to exchange choice for certainty, and to discard what they view as failed ideals (freedom, pluralism, individualism, and democracy in general) if their experience with modernity has been disillusioning. In the twentieth century, the rules of ideological correctness were often a welcome antidote to the disorientation engendered by modernity, and iconoclastic purging had cathartic effects. Texts are brought to the front lines of modern conflicts when distressed groups renounce freedom of choice and individuality for the security of encompassing belief systems. In understanding contemporary extremism and biblioclasm, it is useful to consider how modernity has influenced decisions to relinquish choice and grasp ideology as an all-purpose solution to social woe.

Crisis of choice is a defining characteristic of modernism, which fundamentalism expert Bruce Lawrence (1989, 27) describes as a state of searching for individual autonomy. The quest for individuality is driven by "a set of socially encoded values emphasizing change over continuity; quantity over quality; [and] efficient production, power and profit over sympathy for traditional values or vocations, in both public and private spheres." When an individual's integration of these values leads to greater autonomy and contentment, then modernism is lauded. When the displacement of traditional ideals and behaviors by modern values fails to improve conditions, then alienation, discontent, and fear set in. These are the raw materials of revolution and extremism in modern societies. Disillusionment is channeled into charismatic ideals that leverage attempts to change the playing field and move believers from the edges of society to the center. The more absolute one's ideals, the more black and white one's position in the world, and consequently, the more shape and form one's life has. Dissonance abates as identity comes not from lonely internal struggles but from identification with a group and a totalistic belief system. With the embrace of ideology, the pursuit of individual autonomy is abandoned. As modernism is repudiated, books and libraries, the carriers of humanism and alternate belief systems, enter the danger zone.

Traditional values and the authority of religions have been eroding in Western society since the fifteenth century, when the printing press was invented, vernacular languages emerged in written form, and Martin Luther nailed his theses to the door of Wittenberg Church. As the relationship between God and man was reconceived as a direct one, the desire to use texts for personal growth took flight. During the eighteenth and nineteenth centuries, a new view of man's connection to God through direct access to the scripture formed the basis for modern liberalism, which incorporated the Christian idea that the "redemptive experience of the individual" replaces "obedience to the Law" as the basis of spirituality (Bruce 2000, 110). During the twentieth century, as humanist psychologists explored the idea that the search for knowledge, rather than the pursuit of God, is at the heart of the human condition, becoming fully human became the ultimate value for humankind (Markovic 1974, 236). With knowledge replacing doctrine as the path to transcendence, Western society headed rapidly toward a fervent belief in the ultimate authority of the independent mind. Simultaneously, libraries became important support institutions for secular humanism and its central tenet, that civilization's survival and progress depend upon the preservation and accessibility of written knowledge and the individual's intellectual freedom.

The rise of industrialized secular states brought economic and social changes that further chipped away at the religious foundations of Western society. In many places, organized religion was replaced with an "eclectic spirituality" based on ideas thought to be universal, such as the fundamental equality of all (Bartov and Mack 2001, 3), civil religion (in which there is "the belief in a creator God but not in specific religious creeds"), and secular humanism (Antoun 2001, 12). In democracies and culturally diverse nations, the separation of church and state became the marker of a modern nation, and a certain ethos of tolerance prevailed (Antoun 2001, 12). Religious texts were no longer read as literal truth, but as a collection of metaphors that guided general understanding (Bruce 2000, 66). By the twentieth century, "the relegation of religion to an inconsequential leisure pursuit [became] a peculiarly modern Western phenomenon" (Bruce 2000, 40). For some nations, secularism was imposed by dictators and religion was denounced or brought into line with the regime. For other nations, religious influence and conformity were eroded by humanistic creeds with their tolerance of difference. In these countries, the secular state permitted great liberties to the individual and family in the private sphere in exchange for "something approaching neutrality in the public sphere" (Bruce 2000, 89). For example, a religious group had the freedom to practice religion as it saw fit, but not to impose it on others. The separation of church and state ensured that one group could not "capture" the state. Human and civil rights, rather than religious doctrine, formed the basis of legislation.

Before the Enlightenment, the contents of books were controlled by the elite, whose enforcement of orthodoxy was complete. With Enlightenment-driven ideals providing a platform for revolution and reform, religious censorship decreased, secular texts proliferated, and there was increased access to information. But old notions of the library as something to be controlled have persisted to this day. Indeed, the modern experience has been marked by the continual presence of tension underlying the mission of libraries—the secular humanist tradition of providing information access to a wide range of patrons and thus supporting democracy, diversity, individuality, and scientific advancement versus a persisting image of libraries as exclusive havens for elite segments of the population and as tools for maintaining the power of these groups and the grip of religious or ideological orthodoxy. Each twentieth-century revolution required negotiation of the role of libraries, along with the dismantling of the regime and the premises upon which its institutions are based. Ideologues such as Mao Tse-tung used "elitist" as an epithet, an excuse to attack existing institutions. Reconstructing the state often meant purging books, and then reinventing libraries as ideologically correct tools that served "the people." The key issue determining the lot of libraries was the way "the people" was defined. Unlike secular humanists, who conceived of libraries as pluralistic institutions that served autonomous individuals, autocratic ideologues defined "the people" as a group whose collective interest was best served by strict adherence to ideological imperatives and conforming institutions.

At the dawn of the twentieth century, liberal-democratic sensibilities and the needs of a civilization that thrived on information exchange strongly favored the preservation of libraries, making it difficult for Westerners to fathom their deliberate destruction. The emergence of nationalism over the previous two centuries had brought with it a new role for libraries in creating and nurturing a culture and national consciousness (Harris 1986, 240). Increased public access to education promoted the sense of "imagined community" that binds people into a nation (Anderson 1991). Written knowledge had become deeply valued in Western society, and the replacement of religious texts with secular ones as a source of social inspiration influenced the formation of the fundamental values of modern society: freedom, equality, peace, justice, truth, and beauty (Markovic 1974, 242). Reason and science moved into first place as the engine driving daily activity (Antoun 2001, 46). The Enlightenment idea that the acquisition of knowledge increases human influence over both natural and social forces was commonplace (Markovic 1974, 234). Tyranny was generally associated with ignorance, and literacy with wisdom and progress.

World War I ushered in a new period of social turbulence and change that was exhilarating for those who could adapt (generally the educated and better off) and demoralizing for unskilled lower and middle classes and unemployed workers, especially veterans, who lacked the resources for seizing advantage of burgeoning economic possibilities. The increased freedom from traditional values and lifestyles that accompanied modernization was a hollow victory for those whose lives were disrupted by the accompanying social and economic turbulence. "To be modern," one insightful social scientist has written, "is to experience personal and social life as a maelstrom, to find one's world and oneself in perpetual disintegration and renewal, trouble and anguish, ambiguity and contradiction: to be part of a universe in which all that is solid melts into air" (Berman 1982, 345). Industrialization, massive global wars, and economic depression increased general disorientation and psychological distress in industrialized economies. Tested or broken by trying circumstances, many people felt distanced from traditional social bonds and moral obligations, and lacking in purpose and structure (Piekalkiewicz and Penn 1995, 6).

Distance and lack of purpose fed feelings of vulnerability and alienation. For the beleaguered, options perhaps seemed bleakly simple. They could (1) accommodate to the sweeping changes, no matter the price; (2) privately cling to traditional mindsets and risk having change sweep them to the wayside; or (3) fight back (Bruce 2000, 117). Accommodation meant going with the flow and embracing liberal democracy, the open-ended nature of which brought with it the possibility of new social roles, increased egalitarianism, and the satisfaction of patriotic attachment to a free nation. But frequently the path to democracy was turbulent and contested, and required an acceptance of diversity and the absence of absolutes. Active resistance to modernity, on the other hand, often meant the embrace of extreme ideas and leaders whose promise of resolution depended on mandates of violence. In what was essentially an "escape from freedom" (Fromm 1941), vulnerable groups filled the vacuum of their existence with ideas that were comprehensive, compelling, and absolute. The ideas provided clear mandates for action and the promise, ultimately, of political and social perfection. In part, the allure of an extreme group in the modern world was its ability to fulfill people's need for security and community and to assert their social and economic entitlements.

Marking out the enemy is a common tactic for solidifying intragroup identity, and modernism is a popular target for extremists because it has so blatantly failed them. It is also an extremely dangerous competing force that must be neutralized. It is seen as a threatening package of secular, urban, cosmopolitan, and humanistic values. Liberal democracy (which extremists see as the carrier of modernism) is a creed so powerful that it becomes the logical rival for any absolute belief system, including religious ones. Communist regimes have hated and feared modernism and liberal democracy as competition for their people's minds and souls. In Russia and China, campaigns to inculcate socialism included the purging of these antithetical influences from libraries and narrowly reorganizing their institutions as tools of propaganda. Religious fundamentalists in many regions also fear the contents of books. In Afghanistan in the 1990s, young, uneducated Taliban soldiers were known to burst into libraries and train their machine guns on books in English. Anatomy books and any books with illustrations were purged or burnt in campaigns that pitted the regime against modernization, secularization, internationalism, Westernization, and American imperialism—all of which were seen as "the same evil thing" (Bruce 2000, 111). To the Taliban, the United States—the foremost democratic state—was "the carrier of modernity," a meddling force whose power was "an insult to national pride and a slight on the true faith of Islam" (Bruce 2000, 3). By purifying the country of American influences, the Taliban was purging modernity itself.

Extremist groups exercised their right to rebel against oppressive power structures and alien systems or seek economic and political advantage over rivals. Turbulent social conditions created a ready following for charismatic leaders, who eagerly plugged into discontent and traditional sources of intolerance in order to justify authoritarian measures. Tailoring ideas whose charismatic charge came, in no small part, from their resonance with preexisting social orientations, the Nazi Party offered a revolution that capitalized on the severely reactionary nature of post–World War I Germany. The Taliban similarly bet on the powerful influence of Islam as their best chance for unifying the Afghan people. Pitching ideals at their logical extremes allowed ideologues to overcome passive resistance and generate enthusiasm. Reducing complex moral and ethical issues to simple rules and premises paved a clear path toward utopia. The template of an ideology invited people to relinquish the burdensome aspects of modernity—especially the anomie and cognitive dissonance—in exchange for a clear identity and community. Ideology provided a simple guideline by which to determine who was in the group and, alternately, those to whom there was no moral obligation.

The most destructive twentieth-century ideologies had cult figures at the helm. As the embodiment of statesman, warrior, high priest, and savior, leaders such as Hitler and Mao offered compelling visions of political and social rebirth (Kershaw 2001, 381). Leaders at any level who gain the trust of a marginalized group can provide them with a mission that transforms life into something purposeful. From this premise, it is a short step to accepting as logical and necessary such rituals as race riots, religious pogroms, and book burning—rituals that glorify irrationality, mysticism, and brutality and that enable followers "to work themselves up into state of excitement in which they can either assure themselves of a speedy solution of their problems or ignore them" (Thrupp 1962, 12). Through these rituals, charismatic leaders can effectively channel heightened emotionality into hatred directed at an enemy and its symbols—hatred operating as a "blow-flame," which, as George Orwell (1968, 26) has pointed out, "can be turned in any direction at a moment's notice." Attacking outsiders contributes to a group's cohesion and provides an outlet for feelings of vulnerability and isolation. Snugly ensconced in a community of believers, members of an extremist group are encouraged to perceive outsiders as carriers of dangerous counterideologies (Piekalkiewicz and Penn 1995, 49).

Enemies symbolize the antithesis of one's core values and beliefs and also offer a contrast by which to measure or inflate one's own worth and values (Relyea 1994, 193–194). When aroused by righteous indignation and convinced of a higher morality, followers of an ideology will eagerly give full reign to feelings of enmity and contempt for other groups (Piekalkiewicz and Penn 1995, 47; Koonz 2003, 3). The Serbs' shelling of Sarajevo, which targeted both citizens and cultural institutions, exemplifies the moral blindness (identified by political scientist Hannah Arendt [1964, 276] in her coverage of Adolf Eichmann's war-crimes trial) that enables followers of an extremist regime to commit heinous crimes without any recognition that their actions are wrong. The Serbs' ethnocentric, religious nationalism was inflamed by feelings that they were a "celestial people," victimized by subhuman enemies who sought to extinguish them (Cigar, 1995). Posing the eradication of Muslim cultural heritage as an act of self-defense obfuscated the expedience of cleansing contested territory of institutions and records that testified to the historic presence of Muslims in Bosnia (Knuth 2003). Serbian leaders either denied their atrocities, claiming that they were all pseudoevents created by the Muslims to garner media support (Cohen 1998, 480), or rationalized their aggression as the product not of hatred but despair, and claimed that it was sanctioned by God (Ugresic 1998).

The Serbs were operating on a platform of racist nationalism and religious extremism, a compelling mixture for authoritarian societies that cede power to military establishments and promote intragroup unity by fomenting hatred toward rivals of an ethnic, religious, or political nature. Secular ideologues are susceptible to grafting nationalistic sentiments onto ideological ones because it offers another layer of entitlement. At times, this grafting has been a self-conscious and deliberate choice, as when the Nazis fused National Socialism and nationalism into seamless mandates of racial supremacy and imperialism. At other times, the grafting of ideas occurred below the level of consciousness and may even have been unacceptable to those whose ideology, in fact, rejected nationalism as perverse. The Chinese Communists, who railed against imperialism, could not see that their Sinocization and imposition of socialist transformation on Tibet was effectively the same colonization processes and ethnic cleansing for which they faulted Western regimes.

The goal of ideologues, whether of religious or secular orientation, is to pursue a pristine future. For religious fanatics, the way forward involves a *return* to past traditions and the reestablishment of scriptural authority over both eternal and daily matters (Van Velzen, Thoden, and Van Beek 1988, 14). Across cultures, religious fundamentalism is a reaction to secularization, fueled by fear that the next generation may depart from the traditional way of life. Religious fundamentalists seek cultural authenticity as "followers of a tradition, not the trendsetters of a new one" (Van Velzen, Thoden, and Van Beek 1988, 14). Their protest, too, is one of tradition, and they turn toward "religious explanations for their troubles" and "religious enthusiasm as the solution" (Bruce 2000, 2). Their own texts and doctrines are sacred: for Christian fundamentalists, the Bible is "correct in every detail and complete in its revelation"; for Muslims, the Quran is "God's literal and eternal word" (Bruce 2000, 13). The texts and beliefs of other groups are heretical if they contradict the one "truth." Open-access libraries are humanistic institutions that provide a multitude of perspectives and, thus, are potential Trojan horses.

Because they accept scripture as literal and as the singular basis for all social and political life, religious fundamentalists are appalled at what they perceive as the diminishing presence of the divine in the world (Antoun 2001, 160). They set themselves apart from a trend toward relativism that gained hold in the nineteenth century. The logic of relativism ultimately trivializes religion by deconstructing doctrine, the structure upon which religious faith rests. Popular relativism does not attack any particular interpretation of a religious text. "It does worse: it denies that such texts can have a correct interpretation" (Bruce 2000, 35). The post-Enlightenment mindset—rational, secular, and pluralistic—undermines belief in a supreme being, the truth of divine revelations, and the authority of prophets and moral guidelines that have evolved over time. Those left without religious moorings in a turbulent modern world find that personal salvation and the fate of the world are equally difficult to envision. As the "emissaries of an All-Powerful, All-Knowing Being who has been betrayed by the freedom he granted the modern age," religious fundamentalists are "the last-ditch defenders of God" and their antagonists are any group, institution, or artifact that makes this defense necessary (Lawrence 1989, ix).

When fundamentalists use religious doctrine as the basis for comprehensive programs for public and private behavior, their beliefs become ideology. When charismatic leaders gain control of government, they steer the nation toward theocracy, in which specific ethical dictates derived from scripture gain political and legal enforcement. Flouting these dictates has divine implications as an offense against God, and in some situations offenders are subject to violent retribution. In Afghanistan, where the Taliban's Muslim fundamentalism had full reign, government campaigns to eradicate corruption involved punishing transgressors with beatings or executions, verbally and physically harassing Westerners, and destroying cultural objects that were associated with democratic values (Antoun 2001, 1). By concentrating all the things they do not like into a single force (evil), fundamentalists make it easier to defend any action or campaign because they can "transfer the horror of the greatest threat to the slightest" (Bruce 2000, 112). Beating a woman who appears in public without a male relative is justifiable because that woman is flouting not only Taliban rules but offending God. She is a personification of evil.

Books and libraries can be singled out by religious fundamentalists for many reasons. Prime among them is that the interpretation of their own religious texts as sacred corresponds to recognition of the power of ideas expressed in print. Secular texts that increase "options both for learning and for living" serve to displace religion from the center of life (Lawrence 1989, 232). They carry views that pose scientific knowledge, not spirituality, as the pillar of an examined life. Published records and literature make scientific research possible, and science accelerates change and complexity—a process that is incompatible with a view of the world that "locates values in timeless scriptures, inviolate laws, and unchanging mores" (Lawrence 1989, 232). The contents of libraries sustain complexity and pluralism and threaten the simplistic and homogeneous orientations of fundamentalism.

Libraries are problematic for both religious fundamentalists *and* secular ideologues, the other group implicated in massive cultural destruction. Both sets of extremists demonstrate the uncritical enthusiasm and zeal of the true believer. Rigid adherence to a literal interpretation of ideological tenets is characteristic of secular fanatics and religious fundamentalists alike, as is the potential for violence in the application of these tenets. As so thoroughly demonstrated in the twentieth century, both theocracies and ideocracies have totalitarian potential. Afghanistan's Taliban and the Iranian mullahs, who imposed orthodoxy on their societies, were not so very different from the Nazis and Chinese and Cambodian Communist regimes who all enacted programs of cleansing that included a decided focus on cultural materials as threats to their regimes and their visions of a transformed world.

Secular extremists embrace new or refurbished nonreligious ideas and doctrines that tend to be compatible with the social predisposition of their societies and mimic, or occasionally reinforce, the role of tradition and religion. Hitler's National Socialism, for example, gained a foothold in post–World War I Germany by tapping into existing anti-Semitic and populist currents. Ideologues can accommodate religion when its clerics support the regime and when religion is an important pillar of national identity. In the 1990s, the Christian Orthodox faith was a pivotal force in Serbia's aggression against Bosnia's Muslims, but it functioned within a larger ideology of racist nationalism. The impetus behind secular purification is a compelling transformative vision that dominates other imperatives, even religious ones, as it is translated into specific doctrinal dictates. From these dictates emerge policies that aim to govern thought and behavior as well as membership criteria. Outsiders are considered suspect, inferior, and beyond the moral obligations of the group, and as with religious fundamentalists, the demarcations of believer and heretic are established to build group unity and reinforce ideological solidarity. Secular ideologies have been called "politico-social secularized religions" because their doctrines are revered by adherents as if they were sacred texts and because leaders often acquire the status of a divine figure—such as Hitler, Stalin, and Mao (Gurian 1964; Piekalkiewicz and Penn 1995, 20). These cult figures encourage polarized thinking and the rejection of both traditional values and humanistic norms because they compete with party doctrine. The demand for orthodoxy is no less intense than under a religious regime, and it is held in place through a similarly closed intellectual system and rigid behavioral code.

Like religious fanatics, secular extremists must extinguish or at least attenuate modern forces that compete with their influence on behavior (Taylor 1991, x). But this task is more difficult for secular fanatics because of religion's focus on transcendence from the temporal world. In order for an extremist regime to advance its goals and maintain its influence, it must have its members' allegiance to the ideology and the regime; reason and fact must ultimately give way to faith, and objectivity to subjectivity. In writing about Eastern European Communists, Milosz (1990, 207) explains: "The Party too is a church. Its dictatorship over the earth and its transformation of the human species depend on the success with which it can channel irrational human drives and use them to its own ends." Social violence reaches extremes as the regime approaches success in replacing pluralism with homogeneity, humanism and internationalism with allegiance to doctrine, and critical thinking with zeal. As a regime extinguishes individual autonomy, it also chokes off intellectual freedom, objective scholarship, and unfettered access to books and libraries. A regime demanding total conformity fears books as an invitation to dialogue and dissent.

By the twentieth century, the secular nation-state had become the most common political structure and nationalism, when transformed into an ideology, a frequent precursor to extremism. According to Benedict Anderson (1991), modern people conceive of themselves as part of a community bound together by primordial identities that are shaped by common language, ethnicity, or religion. The emotional power gained from belonging to a beloved nation (especially one with claims to a glorious past) can promote feelings ranging from simple, benign patriotism to virulent militarism, imperialism, and racism—the latter being potential preambles to aggression. At the extreme end of the spectrum, fanatical nationalists seek to transform society by eliminating all competing influences—internal minorities as well as external enemies. Nationalistic ideologues are just as likely to destroy their own books as those of rival nations.

Earlier in this chapter, alienation and disempowerment were discussed in relation to the development of radical positions, the embrace of which offers people the satisfaction of efficacy and influence over their circumstances. Virulent nationalism is particularly attractive to "the insufficiently regarded . . . [who seek] to count for something among the cultures of the world" (Berlin 1991, 261), because its myths of national destiny legitimize aggression. In the last century, when national aggrandizement was pursued through war, the effect on books and libraries was devastating. Striving to secure an empire they believed to be divinely sanctioned yet elusive, Japanese troops during World War II devastated many libraries in China, Korea, and the Philippines. The destruction was the product of both the brutality drilled into the troops and strategies aimed specifically at extinguishing the cultural vitality of subordinate groups. A national sense of victimization by the West grew into a sense of racial superiority that served as a rationalization for the war and effectively prevented Japan from seeing itself as the aggressor it was (Tanaka 1998, 7). Similarly, the Nazis destroyed millions of Jewish books and as many as two-thirds of all the books in Poland, its proposed slave colony. Both Jews and Poles were considered inferior peoples, obstacles standing in the way of the German people's destiny. Racism provides easy justification for exterminating an enemy's culture and dismissing preservation. Because nationalists often burn their own books in rituals designed to link cultural purification with national and racial regeneration, it is not surprising that they resort to burning the books of their enemies. It is a tactic of domination and, when enacted against a rival group, it demonstrates the operating premise that cultural extinction is the ultimate fate of racial and recalcitrant political enemies who stand in the way of ideological goals.

Conservative values are a welcoming host to nationalism, which poses an inspiring, comforting, and familiar antidote to hard times. In the twentieth century, reactionaries had frequent recourse to extreme nationalism when attempts to put into effect Enlightenment-driven, modern ideals and democratic practices failed in societies plagued by ongoing economic crises, social polarization, and the atrophy of traditional and religious bonds (Kershaw 2001, 381). Hard times produced a backlash effect in which a population turned toward authoritarian leaders, traditional values, and the reassuring absolutes of nationalism. An extra emotional charge came from posing the retreat as rebirth and purification. The iconic case, of course, was the replacement of the ideals of the Weimar Republic with National Socialism. The party heroes were Teutonic knights, not French philosophers, and the Nazis' immediate embrace of biblioclasm was inspired by the notion that people express their unique *Geist* (spirit or genius) through their language, literature, and customs. The Nazis extrapolated to suggest that alien influences, vested in written works, compromised the dominance and fulfillment of German genius. At the bonfires in 1933, speeches lauded the German people's turn inward, away from decadence and toward rebirth and purification (Mosse 1984, 150). Images of the fires, which were broadcast around the world, thereafter left book burning associated with a contorted kind of purification, the embrace of social violence, and renunciation of the Enlightenment, humanism, and modernity.

Nazis' precedents of attacking books and libraries because they provide portals through which enemy values can find entry have been reenacted in twentieth-century Latin America. There the self-identified "guardian of public virtues" was often the military. In Chile and Argentina, the people adapted quickly to the authoritarian leadership style of military dictators after civilian regimes proved unable to provide stability. In these countries, a "doctrine of national security" was often the guiding ideology implicated in biblioclasm (Edwards 1984, 20). In Chile in 1973, immediately after a military coup that overthrew Salvador Allende's government, "attacks on books were open, indiscriminate, brutal and often tragicomic" (Edwards 1984, 20). Subversive books, especially Marxist ones, were openly burned; bookshops were raided; and publishers were forced to shred their stocks. These initiatives were rationalized as a defense of internal order against penetration by "foreign" ideas (Edwards 1984).

Social disorganization and political violence may so profoundly affect the people that many welcome a military takeover simply for the resulting imposition of order. In Argentina, 46 years of instability, crises, coups, and profound divisions between the right and left culminated in 1976 with a military coup. As dedicated proponents of a doctrine of national security and "protector of the nation's traditions, well-being, and public order," the junta felt it was its duty to attack alien forces and ideas that sought to undermine unity, Argentinean values, and the nation's internal purity (Staub 1989, 215). The chief enemy were the Communists, whom the regime demonized for using socialism as a new kind of weapon to capture the minds of vulnerable Argentineans, put in place a secular Communist state, and, through that state, endanger Christian civilization and the nation. According to a 1980 government publication on terrorism, Argentina had been targeted for destruction by Communist influences that penetrated every domain, including education. In the eyes of the regime, elementary school teachers who taught "self-education, based on freedom and the search for 'alternatives'" were Communist sympathizers engaged in an attempt to prejudice children and subvert respect for authority (Staub 1989, 216). The new regime quickly targeted books as potential carriers of subversive ideas. In 1976, shortly after the coup, the newspaper *La Razón* reported a book burning that prominently targeted Marxist authors. Lieutenant Colonel Jorge Eduardo Gorleri announced to journalists who had been invited to witness the event, "[We] are going to burn pernicious literature which affects our intellect and our Christian way of being . . . and ultimately our most traditional ideals, encapsulated in the words God, Country and Home" (Staub 1989, 217). In Germany, Argentina, Chile, and states where traditional values were given special stature and militant authoritarianism was the solution to social woes, there was a "contempt for learning" that found expression in violence against books (Stieg 1992, 19).

In Russia, Eastern Europe, and Asia, left-wing revolutionary ideologues, on the other hand, also played on discontent with contemporary conditions, but their proffered millennial dreams did not hold up. They heartily and aggressively rejected tradition as a basis for social decision making. Twentieth-century Communist regimes turned the full force of totalitarian violence at political and economic groups as well as historical, biological, ethnic, or religious groups. Their "crusading, exclusivist" ideology was aimed at the renewal of society along restructured class lines (Kershaw 2001, 381) and Communist Party leaders (Russian, Chinese, Cambodian) vied with each other, internally and externally, in the degree of fanaticism to which they implemented their theories. The Maoist-inspired decimation of China's intellectuals and libraries during the Cultural Revolution was surpassed only by Cambodia's Khmer Rouge regime, which exterminated the educated and urban populations and made books and libraries superfluous to their visions of a pure agrarian Communist state. Communists used the term *revolution* to pose their coups, and subsequent radicalization campaigns, as serious and irrevocable. J. W. Fulbright once observed, "A true revolution is almost always violent and usually it is extremely violent. Its essence is the destruction of the social fabric and institutions of a society, and an attempt, not necessarily successful, to create a new society with a new social fabric and new institutions" (as quoted in Blackey 1982, 405).

During periods of social disintegration, extremists may target books and libraries to challenge their rivals or protest a system that ignores them or violates their beliefs. When discontent reaches revolutionary flashpoint, iconoclasts and anarchists may annihilate libraries to take advantage of the chaos that accompanies regime change. In contrast, those with a plan for replacing a deposed government or system with another, more ideal one are more focused in their biblioclasm. In either case, books are endangered as violence is posed as necessary for sweeping away all that hinders change. Anarchism was advocated in pre–World War I Italy, where Domergue's successors, the Futurists, sought progress by casting off the past and fostering disorder. "Take up your pickaxes, your axes and hammers, and wreck, wreck the venerable cities, pitilessly!" they urged. "Come on! Set fire to the library shelves! Turn aside the canals to flood the museums!" (Berman 1982, 25). In nineteenth-century Russia, *Nihilism* was the name attached to an anarchist philosophy that advocated the violent destruction of social institutions as a path to a new society. Bakunin, its leading advocate, dreamed of "burning down all Russia" (Stites 1981, 3). Dmitri Pisareve advocated random destruction of cultural and historical objects and institutions, arguing (as did the Nazis later) that the worthy would manage to survive. "The breaking up, the smashing of something or other in general . . . is the first step toward culture," wrote the philosopher Rozanov in 1911 (as quoted in Stites 1981, 24). Twentieth-century extremists accommodated and channeled the nihilist sensibility, sometimes allowing it free play and, at other times, muzzling it. Chinese Communist leaders, for example, often disagreed on the issue of preservation and the accommodation of books and libraries into programs of social transformation, a division of thought that replicated the Jacobin-moderate split from the time of the French Revolution: Maoist radicals held that preserving books and libraries was a ploy to curtail the revolution, and moderates pushed for the purification of such materials and their use in promoting a transformed society. In Cambodia, there was no effective moderate group, and the Pol Pot regime had a strong nihilistic bent.

The Enlightenment fostered the idea of man as a rational being whose intellect, developed by learning, could drive sociopolitical reform. The promotion of ideals of free choice, the potential perfectibility of man and society, and change as the engine of progress prepared the ground for revolutions that, ironically, resulted in totalitarian systems that crushed the rights of the individual in the name of the people. The French Revolution "constituted an enormous watershed, ushering in an age in which the concept of revolution as such acquired a life of its own" (Parker 2000, 11). A pattern was set that repeated itself in revolutions for the next two centuries: The turbulent effects of modernization, and especially capitalism, brought instability and demands for reform; when these mandates were ignored or the reforms bungled, the regime's structural weaknesses were exposed and public pressure intensified to the point of explosive confrontation and revolution (Parker 2000, 6–7). Leaders channeled revolutionary furor toward ideological visions and the accompanying blueprint for reordering society and state. The early stages of revolution pose the most dangerous period for cultural objects, although fanatic leaders may recharge iconoclastic impulses whenever they need to revive support for radical programs and provide an outlet for public frustration over insufficient progress toward the promised utopia. The belief system and the leadership's degree of authoritarianism determine to a great extent both the survival of books and libraries and, in the long term, their use. All but the most extreme ideologues believe that if libraries can be sufficiently purged and controlled, then their preservation can be justified by using them as propaganda and as educational institutions for transmitting and supporting their visions. This notion of libraries is a narrowly expedient one that excludes intellectual freedom. Because of the dissident potential of books, ostensible gains from initial purging must be maintained by stringent, ongoing censorship. Ideologues' attitudes toward libraries parallel their attitudes toward individuals: both must be tethered in the interests of maintaining orthodoxy. The relationship is adversarial and profoundly distrustful. Because the contents of libraries can lead the reader astray, they must be controlled as part of programs to control the individual.

In an inversion of contemporary mainstream values, book destruction by ideologues in the twentieth century was staged as purification, an ostensibly constructive move toward a revitalization of the sociocultural environment. Although ideals were used to rally the masses and facilitate their own rise to power and all actions were taken in their name, the leaders' actual commitment to these ideals is difficult to determine. Power is notoriously corrupting, absolute power being absolutely so, as the English historian Lord Acton once pointed out. In the immediate postrevolutionary world, the leaders, the ideology, and the state became one. This conflation made it possible for leaders to rationalize violent excesses against those who would resist their plans. Followers often turned a blind eye to these excesses or justified them as necessary to achieving and maintaining order and reform. Both leaders and followers rushed to form a homogeneous community of like-minded people, to embrace practical values, and to substitute extremism and social solidarity for the alienation and impotence associated with freedom and modernity. Book destruction became a repudiation of the risky freedom made possible by critical thinking and intellectual autonomy.

Enlightenment notions of reason and rationality assumed that explanations (rationales) should be grounded in reason or fundamental principles. The rationales of extremists can more appropriately be seen as rationalizations, that is, explanations that, although seemingly based on reason, function primarily to justify questionable acts or beliefs. Extremists of the last century were enamored of the heady entitlement conferred by reason and translated the practice swiftly into an ability to rationalize and normalize any action in the interests of society, although, of course, they acted primarily in their own interest. In their ritual bonfires and public ceremonies, the Nazis even rationalized irrationality and celebrated its power to effect change. Modern extremists wielded rationalizations like weapons. Their discourse referenced religious doctrines, racial destiny, national security, and political beliefs (including democracy) as they pursued narrow agendas of dominance, and their rhetoric characterized all their actions as morally justifiable. While glorying in the ability to use ideas and beliefs to construct improved societies, they immediately foreclosed these privileges to others. The new autocrats returned to book destruction and censorship, the legacy of past tyrants, as a means to lock down society and enshrine their ideas as absolutes.

REFERENCES

Anderson, Benedict. 1991. *Imagined Communities: Reflections on the Origin and the Spread of Nationalism.* Revised Edition. New York: Verso.

Antoun, Richard T. 2001. *Understanding Fundamentalism: Christian, Islamic, and Jewish Movements.* Walnut Creek, Calif.: Altamira.

Arendt, Hannah. 1964. *Eichmann in Jerusalem: A Report on the Banality of Evil.* New York: Viking Press.

Avrich, Paul, ed. 1973. *The Anarchists in the Russian Revolution.* Ithaca, N.Y.: Cornell University Press.

Baczko, Bronislaw. 1989. "Vandalism." In *A Critical Dictionary of the French Revolution*, eds. François Furet and Mona Ozouf, trans. Arthur Goldhammer. Cambridge, Mass.: Belknap Press, 860–868.

Bartov, Omer, and Phyllis Mack. 2001. "Introduction." In *In God's Name: Genocide and Religion in the Twentieth Century*, eds. Omer Bartov and Phyllis Mack. New York: Berghahn Books, 1–19.

Berlin, Isaiah. 1991. *The Crooked Timber of Humanity: Chapters in the History of Ideas.* Ed. Henry Hardy. New York: Alfred A. Knopf.

Berman, Marshall. 1982. *All That Is Solid Melts into Air: The Experience of Modernity.* New York: Simon and Schuster.

Blackey, Robert, ed. 1982. *Revolutions and Revolutionists: A Comprehensive Guide to the Literature.* Santa Barbara, Calif.: ABC-Clio.

Bruce, Steve. 2000. *Fundamentalism.* Malden, Mass.: Polity.

Chartier, Roger. 1991. *The Cultural Origins of the French Revolution.* Trans. Lydia G. Cochrane. Durham, N.C.: Duke University Press.

Cigar, Norman. 1995. *Genocide in Bosnia: The Policy of "Ethnic Cleansing."* College Station: Texas A&M University Press.

Cobban, Alfred. 1960. *In Search of Humanity: The Role of the Enlightenment in Modern History.* New York: George Braziller.

Cohen, Roger. 1998. *Hearts Grown Brutal: Sagas of Sarajevo.* New York: Random House.

Curtis, Michael. 1979. *Totalitarianism.* New Brunswick, N.J.: Transaction Books.

Edwards, Jorge. 1984. "Books in Chile: How the Censorship of Books Has Evolved since 1973." *Index on Censorship* 13:20–22.

Einaudi, Mario. 1968. "Fascism." In *International Encyclopedia of the Social Sciences*, Vol. 11, ed. David L. Sills. New York: Macmillan Company and Free Press, 334–341.

Fromm, Erich. 1941. *Escape from Freedom.* New York: Holt, Rinehart and Winston.

Gamboni, Dario. 1997. *The Destruction of Art: Iconoclasm and Vandalism since the French Revolution.* New Haven, Conn.: Yale University Press.

Gay, Peter. 1969. *The Enlightenment: An Interpretation*, Vol. 2. [The Science of Freedom]. New York: W. W. Norton.

Gurian, Waldemar. 1964. "Totalitarianism as Political Religion." In *Totalitarianism*, ed. Carl J Friedrich. New York: Grosset and Dunlap.

Harris, Michael H. 1986. "State, Class, and Cultural Reproduction: Toward a Theory of Library Service in the United States." In *Advances in Librarianship*, Vol. 14, ed. Wesley Simonton. London: Academic Press, 211–252.

Kershaw, Ian. 2001. "Afterthought: Some Reflections on Genocide, Religion, and Modernity." In *In God's Name: Genocide and Religion in the Twentieth Century*, eds. Omer Bartov and Phyllis Mack. New York: Berghahn Books, 372–383.

Knuth, Rebecca. 2003. *Libricide: The Regime-Sponsored Destruction of Books and Libraries in the Twentieth Century*. Westport, Conn.: Praeger.

Koonz, Claudia. 2003. *The Nazi Conscience*. Cambridge, Mass.: Belknap Press.

Lawrence, Bruce B. 1989. *Defenders of God: The Fundamentalist Revolt against the Modern Age*. San Francisco: Harper and Row.

Leys, Simon. 1977. *Chinese Shadows*. New York: Viking Press.

Lokke, Carl. 1968. "Archives and the French Revolution." *American Archivist* 31 (1):23–31.

Markovic, Mihailo. 1974 . "Violence and Human Self-Realization. In *Violence and Aggression in the History of Ideas*, eds. Philip P. Wiener and John Fisher. New Brunswick, N.J.: Rutgers University Press, 234–252.

Martin, Henri-Jean. 1993. "The French Revolution and Books: Cultural Break, Cultural Continuity," trans. David Skelly and Carol Armbruster. In *Publishing and Readership in Revolutionary France and America: A Symposium at the Library of Congress, Sponsored by the Center for the Book and the European Division*, ed. Carol Armbruster. Westport, Conn.: Greenwood, 177–190.

Marx, Karl. 1963. *The 18th Brumaire of Louis Bonaparte*. New York: International Publishers.

Milosz, Czeslaw. 1990. *The Captive Mind*. Trans. Jane Zielonko. New York: Vintage International.

Mosse, George L. 1984. "Bookburning and the Betrayal of German Intellectuals," trans. James W. Jones. *New German Critique* 31:143–156.

Orwell, George. 1968. *The Collected Essays, Journalism and Letters of George Orwell, Vol. 2: My Country Right or Left 1940–1943*. Eds. Sonia Orwell and Ian Angus. New York: Harcourt, Brace and World.

Panitch, Judith M. 1996. "Liberty, Equality, Posterity?: Some Archival Lessons from the Case of the French Revolution." *American Archivist* 59 (1):30–47.

Parker, David. 2000. "Introduction: Approaches to Revolution." In *Revolutions and the Revolutionary Tradition in the West, 1560–1991*, ed. David Parker. London: Routledge, 1–14.

Piekalkiewicz, Jaroslaw, and Alfred Wayne Penn. 1995. *Politics of Ideocracy*. Albany: State University of New York Press.

Posner, Ernst. 1940. "Some Aspects of Archival Development since the French Revolution." *American Archivist* 3 (3):159–172.

Relyea, Harold C. 1994. *Silencing Science: National Security Controls and Scientific Communication*. Norwood, N.J.: Ablex.

Staub, Ervin. 1989. *The Roots of Evil: The Origins of Genocide and Other Group Violence*. Cambridge: Cambridge University Press.

Stieg, Margaret F. 1992. *Public Libraries in Nazi Germany*. Tuscaloosa: University of Alabama Press.

Stites, Richard. 1981. "Iconoclasm in the Russian Revolution: Destroying and Preserving the Past." Kennan Institute for Advanced Russian Studies, Occasional
Paper Number 147. Conference on the Origins of Soviet Culture. May 18–19,
1981. Washington, D.C.: The Wilson Center.

Tanaka, Yuki. 1998. *Hidden Horrors: Japanese War Crimes in World War II.* Boulder,
Colo.: Westview Press.

Taylor, Jay. 1993. *The Rise and Fall of Totalitarianism in the Twentieth Century.* New York:
Paragon House.

Taylor, Maxwell. 1991. *The Fanatics: A Behavioural Approach to Political Violence.*
London: Brassey's.

Thiem, Jon. 1979. "The Great Library of Alexandria Burnt: Towards the History of a
Symbol." *Journal of the History of Ideas* 40 (4):507–526.

Thrupp, Sylvia. 1962. "Introduction: Millennial Dreams in Action: A Report on the
Conference Discussion." In *Millennial Dreams in Action: Essays in Comparative
Study*, ed. Sylvia L. Thrupp. The Hague: Mouton and Co., 11–27.

Ugresic, Dubravka. 1998. *The Culture of Lies: Antipolitical Essays.* Trans. Celia
Hawkesworth. University Park: Pennsylvania State University Press.

Van Velzen, H.U.E. Thoden, and Walter E. A. Van Beek. 1988. "Purity: A Greedy
Ideology." In *The Quest for Purity: Dynamics of Puritan Movements*, ed. Walter
E. A. Van Beek. Berlin: Mouton De Gruyter, 3–33.

Part I

Grappling for Voice and Power

Modern sociologists have characterized societies as having a center and peripheries. At the center is government and the belief system upon which the government acts. A government's authority—its grip on power and control of the central belief system—depends on its ability to rally the population (especially minority groups that exist at the outer edge of society) around a set of values that are accepted as fundamental, even sacred. This value system is the font of power, and in every society there are peripheral groups that struggle to influence it. When alienated groups come to be led by extremists, they will renounce such values as pluralism and democracy with the ultimate goal of displacing the central value system with their own. By attacking a library, they may seek political influence, as was the case in Amsterdam (Chapter 3). Or, if there is ethnic polarization (as in the three Asian regions discussed in Chapter 4), an extremist group may destroy its rivals' libraries as a means of defeating another group's influence on society. Biblioclasm is a tactic for capturing the center.

CHAPTER 3

Political Protestors and Amsterdam's South African Institute, 1984

It is belief in absolutes, I would hazard, that is the great enemy today of the life of the mind . . . [H]istory suggests that the damage done to humanity by the relativist is far less than the damage done by the absolutist—by the fellow who, as Mr. Dooley once put it, "does what he thinks th' Lord wud do if He only knew the' facts in th' case."
—Arthur Schlesinger Jr., "The Opening of the American Mind"

On January 19, 1984, the afternoon calm of Amsterdam's South African Institute was suddenly disrupted as four young people, ostensibly using the library for research, blew a whistle and then opened a secured door to the street. Fifty associates wearing black stockings over their heads rushed in, cut the telephone wires, pulled over bookshelves, and smashed the microfiche reader and copier. In a matter of minutes, the books and documents (including archival clippings), the library's walls and furnishings (including artwork), and the building façade were splashed with "paint bombs"—little bags filled with tar, printer's ink, cooking oil, and black paint that burst on contact. The attackers appeared to be well informed, well organized, and working against the clock (Ester 1984). While some wreaked havoc on the first floor, others headed straight to the valuable Africana collection in the basement and began hurling the contents into the street and an adjacent canal. Rare editions of sixteenth- and seventeenth-century travel descriptions of southern Africa, documents from the time of the Boer Wars, as well as contemporary materials, disappeared into the fetid water. No resistance was offered, and no one was physically hurt. During the raid, the perpetrators said little by way of explanation except to declare that the institute supported apartheid ("*SA skatte verniel*" 1984).

The river police rescued some of the books from the Keizersgracht, a nearby canal, and a group of divers extended the search and monitored the locks of the waterways ("*Soektog na*" 1984). In the end, a total of six large postal bags were filled with sodden rescued books. Wim De Haan, a student majoring in Afrikaans at the University of Amsterdam, led an effort to separate the books and unstick their pages ("*Soektog na*" 1984), and bookbinders were called in to lend their expertise. A saving grace was that the chemical composition of the ink in the older, more valuable books was more resistant to water than the ink used in more contemporary books ("*Soektog na*" 1984). It was difficult to determine losses because the entire 10,000-volume-collection was in chaos; scattered books and index cards that ended up in the street were mangled by traffic, an unknown number of books had disappeared into the canal, and hundreds of books were water-soaked or covered in paint and oil (Ester 1984). G. J. Schutte, historian and chairman of the affiliated *Nederlands-Zuidafrikaanse Vereniging* (NZAV), despaired: "The books which have been retrieved were mostly on the same shelf. They were old, rare books from the 18th or 19th century. . . . Unfortunately, the shelf beside it is still empty. And it also contained old volumes with unique material, for example a photo album from the 19th century" (Van Seeters 1984c). P. E. Westra, director of the South African Museum, was particularly concerned about the archival collection, which contained some documents (without duplicate copies) from before the Second War of Freedom. He referred to damage to the writings as a "cultural disaster" ("*SA skatte in*" 1984). In a preliminary assessment, 80 books were sent to the restorers; another 100 so badly damaged they had to be discarded; 200 damaged by paint; and 400 damaged by oil. Hundreds of books, many rare or irreplaceable, were gone entirely. Also lost (presumed stolen) was a medal rack with 16 bronze and silver coins commemorating Dutch-South African or South African historical events. The library's immediate losses would soon be compounded by expenditures for restoring the facilities and recataloguing, reorganizing, and conserving damaged materials. Redoing the archive alone, only recently organized by a specialist, required hours of professional time (De Waard-Bijlsma 1984). The library was temporarily shut down in response to the devastation, causing a loss in research hours that could not be quantified.

A group of anti-apartheid protestors calling themselves the "Amsterdammers against Racism and Discrimination" (AARD) claimed responsibility for the library's destruction. The AARD was confronting the *Nederlands-Zuidafrikaanse Vereniging* (NZAV), a group that sponsored the library and fostered cultural links between South Africa, the Netherlands, and affiliated private cultural organizations that maintained relations despite anti-apartheid boycotts. The most overt of these groups was the *Nederlands-Zuid-Afrikaanse Werkgemeenschap*, founded in 1963 by reactionary politicians and clergymen who used letter campaigns to defend apartheid (Grundy 1974, 12). The AARD protestors were also sending a message to the Dutch government and a complacent public whose interaction with the South African regime, in the eyes of the protestors, kept apartheid in place. Their attack triggered an intense reaction that condemned library destruction as ignorant and fascist and that, for the most part, drowned out the original issues. The perpetrators angrily differentiated themselves from fascists (Nazis in particular) because they were not selecting books to be destroyed based on "race or conviction" (Van Dis 1984a). Instead, they said, they were protesting repressive ideas and an organization that used its resources, including a library, to support the consummate evil of apartheid (Van Seeters 1984a). For the AARD, the library was a "tool" of the enemy.

While portraying the material, financial, and cultural losses, this chapter focuses on the context, motivation, and implications of the attack. It is a complicated case and must be approached with both a wide lens and an eye for specificity. Although ostensibly a "localized" conflict (relatively small, and confined to a single library and single incident), it was generated by a political controversy over apartheid that spanned the globe. The origins of both apartheid and the global anti-apartheid movement are covered, and the perpetrators, their target, and the public's responses to the incident are situated within the contemporary political and social environment of the Netherlands. A spotlight is trained on the AARD, its rationalizations, and the social movements from which it sprang, as well as on the target institution, its sponsor and affiliations, and the specific nature of its collection. An argument could be made that both the anti-apartheid perpetrators and their intended target (the apartheid establishment and its supporters) were on the path of extremism, and this incident was a skirmish between two peripheral groups over respective beliefs. Certainly, the perpetrators of the attack sought to draw public attention to their cause and force resolution of the issue of Dutch involvement with the South African regime.

The case poses several questions that perhaps overshadow those intended by the attackers. An obvious one: How could an attack on an important research library occur in a literate, democratic country in 1984, almost 50 years after the trauma of Nazi book burnings had seared into global consciousness a renunciation of such actions? And, a little deeper: How did moral antipathy come to serve as political strategy and justification of biblioclasm by a liberal, countercultural group? The dynamics of this case offer a unique view of the processes of biblioclasm committed in the name of protest and of responses that resolutely link respect for libraries with tolerance and intellectual freedom.

The South African Institute (SAI) had the distinction of being one of the most outstanding libraries in which to study the history and literature of South Africa. The material losses, temporary shutdown, and subsequent limits on access were significant blows to a community of scholars. According to one, "It is the most important library on the subject of South Africa outside of

South Africa itself and in the area of Africana it is unique in many regards, including manuscripts" (Van Dis 1984a). The collection consisted of roughly 22,000 objects, many dating from the eighteenth and nineteenth centuries. The library contained all of the books published in South Africa before 1900, and its many original historical documents included the correspondence of Boer War leader Paulus Kruger (1825–1904) and his secretary. It held many of the first texts in the Afrikaans language—little books printed on poor-quality paper and looking cheap, "ostensibly worthless little pamphlets" that nevertheless offered "insight into the language struggle of the farmers who resisted the bondage of the English rulers" (Van Dis 1984b). The Afrikaans language, which had evolved away from the original Dutch, was one of the first expressions of Boer emancipation and the beginning of their consciousness as Afrikaners (Van Dis 1984b). Thus, materials in the library allowed study of the political-cultural movement of Afrikaner nationalism, which eventually pro-duced the doctrine and system of apartheid (O'Brien 1987, 444).

In addition, the library housed important contemporary materials. Many were from the South African regime, which had justified its racist policies through a prolific stream of books, pamphlets, maps, and other materials prepared deliberately to promote the white Afrikaners' view of history and geography. These documents declared that South Africa was uninhabited when the Dutch arrived in the seventeenth century, ignoring or distorting archeological research that confirmed extensive African settlement as far back as the Early Iron Age (Lane 1990). The moral justification of both the black homelands policy and of apartheid itself rested on claims that the black major-ity had never lived in any of the 87 percent of South Africa designated, in the twentieth century, as "white homeland" (Laurence 1987, 155). According to John C. Laurence (1987), the entire policy of apartheid was based on a deliberately fictionalized version of history so successfully disseminated that it led to global misunderstanding of the situation in South Africa. But the SAI library housed both regime-generated materials and the historical documents that countered these versions. Also, in contradiction to the cultural disenfran-chisement of South Africa's black population, this library contained not only the first editions of works by distinguished Afrikaans authors, but also one of the largest collections of contemporary works by black-African authors. The library regularly purchased books and journals from South African publishers who complied with government censorship and from external publishers who objected to the apartheid regime (Van Dis 1984a).

The scope of the collection resulted from the synergy of its two parts. The older and smaller part belonged to the NZAV and was set up when that organization was founded in 1881. It contained about 5,000 books, articles, and pamphlets, and valuable historical and cultural items related to the Freedom War, the Boer Republics, and the two language movements ("*Soektog na*" 1984). The other part was the South African Institute, a library created in 1930 as part of the University of Amsterdam. The mission of this branch was to support South African Language and Literature studies. After the war, a lack of funds forced the university to place the library under the aegis of the NZAV, where it functioned as "legally independent" of the NZAV while closely connected administratively (Van Dis 1984b). The university maintained ties through students and researchers; indeed, after the attack, Dr. Ernest Braches, director of the university library, joined in the outcry and pointed out that the library was used by the university as a valuable source of information on the intersection of Dutch and South African history (Van Dis 1984a).

The special nature of the collection, with its focus on South Africa and links with an organization that promoted cultural ties to that nation, raised the question of whether or not it was a propaganda library for the white apartheid government. Institute spokespeople vigorously refuted this suggestion on the grounds that, for more than 80 years, the library had provided the Dutch and European people with an objective view of South Africa by purchasing publications that presented diverse views of South African society (South African Embassy 1984). According to Dr. Schutte, the library reflected the whole of South Africa; its collections included "government publications and publications banned in South Africa [standing] side by side in a brotherly fashion" ("*Mogelijke*" 1984). Indeed, the library was often used for research by anti-apartheid movement members. In an article about the attack, the independent journalist and scholar of Afrikaans Adriaan Van Dis corroborated the library's accessibility to all:

The library was mainly used by researchers and students critical of the country [South Africa] . . . books of all kinds about and from South Africa were collected in the library; also works by the African National Congress which were forbidden in South Africa. . . . And that is why it was the only place where South African literature could be studied [systematically] in its entirety. . . . This is now no longer possible and in that way the study of and fight against the apartheid phenomenon has been dealt a great blow. (Van Dis 1984b)

In his article Van Dis went on to distinguish between the SAI and the NZAV, a distinction that the perpetrators did not make but that emerged in full after the attack focused attention on these two relatively unknown institutions. The South African Institute was first and foremost a library; its goals and objectives had to do with supporting knowledge. The NZAV was an organization with a broader cultural mission. It maintained an interest in the library as part of wide-ranging activities in support of Dutch-South African relations. The NZAV was founded in 1881 at the time of the Boer Wars, when the Dutch were still wholeheartedly behind the Afrikaner Boers in their fight against British imperialism and their struggle to retain their own Dutch-based culture. The Afrikaners, after all, were the descendants of Dutch settlers who arrived at the Cape of Good Hope in 1652 and thrived under the mantle of the Dutch East Indies Company until 1806, when the British assumed control. "Help for and strengthening of the kinsman," the Dutch-Afrikaner element in South Africa, remained a central goal of the NZAV in the twentieth century (Fennema 1984b). By the 1980s, members of the NZAV consisted mainly of people who were interested in South Africa either from this traditional point of view of shared cultural roots or from the more distanced view of scholarship. Those with family ties took pride in being the "friends of South Africa, and in particular of that section of the people who fought for freedom in 1881," said Professor Frits De Waard, former chairman and a prominent NZAV member, who added, "We are happy that the Afrikaner people have been able to prove their vitality in the past hundred years" (Fennema 1984a). Despite South Africa's pro-Nazi proclivities during the 1940s, when the Netherlands was at war with Germany, and the current regime's embrace of reactionary and racist policies, ties between the two countries remained strong. The NZAV promoted exchanges, provided teachers and teaching materials to Dutch and South African schools, encouraged Dutch emigration, and cosponsored cultural activities with the South African Embassy. In 1982, De Waard went on record as saying that the organization was trying to "neutralize" the negative image of South Africa in the Netherlands through communication. Others stressed the position of the organization as "neither pro nor anti-apartheid" (Grundy 1974, 2).

The NZAV played a dominant role as liaison between the two countries until a South African Embassy was established in the Netherlands in 1972 ("*Pres. Steyn*" 1984). Thereafter, the NZAV's functions were formalized in an official Cultural Agreement between the Dutch and South African governments. Both governments provided money for cultural interactions, and the NZAV became the "de facto executor of the Agreement on the Dutch side" (Fennema 1984a). The main rationales of the Cultural Agreement were that familiarity with the Dutch culture and way of life was desirable for South Africans (Heldring 1984) and, similarly, that Europeans benefited from contact with South African culture (Fennema 1984a). However, as the anti-apartheid movement gained ground in the Netherlands in the 1970s, relations with South Africa deteriorated and the Dutch government was pressured to cut official ties with South Africa's government. Despite the lobbying efforts of NZAV members, the Cultural Agreement was frozen in 1979 and officially nullified in 1982, when the Dutch government decided that the benefits of the sponsored cultural programs did not extend equally to both races and, for that reason, it would no longer facilitate or tolerate racist policy (Bosgra 1984).

The officers and most active members of the NZAV rejected a complete cultural boycott, which seemed to them like "an abortion of the influence which Dutch culture can have on South Africa" (Van Seeters 1984b). Instead, they quietly exercised what they felt was a private mandate to maintain ties with the "outlaw state" and, through cultural intercourse, influence its reform. It was this decision that put the organization on a path that diverged from that of the anti-apartheid movement, global public opinion in general, and a small group of Dutch radicals in particular. NZAV members believed that they were engaged in relatively neutral cultural interactions, not political activities; some may even have felt that their actions amounted to a positive, quasi-therapeutic dialogue with a troubled sister state whose reform was more likely to result from engagement than from isolation. This interaction did not sit well with members of the anti-apartheid movement who saw isolation as the primary weapon in the fight against apartheid and who viewed any contact with South Africa as legitimizing the state's racist policies. The conflict over these contradictory approaches to South Africa and its policies, as played out in the Netherlands, resonated with similar debates around the world regarding the relative efficacy of dialogue versus isolationism in promoting apartheid reform. As the anti-apartheid movement radicalized, extremists increasingly foreclosed this debate and conflated any form of involvement with South Africa with active racism. They divided the world into those who were against apartheid and those who were for it. Those who were deemed pro-apartheid were racist and therefore beyond the pale. They had to be confronted.

The term *apartheid* was first used in South Africa's parliament in 1944, when D. F. Malan, leader of the Nationalist Party, spoke of it as a policy "to ensure the safety of the white race and of Christian civilization" (Shepherd 1977, 3). Later, in a solicited letter describing apartheid to American church leaders, Malan (1987, 94) attributed the deep-seated color consciousness of white South Africans to fundamental differences between the races and fear of being overrun by an inferior majority. "The difference in color [between white and black South Africans]," he wrote, "is merely the physical manifestation of the contrast between two irreconcilable ways of life, between barbarism and civilization, between heathenism and Christianity, and finally between overwhelming numerical odds on the one hand and insignificant numbers on the other." Apartheid was formally introduced as policy in 1948, although it was not rigorously pursued until H. F. Verwoerd became prime minister in the 1950s. For Verwoerd, apartheid's slogan, "Keeping It White," meant one thing: "namely White domination, not leadership, not guidance, but control, supremacy" (Grundy 1991, 8). The white government passed laws that institutionalized the dominance of its race and the complete separation of the black majority. According to activist-scholar Breyten Breytenbach (1987, 29), the state's totalitarianism rested on structural and official racism and violent control of its own citizens; he judged it a conscious banalization of humanity. Its sole aim was to perpetuate itself.

With its adoption of apartheid and minority rule, South Africa fell out of step with world values at precisely the time when principles of self-determination and racial equality were gaining acceptance as international norms. Public opinion favored immediate decolonization, and South Africa's recalcitrance sparked protests that coalesced into an anti-apartheid movement that spanned the globe. For many, including the AARD, it was a cause in which making a difference was truly possible and the issues were refreshingly simple: South Africa's inhumane and exploitative policies clearly exposed its segregation and systematic discrimination as immoral (Grundy 1991, 21). The movement gained ground in the late 1950s and maintained its commitment to peaceful action until the mid-1960s, when younger, more radical groups, particularly in Great Britain, brought in ideas of liberation and new modes of protest: boycotts, demonstrations, strikes, and civil disobedience that sometimes turned violent (Shepherd 1977, 37). In the United States, anti-apartheid was a fundamental part of the civil rights movement as it radicalized during the 1960s and 1970s. In both the United States and Great Britain, racial discrimination became an emotional issue, and demonstrations of moral outrage over the situation in South Africa were commonplace (Grundy 1974, 24). In a relatively unprecedented sign of solidarity, churches and colleges joined the cause. Activists used investigative techniques to expose government and corporate connections to the South African government and urged across-the-board divestment, cancellation of subsidies, and isolation of the state as a pariah regime.

As South Africa was condemned to a growing "moral loneliness" (Vandenbosch 1970, 259), the regime became more and more entrenched in institutionalizing white domination. Conservative white South Africans were intensely frustrated by the isolationist stance. For them, apartheid policy was simply a "cool-headed response to the logic of an inherited situation" (Manning 1972, 598). In the journal *Foreign Affairs*, commentator George F. Kennan (1971, 220) described the Afrikaners' belief that they were

confronted with a very real problem when it comes to maintaining, in the face of a large black African majority, their own historical and cultural identity. It is a remarkable identity, forged and affirmed over the course of centuries, at times in struggle and diversity, and against a background of circumstances in some respects different from that which any other people has ever had to face. It is an identity in which, as in the case of the Israelis, national components are mixed, for better or for worse, with religious ones; and the Afrikaners are not more inclined to jeopardize it.

Scholar Kenneth Grundy (1991, 18) theorizes that single-minded dedication to apartheid was part ideological and part desperation: the leadership, although "the enlightened among them realize that apartheid has failed them," simply did not know what to replace it with.

Indeed, within South Africa, the regime actively discouraged alternate visions and sociopolitical solutions that threatened its power. The contents of South African libraries were subject to censorship, and all aspects of publishing and scholarship were highly constrained. The legitimacy of white rule and entitlements depended on Afrikaner versions of history that scholars refuted at their peril. In 1979, at a theological conference at the University of South Africa, distinguished historian Floors Van Jaarsveld was tarred and feathered when he challenged aspects of the nationalist version of Afrikaner history (upon which apartheid was erected) (O'Brien 1987, 449). Misunderstood and bitter that South Africa was apparently "the most loudly and systematically hated country in the world today" (Manning 1972, 603), Afrikaners generally reacted defensively to external criticism and what they perceived to be a hysterical and hostile international community (Manning 1972, 598). Through diplomatic channels and the media, they officially protested against anti-apartheid activities. They ran campaigns to educate the global public about the necessity and efficacy of apartheid and to pose white Africans as victims of international vilification campaigns. One sympathetic British professor emeritus protested, on their behalf, that "the build-up of Pavlovian disapproval among the highminded is now so formidable as to recall the comparable animus in Nazi Germany against the Jews, an animus engendered and kept ardent, in the main, by similar techniques" (Manning 1972, 606). White South Africans were especially quick to counter negativity from the Dutch community because historic ties with the Netherlands made the criticism more personal, almost a betrayal (Worrall 1972, 580).

Global anti-apartheid activism achieved its greatest success with its campaign to exclude South Africa's all-white athletic teams from all international competitions, including the Olympics. In the late 1960s, after large and often violent grassroots demonstrations and the active involvement of approximately 90 nations, South Africa was expelled from the International Olympic Committee and either expelled or suspended from international competition in sports that included soccer, boxing, tennis, and gymnastics (Lapchick 1975, 197). Although decade-long policies of polite remonstrance had achieved nothing, absolute isolation in international sporting competitions had finally inspired internal protests against regime policies and some movement toward the racial integration of South African sports teams (Lapchick 1975, 205). These successes were not lost on activists, who interpreted the expulsions as validating their belief that any contact with South Africa, no matter how benign in appearance, supported the apparatus of apartheid. This premise would thereafter drive the movement's activities and quell, within the movement, the controversy over bridge-building versus isolationism.

However, acceptance of this premise did not extend outside the anti-apartheid movement, and a division of approaches to the problem of apartheid persisted for another two decades. Activists favored total political and social disengagement from South Africa (and parallel support for liberation movements) in order to increase opposition to the regime and undermine white domination. Those outside the movement yet somewhat sympathetic to its goals, by contrast, favored engagement, because they thought that aggressive techniques like isolation created a resistant and defensive mentality, while also weakening the condition of the Africans themselves (Shepherd 1977, 143). They reasoned that disengagement and isolation may "cleanse the soul," but do not necessarily end apartheid (Grundy 1991, 99). This approach was favored by the governments of (non-African) trading partners, such as the United States and Great Britain. In a battle over public opinion in the West, the anti-apartheid movement and the apartheid regime both claimed that the other used psychological warfare to either attack or maintain South Africa's legitimacy (Shepherd 1977, 208). The apartheid regime, its adherents, and even some gradualists posed white South Africans as the misunderstood victims of this psychological war. Isolationists within the United Nations did not relent in efforts to keep the South African state, which "reject[ed] the very concept of mankind's unity," from benefiting from the "strength given though friendly international relations" (Barratt 1972, 558). In 1979 alone, 18 General Assembly resolutions against apartheid were passed, each of which expressed the idea that all international connections with South Africa (political, economic, or cultural) helped to maintain the status quo in that state and thus to sustain racial tyranny (Shepherd 1977, 152). Critics pointed out that visits by prominent figures demonstrated that the domestic racial détente was working; foreign visitors thus unwittingly contributed to perceptions of South African policy as credible.

International and local pressure to cut ties with the South African government continued from the 1960s through the 1980s. The Dutch government found breaking off relations with the South African state economically unfeasible, as well as socially difficult. Political developments were still influenced by the descendants of seventeenth-century Dutch emigrants, the Afrikaners or Boers, who maintained ethnic and cultural identification with the Netherlands. The connection was at the basis of Boer identity, which had developed in response to policy changes that occurred as a result of a British takeover in 1795. In the Netherlands, the anti-apartheid movement effectively promoted the idea that *all* interaction with South Africa legitimized apartheid. The argument was that Dutch trade and the steady influx of Dutch white-collar workers into South Africa benefited the economy of that country and, thus, the regime. Similarly, Dutch emigration widened the constituency of the sympathetic within the Netherlands, effectively serving as a propaganda agent for the regime (Grundy 1974, 14). In a "mounting crescendo of disharmony," activists tried to discourage the Dutch government from both trade and traditional subsidies to emigrants (Grundy 1974, 10). Throughout the 1960s, the Dutch government clung to the position that continued relations and dialogue with South Africans would offer better prospects for change than isolation. But as time passed, more and more public pressure was exerted on the Dutch government to acknowledge that its policy of dialogue had failed to yield results in South African policy. The pressure came from without and within. Throughout the 1970s, as the generally liberal, outward-looking, and internationalist Dutch people began to reject supposed "blood ties" and differentiate themselves from the Afrikaners, the Afrikaners became further entrenched in their role as a "self-proclaimed tenacious people" (Grundy 1974, 14). Most Dutch citizens now rejected the idea that they should protect their "brothers and sisters" and "cushion their contact with a hostile world," and even the idea, previously embraced by some, that those brother and sisters were an embarrassment and "must be guided to a more humane, contemporary world view" (Grundy 1974, 15). As detachment and condemnation set in, it became stylish in Dutch intellectual circles to criticize South Africa (Grundy 1974, 29). Anti-apartheid activists sharply differentiated themselves from avidly pro-apartheid organizations, an ambivalent government, and a hostile public. Occupying the middle ground was the NZAV, which quietly lobbied the government for the extension and activation of cultural ties (Grundy 1974, 12) but professed to be neither for nor against apartheid.

Whether or not the NZAV was truly neutral on the issue of tolerance of the segregationist policies of the South African regime is arguable. Anti-apartheid advocates saw the NZAV as part of a complex network of indepen-dent pro-South African organizations whose common members and officers and communications networks formed a tightly knit structure (Fennema 1984b). Indeed, the NZAV housed several other organizations that funded emigration loans and gave study grants to South Africans. Although it was possible to make the case that the NZAV was itself a relatively independent, relatively inactive organization that charitably sought constructive dialogue with South Africa, a case of guilt by association could also be made, especially as public tolerance for contact dwindled (*"Deel Bibliotheek"* 1984). In a sense, the NZAV was caught between those who thought it did too little to support apartheid and those who thought it did too much.

After the Cultural Agreement was nullified in 1982, the NZAV quietly con-tinued cultural relations with South Africa and promotion of Dutch influence there (*"Nederlands-Zuidafrikaanse Vereniging"* 1984). The Dutch government had not prohibited private organizations from doing so and neither had it terminated trade relations with South Africa, making its nullification of the Cultural Agreement a relatively empty gesture (Heldring 1984).

Social movements are a form of collective action undertaken to change exist-ing cultural patterns at the levels of individual behavior, social institutions, and structures (Jennett and Stewart 1989, 4). Movement activists generally display a deep idealism. Participants promote reform by asserting the moral superi-ority of their views and by changing people's hearts and minds rather than capturing elections or fomenting revolution (Jennett and Stewart 1989, 16). The ultimate objective, of course, is to change central belief systems. Social movements tend to be loose in structure; often they form quickly and then dis-appear (Jennett and Stewart 1989, 1). Membership is open and, indeed, move-ments provide a niche for activists with a range of political positions, from liberal to anarcho-individualist (Jennett and Stewart 1989, 12). Because social movements coalesce around values that are not open to compromise, there is a potential toward fundamentalism in all movements (Cohen 1985). What outsiders perceive as irrationality sets in when mindsets become extreme, and radical members reject governmental structures (such as the law) as institu-tionalized oppression, pose the establishment as violent, see themselves as conducting a crusade, and begin to measure reality against an ideal that is "the morality of the movement, which is assumed and claimed to be [absolutely] right" (Eder 1985, 884). In the face of official and public indifference to their cause, protestors may channel impotence and alienation into violent action and easily rationalize tactical and ideological vandalism.

Known since the 1960s for its "imaginative and playful" counterculture, Amsterdam, by the 1980s, had developed into a key site for social protest (Katsiaficas 1997, 115). It was the center for various overlapping causes that were promoted by networks known as social movements or, by sociologists in search of greater precision, as *new* social movements. During the 1960s and 1970s, countercultural groups with strong anti-institutional views committed civil disobedience in the name of democracy and found community among movements that were fighting colonialism, racism, patriarchy, capitalism, and economic exploitation (Jennett 1989). A "squatter movement" materialized in response to a pronounced housing shortage, which was blamed on municipal policies of liberalization, deregulation of housing, and decreased commitment to low-cost housing. When, beginning in 1965, squatters occupied vacant houses that were scheduled for demolition, they met with a degree of public sympathy and social accommodation, their activity perceived as a constructive reaction to a very real housing shortage. As a result, the laws pertaining to housing became quite liberal: once a table, a chair, and a bed had been moved into a vacant apartment, the occupant was legally entitled to stay (Katsiaficas 1997, 117).

By the mid-1970s, squatters numbered in the thousands and had formed a new social movement that took the form of an informal network. The squatters were not the usual homeless poor; many were young, well educated, and employed. There was no central organization or spokesperson, but a deepseated, common set of alternative values, plus consensus as to what they were against, ensured unity among the autonomous members (Melucci 1985, 793). Volunteers served the community in various ways. In some squatted properties, their rudimentary information centers dispensed advice, manuals on squatting, a monthly journal, and books. There was a squatters' newspaper and radio station, and in many cases, a press team, a propaganda team, and an information team was formed for a particular "action" (Draaisma and Van Hoogstraten 1983, 408). The squatters eventually assumed a Robin Hood persona as they formed networks and distributed "liberated" housing as they saw fit (Priemus 1983, 420). In the 1980s, sociologists even began to study the groups and the myths that surrounded these protagonists of "urban struggles" (Castells 1983, 405).

This persona, however, also led to escalating conflicts over squatted properties and a crisis that resulted in violent confrontations with the police during demonstrations in 1975. Thereafter, city officials became more conciliatory, and the next five years passed in relative calm as squatters consulted with municipal officials on solving housing issues (Anderiesen 1981, 83). By the end of the decade, the number of people on waiting lists for housing had climbed to 50,000 (even though fewer than 800,000 people lived in all of Amsterdam). Progress toward solving housing problems had clearly stalled. Still, Amsterdam residents were stunned when on December 19, 1979, a group of squatters disrupted a meeting of the municipal council, declared that "the limit was reached," and set off smoke bombs to break up the meeting (Anderiesen 1981, 84). This event signaled a new period of radicalization. Squatters aggressively occupied buildings and resisted eviction, erected barricades in and around contested properties, and engaged in turbulent clashes with the police. They saw themselves as defending their rights against a violent and uncaring power structure that was bought and paid for by a greedy opportunistic elite.

As the violence "gained an independent status beyond the purpose of the direct defense of squatted properties" (Draaisma and Van Hoogstraten 1983, 412), public sympathy and support quickly eroded. It would decline precipitously after squatter participation in riots during the coronation of Queen Beatrix in April 1980. At this time squatters protested the $25 million cost of the celebration with the slogan "No place to live, no coronation" and provoked a physical confrontation with the police; they fought so tenaciously that the police lost control of the situation and several officers were hurt and traumatized (Katsiaficas 1997, 116). In March, in a show of "military overkill," tanks and armed cars with more than 1,000 insurgency police were sent in to remove squatter barriers in front of buildings at the corner of Constantijn Huygensstraat and the Vondelstraat (Anderiesen 1981, 83). The message that the extremists thought they were sending, of principled protest, was increasingly perceived to be that of undisciplined hooliganism.

The squatters were able to control the streets for a while, but eventually Dutch tolerance became "tempered with a new edge of legal reprimand and revengeful violence" (Katsiaficas 1997, 116). Average citizens, football teams, and neo-fascist groups formed committees and donned steel-tipped boots and helmets to assist police in clearing buildings. As the incidents became increasingly ugly, squatters escalated their deviance and vandalized some contested properties, burned a streetcar, destroyed a historical statue, and threw smoke bombs at the mayor's house. In 1982, when they placed bombs in brokers' offices and threatened the homes of councillors, response stiffened further and the media began describing the movement's activities as "political terrorism." Police attempts to clear a squatted villa resulted in a pitched battle and the suspension of civil rights in Amsterdam for three days. At this point, the radical squatters came to be viewed by authorities as "a savage hoard" (Draaisma and Van Hoogstraten 1983, 409) and "a threat to public order" rather than a symptom of a housing problem (Anderiesen 1981, 88). They were subjected to violent beatings in encounters with the police.

Within the squatter movement as a whole, there appeared to be a split between *bona fide* squatters and the rioters who increasingly grabbed the headlines. Although there was some internal criticism of the momentum toward militancy, the more moderate squatters—those who practiced squatting as self-help or as a protest against specific urban-development policies—did not openly denounce the violence or distance themselves publicly from those who embraced anarchy as a response to authority, capitalism, and Dutch society (Priemus 1983, 424). What had begun as a peaceful social movement had descended into threat and violence (Draaisma and Van Hoogstraten 1983, 412). It had also spawned an activist group, "Amsterdammers against Racism and Discrimination (AARD)," whose members empathized with the blacks in South Africa and saw themselves as similarly victimized by corrupt government policies, police violence, and a right-wing populace.

Public opinion in the Netherlands became increasingly polarized. The AARD was responding to an atmosphere of violence that was also fed by the rise of an extreme right-wing presence. The squatters were an idealistic group; their response to a deteriorating socioeconomic environment was to form a social movement that was committed to housing reform. Many, like AARD, were "multi-purpose liberationists." They also participated in a constellation of sister movements—anti-apartheid, world peace, nuclear disarmament—and sought to transform the values underpinning Western political and economic decisions (Jennett 1989, 104). Other Dutch citizens, alienated by urbanization, social unrest, and economic disparities, chose to respond to hard times by embracing the political right. This "new right" was patriotic, xenophobic, and conservative, and sought reform through political means rather than civil disobedience and protest. To gain votes, its political candidates appealed to populist sentiments of aversion to the immigrants, asylum seekers, and foreign workers who had become a prominent feature of urban life. Indeed, between 1970 and 1983, immigrants from former Dutch colonies had poured into the Netherlands by the thousands. They were reacting to depressed economies and political unrest at home and were drawn to the cultural environment of Amsterdam. In less than 15 years, the number of residents from Surinam had quadrupled to about 190,000, and there were 35,000 immigrants from the Dutch Antilles. Turks and Moroccans numbered 155,000 and 106,000, respectively. By associating these groups with problems such as unemployment, crime, disease, national decline, and so on, the extreme right made them scapegoats for the country's problems (Hainsworth 1992). As the economy slowed and the standard of living declined, right-wing political parties gained support by advocating repatriation and restrictions on immigration, and urged the government to protect the native Dutch population from foreign "occupation" and domination.

The political racism of the right was not lost on members of Amsterdam's countercultural social movements, especially when a group sponsored by the short-lived *Nationale Centrum Partij* (National Center Party) raided an Amsterdam church purported to be sheltering illegal immigrants and beat them up (Mudde and Van Holsteyn 2000, 147). After a storm of protest, this party dissolved and one week later reformed as the *Centrum Partij*, the Center Party (CP). The CP had "a clear ethnically exclusionist appeal though without the connotations of outright extremism and the neo-Nazism" associated with earlier right-wing parties (Husbands 1992, 111). The party's argument was simple: "500,000 foreigners in our country and 500,000 unemployed" (Harris 1990, 41). In 1984, the party captured almost 10 percent of the vote and two seats in a municipal election. The squatters, already antagonized by run-ins with ultra-right gangs who "defended" properties they had attempted to claim through squatting, labeled all those they saw as right-wing as "fascist racists," lumping into a single category groups that ranged from Dutch street gangs and the CP to South Africa's apartheid regime itself. On January 16, 1984, three days before the attack on the South African Institute, a group of squatters (some of whom later identified themselves as members of AARD) made headlines by storming into the Council Chamber in Almere and using their fists to disrupt the inauguration ceremony of the newly elected CP councillors. A disgusted journalist reported the scene: "The councillors were hit on the head with beer bottles, and their clothes, as well as those of the bystanders and police, were covered with paint, all this under the guise of—as the people carrying out this violence explained—expressing a dignified and peaceful protest [*sic!*]" ("*Anti-fascisten horde*" 1984). A later interview with a perpetrator, who identified himself as a squatter, provided clues to the group's motivation and attitudes:

[S]hould we wait until the foreigners are shoved into trains and deported? We have nothing to lose. Our actions make it clear that the Center Party is no good. Our people will always assault people from the Center Party. Now that the Center Party is legal I don't mind warning potential members that their windows will be broken if they openly adhere to the party. It should be normal that somebody who is singing drunken racist songs in the pub is thrown out. We must undertake timely and strong action against racism. The newspapers are afraid of fighting in the street. But that has been around for a long time. Gangs from the right have been active for many years already. And they're saying we can't beat up a couple of members of the Center Party from time to time? (Van Seeters 1984a)

Reactions to the Almere incident were diverse. In one newspaper, a commentator deplored the Center Party but nevertheless warned squatters of the dangers of fighting fire with fire (De Kok 1984). A new committee calling itself "Almere Knows Better" saw the squatters as violating democratic boundaries through a sort of leftist fascism ("*Anti-fascisten horde*" 1984). Its concern was mirrored in incensed letters to the editor that appeared in Dutch newspapers. One irate citizen pointed out that "the public jolly well knows that the real fascism, the Nazi-methods, have never been applied by the CP, but they have been by the so-called anti-fascists" ("*Anti-fascisten horde*" 1984). Another concerned citizen quoted the famous prediction of Dutch scholar Sam De Wolff (1878–1960): "If fascism makes a comeback, it will present itself as anti-fascism," comparing the Almere perpetrators to prewar Nazi paramilitaries who used the same arguments to silence opposing viewpoints ("*Anti-fascisten horde*" 1984). Still others who defended the squatters and equated the CP with the Nazis held that although the squatters' methods were unpleasant and excessive, they were necessary in fighting for an anti-fascist society. For a radical subsection of the squatter's supporters, the deeds were "praiseworthy" and a desirable alternative to "giving that scum [the Nazis] space again" ("*Anti-fascisten horde*" 1984). Indeed, to this group, the protest was insufficient in light of recent right-wing attacks on colored immigrants, including the attack in the church (Van Seeters 1984a).

The squatters who demonstrated at Almere believed that the Center Party's racism had forfeited its members' right to freedom of speech, to organize, and to participate in politics. When accused of being undemocratic, a squatter stated defiantly:

Honor democracy? Do I have to do that for a democracy that subsidizes the Center Party and gives it broadcasting time? In doing that, the taboo on racism is broken. The Center Party becomes a highly respectable party . . . [it] can build up a framework. I do not want to allow that. I cannot talk to Vierling [the CP leader]. As far as I am concerned there is only one solution for that man: out with him. I don't want to have a reasonable discussion with him. He is an intelligent man, which is why he is so dangerous. (Van Seeters 1984a)

This statement reveals a common weakness in social movements, identified by sociologist Alain Touraine (1985, 779) as runaway intolerance that threatens the very foundations upon which the movement is based. In terms of the squatter and anti-apartheid movements, the foundations were equality, democracy, intellectual freedom, and freedom of speech and assembly. Rationalizing violence against anyone whose opinions differed from its, a splinter group within the squatter movement moved from idealism, pacific activism, and democratic methods to quasi-ideological intolerance for any organization remotely associated with apartheid. The firestorm of universal condemnation that followed its attack on the library, like the Almere incident, involved general rejection of its methods but spawned controversy. There was confusion over the fundamental missions and ethics of the AARD, the anti-apartheid movement in general, the NZAV, and the apartheid regime that it seemed to support. In the uproar, whether or not the protestors had successfully indicted the Dutch government and population for their role in festering social conflict became a moot point. In fact, the group seemed merely to have fed social chaos, clouded issues, and contributed not only to its own marginalization, but to the continued peripheral status of its causes.

Newspapers exploded in condemnation of the attack on the library. A public dialogue was conducted in editorials, features, and letters to the editor in newspapers in the Netherlands and South Africa alike. This dialogue included the usual humanistic laments on the sanctity of libraries and the barbarism of those who destroy them, as well as a wide-ranging, though shallow, discussion over contemporary issues and values. On the table were such topics as freedom of speech, intellectual freedom, tolerance, democracy, apartheid, morality, the boundaries of protest, norms that protect cultural institutions, and the meaning of libraries. The discourse was animated by the individual voices that emerged: those of the indignant perpetrators and their defender, poet Julian With; concerned South African and Dutch citizens; as well as journalists and commentators such as Adriaan Van Dis and Wilfried Fennema, anti-apartheid activist Boudewijn Buch, and NZAV chairman G. J. Schutte.

In South Africa, newspapers responded to the attack on the library with out-rage and moral indignation. However, white journalists professed little surprise, because of "the climate of almost paranoid interference with South Africa" that the Dutch anti-apartheid groups had fostered in the Netherlands ("*Vandalisme in Amsterdam*" 1984a). "These young vandals from Amsterdam only did what their older generation has been preaching for years," an Afrikaner newspaper declared ("*Aartjies na*" 1984). However, at least one commentator left open the question of whether the "spirit of intolerance and blind enmity" was shared by all Dutch citizens: "First it was the Germans, and now this is an occupation by the riff-raff. If the silent majority would speak out, then a group such as this one would never have been able to do this" ("*Vandalisme in Amsterdam*" 1984b). From the South African perspective, the Dutch population as a whole was guilty of collaboration with radicals because it had allowed one group to dominate discourse, flout the law, and employ coercive techniques to impose its will. Identifying within the perpetrators a "desire for destruction which one would only expect from barbarians lacking in any sense of culture or supporters of a desperate and blinkered ideology [*anti*-apartheidism]," South Africans were able to use the criticism of blind ideological allegiance that so often had been levied at them (South African Embassy 1984). For Afrikaners, ignorant idealism was an important explanation for what they viewed as the excommunication of South Africa from the world community (Rhoodie 1969, 48). Their press appeared eager to reinforce this explanation and divert critical attention from apartheid by identifying the perpetrators of the attack as representative of the "fanatic" and "stupid" opposition. No doubt it was a relief for white South Africans to find community again with the rest of the world; editors of the newspaper *Die Burger* found it "cheering" to see that the whole world condemned this act of cultural terror ("*Vandalisme in Amsterdam*" 1984a).

To be sure, the reaction in South Africa matched the general climate in the Netherlands, where journalists and most of their readers decried the incident as violent and stupid. A statement by the South African Embassy (1984) in the Netherlands reflected a general consensus that the destruction of a library, especially a rich and historical library, is "despicable" and "uncivilized" under any circumstances. Libraries maintain the historical record, it was argued, and sustain the objective inquiry and intellectual freedom that are the foundations of a democratic society. They must, as far as possible, stand apart from ideol-ogy and fanaticism. "A library collects. That is the only thing it should be doing" (Van Dis 1984a). Others pointed out the danger of the destruction of politically or socially "incorrect" texts. If moral antipathy justifies destruction, then no library is safe: the papers of the Inquisition, anti-Semitic writings, pornographic collections in France's *Bibliothéque Nationale*, colonial archives (whose materials reveal imperialist excesses, or contradict the founding myths of postcolonial nations), Muslim materials, Christian materials, and so on ("*Anti-fascisten horde*" 1984). Underlying some of the condemnations was a tone of incredulous bemusement. To educated people with an appreciation of

books and scholarship in general, the squatters seemed almost criminally ignorant. In an emotional commentary, writer Adriaan Van Dis (1984b) declared
that the perpetrators were not smart enough to know that attacking the library
of an enemy offends norms of civilized behavior and triggers recriminations,
far inferior a strategy than discovering the enemy's weaknesses by studying his
writings. Van Dis (1984a) took the "book barbarians," a "sad, stupid lot," to task
for their shortsightedness. In their haste to dismantle apartheid, he claimed,
they had played into the hands of the South African regime: they had attacked
a library whose collections (which included anti-apartheid publications) could
have served as an indictment of the regime for many years to come. Hans Ester
(1984), a scholar whose research was interrupted by the attack, also lamented
the AARD's naivité and pointed out that the net result of the destruction was to
impede access to sources that might have supported thoughtful and different
solutions to the difficult problem of apartheid: "The situation in South Africa
has become so complex (and has been made so complex) that wild war cries
have no effect, not here or there. Before determining any position, [a] careful
information gathering process must take place. For this we need the books
which have now ended up in the water."

Van Dis emerged as an articulate insider spokesman for those who felt the
loss of the library most poignantly and understood the cultural and scholarly
ramifications of biblioclasm. His perspective was particularly valuable because
he was a scholar of book destruction, a member of the NZAV, a dedicated user
of the library, and, at the same time, a vocal opponent of apartheid. He had
started his studies in South African Language and Literature at the University
of Amsterdam because of a love for the poetic Afrikaans language, but the
politics of apartheid had quickly brought him to indignation (Van Dis 1984b).
Although his interest in the country and its language endured, early in his academic career Van Dis became skeptical about the possibility of communication with contemporary South Africans: "My correspondence with Afrikaner
authors ends up in mutual reproach. Our 'dialogue' seems to confirm our own
sense of being right" (Van Dis 1984b). He became a self-proclaimed "inde-
fatigable opponent" of apartheid politics but, after the attack, retrospectively
defended the presence within the SAI library of even the most slanted pro-
apartheid materials out of his belief that one must learn about evil in order
to defeat it. Van Dis (1984a) felt that the preservation of such materials was
important to future generations. His commentary on the attack brought him
to the forefront of the debate because he was able to articulate the rationales
behind taken-for-granted values that hold libraries to be worthwhile, even
sacrosanct, institutions.

One Dutch analyst, heaping "complete shame" on the perpetrators, stated
categorically that there could be no democratic consideration of the library's
destruction on its own merits: "Any argument apart from the observation that
this terror is, on principle, at all times unacceptable is totally superfluous"
(De Vogel 1984). But condemnation of an attack on a library did not forestall
the further widening of differences of opinion, emerging after Almere, over

the use of rationalized violence as a tactic of protest. Whereas the earlier incident had focused criticism on the squatter movement, the destruction of the SAI library cast the entire anti-apartheid effort in a negative light. As in South Africa, those who resented the moral smugness of the anti-apartheid movement seized the opportunity to accuse activists of intolerance and characterize them as fascists. "Apparently, according to this leftist group, you can be opposed to discrimination, but you have the right to discriminate against your opponents and destroy their property. Did not the same thing happen at the start of the Nazi-era in Germany?" (De Groot 1984). Comparisons of the library destruction to the Nazi book burnings of 1933 were frequent: "In principle, there is no difference between burning books and throwing them in the canal. It comes forth from a perfidious mentality which . . . must be branded as fascist" (*Een Schanddaad* 1984). Both the protestors and the Nazis, after all, were targeting intellectual freedom and its supporting institutions. According to one concerned citizen:

this group of people has shown what a mass of people blinded by hatred is capable of when incited by organizations which do not shrink from any means of achieving their ends. This act of terror, carried out by a number of cowardly vandals, shows how fragile our democracy really is. A government which fails to put an end to these criminal practices is also guilty of the fact that soon the boots will be droning through our streets again. . . . We see here that those who are shouting most loudly that they are fighting against fascism are in fact, by dint of their intolerance, the greatest fascists. (Van Der Graaf 1984)

One commentator lamented that a generalized atmosphere of intolerance had gained ground in Dutch social movements:

In South Africa customs and experiences of many years were exalted into a hard and . . . [un]friendly legal system, while conversely in the rest of the Western world there was actually a development in the opposite direction. It was from that point of view that apartheid was—justly—contested. However, if one adopts a similar intolerance, one is pursuing something wrong . . . in a stupid way. You can't rub out history or the present reality by throwing historical works in the water[;] no systems can be fought against by book burning. (De Kok 1984)

The attack on the library and the NZAV and the AARD's disavowal of pluralism and intellectual freedom, mainstays of democracy, reflected on the tolerance of the anti-apartheid movement as a whole. Movement members were reported to have made such statements as "Democracy is failing if an institute such as the Dutch-South African Association is tolerated" (Van Seeters 1984a). The NZAV members, in turn, discovered with horror that "some elements in the Netherlands no longer take any notice of legal order. Carrying the name 'South Africa' is evidently enough excuse to carry out violence, theft and destruction" (*Anti-fascisten horde* 1984). In the aftermath of the attack, the NZAV's basic commitment to dialogue was affirmed. The NZAV provided a safe space for members to articulate contradictory views such as those of Mr. J.L.A. Pfundt, who said at an annual meeting that the isolation policies were "a petty-minded method to express aversion to South Africa" (as quoted in Van Seeters 1984b). On the other hand, he continued, it was no longer an undivided pleasure to say that he was committed to Dutch-South African relations. Discussions following the attack defended the rights of the Center Party, the NZAV, and indeed any group, to hold its own opinions without becoming prey to demagogy.

In spite of nearly universal public condemnation of the attack on the library, the squatters achieved some order of success in "exposing" and discrediting the NZAV. Although anti-apartheid newspapers distanced themselves from the perpetrators, they nevertheless took a critical stance against the NZAV by publishing incriminating documents (letters and memos) stolen during the attack. Selected letters and memos appeared, along with critical commentary, in the squatter's paper *Bluf* and in *Amandla*, an anti-apartheid publication. *Amandla* cited letters written by and to NZAV officers as proof that the NZAV was a "political lobby-club" that worked against international sanctions, promoted contacts with South Africans, and kept company with the extreme right while trying to project an image of respectability (Fennema 1984a, 1984b). Other documents showed that NZAV members were in regular contact with the apartheid regime and visited regularly with the South African ambassador to the Netherlands; annual donations to the group from the South African Embassy also came to light. *Amandla* quoted the NZAV chairman of the board as having written in March 1983: "We are sufficiently active behind the scenes because we cannot do much in public," and adding in April 1983: "The NZAV is, as it were, maneuvering in a minefield" (Fennema 1984b). These comments indicate a level of awareness on the part of NZAV leaders that they might be condemned as extremists—their programs, grounded in nonnormative ideals, could be construed as deviant.

The documents also indicated that some of the members had decidedly pro-South African views: for example, one purloined NZAV letter criticized a member of the Dutch government for being "extremely unsympathetic about the present regime [in South Africa]" (Fennema 1984a). The press interpreted some comments as both right-wing and racist. In his review of the documents, anti-apartheid activist Boudewijn Buch (1984) detected a clear shift to the right in 1981 by the NZAV board and its secretary, Mrs. Johanna De Waard. His article included a letter in which De Waard described Adriaan van Dis as "a coloured person—very anti South Africa." Buch characterized her remarks about a fellow NZAV member as racist, stupid, and providing "a nice insight into the way Mrs. De Waard and all the little clubs on the Keizersgracht think" (Buch 1984). Buch (1984) reported Van Dis's incredulity at Mrs. De Waard's comment: aside from being both irrelevant and crypto-fascist, he had said, it was also simply erroneous because he was pure Caucasian (Buch 1984). Later, in an article entitled "Reluctantly Written," Van Dis (1984b), himself a member, described the NZAV as an association that "takes a mild stance regarding South Africa" and rather simplistically differentiated between members, elderly and "impressively calcified," and leaders who are "cunning" and have dubious contacts. In his article, Van Dis indicated concern about his access to the library in the future because he was speaking out so publicly. The publication of the documents and commentary contributed to the polarization of social dialogue around responses to apartheid.

The publication of archival material and letters brought other issues of intellectual freedom to the surface. For Buch (1984), the views expressed in De Waard's letter, which was written on official NZAV writing paper and filed in the archives, were by implication fairly attributed to the NZAV as a whole. NZAV chairman Schutte distanced himself from Mrs. De Waard's letter, saying that it was a strange, "rattling" way of thinking (Buch 1984). Pointing out that the letter was private, however, he expressed surprise that a paper like *Amandla* would take "the role of thief and accomplice" and criticized the unauthorized publication of their private correspondence and resulting defamation of committee members (Van Seeters 1984b). Although disclosure of the stolen documents and exposure of the NZAV officers' views appeared to serve the interests of anti-apartheid activists, it raised again the question of what methods of protest are acceptable in a democracy and what boundaries, if any, should be applied to freedom of expression (Van Seeters 1984b).

In general, the idealism of the AARD and its rationalizations found little sympathy among the Dutch public (Van Dis 1984b). In fact, even the independent *Parool*, while lauding the group's aversion to racism and discrimination, nevertheless judged the 50 activists as guilty of terror. Condemning the vandalism, the paper stated that "not even the most ardent opponent of that odious apartheid system in South Africa can approve of this" (Jansen 1984). Indeed, within the squatter and anti-apartheid movements, some members acknowledged the problematic nature of recent attacks by seeking distance from the perpetrators and criticizing trends toward radicalization by internal splinter groups. Moderate members of a counterculture that valued unity, solidarity, and pluralism were shaken as they confronted the degree to which they had embraced the "strange coalitions of often unexpected bedfellows" that were drawn to the "high-profile emotion-laden issue" of apartheid (Grundy 1991, 85). Some years after, a sociologist made the observation that activists may oversimplify South Africa's dilemmas and issues, and thereby force them into

a neat progressive-reactionary model. In other words, we insert our political ideologies into the South African drama . . .[and that] badly distorts reality. Apartheid offends our democratic values, as it should; so we subconsciously assume that all of those fighting apartheid must share our political commitment to the democratic-liberal values . . . when, in fact, some may be radical, socialist, or violently antidemocratic as well as anti-apartheid. (Grundy 1991, 22)

The incident shook the faith of some apartheid opponents, who realized that there were limits to protest: carrying the logic of isolationism to extremes could exact unacceptable social costs and be counterproductive. Others dug in their heels and held fast to premises that *any* contact at all with apartheid conferred complicity and that the library was a legitimate target for violence because of its association with "the anti-apartheid lobby on the Keizersgracht" (Fennema 1984b).

A single educated spokesperson emerged to defend the AARD. Dr. Julian S. With, a black Surinam-born poet and psychologist whose thoughts on Dutch society regularly appeared on the *Utrechts Nieuws* opinion page, reacted to the action "with great pleasure" because it reassured him that "there are still white people around who are credible in their rejection of the racism in South Africa" (With 1984a). "Well done, boys!" he praised them (With 1984b). Dr. With saw the AARD's actions as a laudable attempt to end the repression of black people and the general public's rejection of its deeds as primarily color-based. "The Netherlands is composed of 96% white people and a large proportion of them are in sympathy with the apartheid system in South Africa" (With 1984b). In With's opinion, those who thought violence and vandalism to be less effective than dialogue in swaying public opinion were historically shortsighted (With 1984b).

De Volkskrant [a newspaper] excels itself in stupidity and naiveté by branding the action as political nonsense and repugnant. If one feels kicked in the balls so easily that one uses words like repugnant for an action in a library, which word is then still left to describe the behavior of white people in South Africa? This reaction suggests that one should take moderates into consideration when one undertakes action against apartheid. What would need to happen in South Africa before the moderates review their point of view on this matter? Probably the use of an atom bomb on their homelands. (With 1984b)

Five AARD members, four men and one woman between the ages of 22 and 30, allowed a journalist to interview them in order to explain their actions. Because they, like all the rest, were never tracked down and prosecuted for the attack on the library, their comments offer the only available direct insight into the group's aims and beliefs. The reporter characterized the hour-long interview as "one long complaint," in which they all indignantly talked at once (Van Seeters 1984a). They were incensed at the "disgusting" way the press had portrayed their protest and felt deeply hurt and misunderstood:

It is sickening and stupid that our action is being compared to the book burning. The Nazis were pursuing a systematic destruction of books with liberating ideas . . . in a fight against writers. We wanted to undertake a symbolic action against repressive ideas, against an organization which makes propaganda for a fascist and murdering regime and uses different methods to achieve that end: a library, loans, promoting emigration. It is an every day practice in South Africa for [black] people to be evicted from their homes and expelled from their country with all their possessions. We wanted to send this Institute to its home: the canal. (Van Seeters 1984a)

When queried about their tactics, they responded that it was ironic that their actions were singled out as violent, while racism and discrimination, "violence in a suit," were ignored (Van Seeters 1984a). However, they seemed to acknowledge that their attack had dubious aspects when they said that they were not really "crazy about violence" and had spent a lot of time on the question of attacking a library. One member said that he had hurled the "beautiful" books into the water with a heavy heart, but justified his actions by saying that the library was an active part of the apartheid regime's propaganda machine. The group members saw themselves as very conscientious about weighing the ends against the means and avoiding gratuitous violence. They had agreed beforehand that the institute's pet dog would not be hurt, and they had an AARD member, wearing a suit, reassuring the building occupants. "Nobody was hurt and we didn't set fire to the building, we only carried out a task" (Van Seeters 1984a). The AARD felt that its actions in Almere and at the SAI library were justified because other means of protest were no longer effective. With Dutch politicians dragging their feet over the issue of condemning South Africa and breaking off contact, progressively violent steps were warranted (Van Seeters 1984a). The group members felt that their actions were moral, a necessary act of protest, and that they had simply followed the logic of anti-apartheidism to its rational conclusion. They were blind to the difference between carrying something to its rational conclusion versus to its logical extreme.

In retrospect, how can we classify the behavior of these young vandals? If we apply the criteria presented in the first chapter, their vandalism appears to be somewhat vindictive in character: the attack was an alternative to attacks on humans; the choice of target was not arbitrary; and the perpetrators were lashing out at a symbolic stand-in for the apartheid regime. It was tactical, planned to achieve the goal of disabling a tool of apartheid, and it was also ideological, a desperate attempt at communication that was oriented toward drawing attention to the cause of anti-apartheidism. In its entirety, it was a classic case of biblioclasm, an attack on books by those seeking to undermine an antithetical belief system, power structure, and despised enemy. The attack was an act of both renunciation (of an evil policy and the toxic values that underlay it) and affirmation (of the superiority of the anti-apartheid movement and its ideals). The case illustrates poignantly the clash of belief systems between extremists and the larger social community. It provides insights into those who, at a grassroots level, see the destruction of a library as an acceptable tactic of social and political protest—it is, in their minds, a rational, purposeful, and even laudable means of effecting social change. It did not involve violence to human beings or affective elements such as hedonism and joy in destruction. This is in stark contrast to many of the attacks that are discussed throughout this book. But, like many of those cases, it was calibrated so as to escape legal consequences and the full wrath of the authorities.

Was the attack successful by the goals the AARD had set for itself? No one was hurt. The library was put out of action, temporarily at least. The attack garnered a tremendous amount of public attention, as it was meant to. But most of the attention was not directed toward the horrors of apartheid and the regime and supporters that kept it in place. The attack on the SAI may even have been a tactical error. The AARD may have inadvertently offended a consensual value in a democratic society (the sanctity of libraries) powerful enough to elicit support from all sides of the Dutch political and social spectrum. In effect, the attack cemented the opposition and compromised the AARD's legitimacy as social reformers. Even in a climate of eroding tolerance and increasing polarization, attacking a library struck a central nerve. For the squatters, the library was primarily a symbol of repressive ideals and hated policy. For almost everyone else, the library symbolized cultural memory and civilization, and represented the possibility of democratic inquiry and reason. Biblioclasm, not apartheid, was condemned as a result.

Media coverage of the attack affirmed the value of libraries per se and the violation felt at the loss of the SAI library in particular. Although the discussion was wide-ranging, an overriding emphasis on the perpetrators' misplaced zeal may have taken priority over more substantive issues, such as the seductive nature of righteousness, orthodoxy, and extremism, and the occasional inability of democratic societies to respond effectively to the warning salvos of those who protest structural problems. The dialogue brought some recognition to the library's role in supporting inquiry, critical dialogue, and intellectual freedom, but the overall tenor of the coverage was one of moral judgment: intelligent people distancing themselves from the AARD by focusing on the group's "stupidity." Categorizing the perpetrators as stupid negated what had been, for the group, a desperate attempt at communication. Like other kinds of vandalism, the attack was both retaliation (against the apartheid forces) and a "call to society to recognize its culpability" regarding apartheid (Fisher and Baron 1982, 185). The protestors saw their actions as challenging not only South Africa's apartheid policies but Western political and social organization in general. This challenge was not acknowledged by the press and public opinion. Neither was the drift away from basic humanistic and democratic ideals that had been building throughout Dutch society and had created a context for violence.

Among issues that could perhaps have been addressed with greater depth, but were not, was the fact that the Dutch social climate had grown so toxic that protestors and police battered each other in the streets, a right-wing ethnocentric party had gained significant electoral inroads, and members of social groups ostensibly dedicated to peace, justice, and equality were enforcing an orthodoxy that defied humanistic and democratic norms. One could argue that the incident at Almere and the destruction of the SAI did, in fact, serve as a wake-up call to many in their recollection of the Nazis and the misery that comes from silencing alternate voices with violence, and it may have sparked some introspection. However, although "fascist" was used as an epithet by all sides, there was little discussion of the fact that other forms of absolutism also linked unwavering beliefs and violent action. Despite the fact that the first half of the twentieth century—the bloodiest period in world history—had demonstrated the fatal nature of succumbing to righteousness, imposition of group-think, and extremism, there was little engagement, in the Netherlands in 1984, in wrestling with how easily beliefs can crystallize and polarize and how social agreement can lock out tolerance while providing entry to violence.

What makes the Amsterdam incident so interesting is that it demonstrated that libraries can be destroyed because of a "good" cause (in this case, anti-apartheidism, which aligns with international values) and because it occurred in a modern, democratic nation. The Netherlands in the second half of the twentieth century was, of course, not the only democratic nation to host countercultural extremists and it, like others, was able to weather the storm. In theory, the health of a democracy is dependent on pluralistic alternatives and dissidence as a catalyst for change. The status quo resists change while societal equilibrium and the degree of credence given to various groups by public opinion fluctuates. When society is sufficiently unbalanced, dissidents with no outlet and a messianic cause may turn to extremism and channel their alienation and frustration into vandalism and terrorism. Acts of violent protest, especially those with a symbolic component, are attempts at communication that society ignores at its peril. However, the loss of the South African Institute Library also demonstrates that moral antipathy as political strategy is risky. Biblioclasm, like vandalism, sends a message, but that message may not be the one intended by the perpetrators.

REFERENCES

"*Aartjies na vaartjies*" [Chips Off the Old Block]. 1984. *Beeld*, 23 January.

Anderiesen, Gerard. 1981. "Tanks in the Streets: The Growing Conflict over Housing in Amsterdam." *International Journal of Urban and Regional Research* 5 (1):83–95.

"*Anti-fascisten horde barbaren*" [Anti-fascist Load of Barbarians]. 1984. *Het Parool*, 11 April.

Barratt, John. 1972. "South Africa's Outward Policy: From Isolation to Dialogue." In *South African Dialogue: Contrasts in South African Thinking on Basic Race Issues*, ed. N. J. Rhoodie. Philadelphia: Westminster Press, 543–561.

Bosgra, Sietse. 1984. "*Zuid-Afrika*" [South Afrika]. Letter to the Editor from the *Komitee Zuidelijk Afrika* [Committee Southern Africa]. *NRC*, 10 April.

Breytenbach, Breyten. 1987. "The South African Wasteland." In *The Anti-Apartheid Reader: The Struggle against White Racist Rule in South Africa*, ed. David Mermelstein. New York: Grove Press, 27–38.

Buch, Boudewijn. 1984. "*Zuid-Afrikaans Instituut Bekent Kleur: Perverse Gedachtengang Zwart Op Wit*" [South African Institute Admits Color: Perverse Thought Process in Black and White]. *Amandla*, April.

Castells, Manuel. 1983. "Squatters in the Netherlands: Elements for a Debate." *International Journal of Urban and Regional Research* 7 (3):405.

Cohen, Jean. 1985. "Strategy or Identity: New Theoretical Paradigms and Contemporary Social Movements." *Social Research* 52 (4):663–716.

De Groot, Max. 1984. "*Is Dit Geen Discriminatie?*" [Is This Not Discrimination?] *HA*, 25 January.

De Kok. 1984. "*De Verbeelding Aan De Macht?*" [Imagination in Power?]. *Commentaar* [Commentary]. *Haagsche Courant*, 20 January.

De Vogel, Steven. 1984. "*Gezwel*" [Tumor]. Letter to the Editor. *De Volkskrant*, 28 January.

De Waard-Bijlsma, J.C. 1984. Letter from *Nederlands-Zuidafrikaanse Vereniging* [Dutch-South African Association] Secretary to Members, 24 January.

"*Deel Bibliotheek in De Gracht: Vernielingen in Pand Van Z-Afrikaanse Vereniging*" [Part of the Library in the Canal: Destruction in the Premises of South African Association]. 1984. *De Volkskrant*, 20 January.

Draaisma, J., and P. Van Hoogstraten. 1983. "The Squatter Movement in Amsterdam." *International Journal of Urban and Regional Research* 7 (3):406–416.

Eder, Klaus. 1985. "The 'New Social Movements': Moral Crusades, Political Pressure Groups, or Social Movements?" *Social Research* 52 (4):869–890.

"*Een Schanddaad*" [A Shameful Act]. 1984. *Commentaar* [Commentary]. *Trouw*, 28 January.

Ester, Hans. 1984. "*Boekverdrinking was Puur Vandalisme*" ("Book Drowning Was Pure Vandalism"). *Trouw*, 2 February.

Fennema, Wilfried. 1984a. "*Onfrisse NZAV-Praktijken (Deel 2): Op De Bres Voor De Broedernatie*" [Unsavory NZAV-practices (Part 2): Into the Breach for the Brother Nation]. *Amandla*:16–19, April.

Fennema, Wilfried. 1984b. "*Zuid-Afrika Subsidieert Nederlandse Stichtingen: Een Huis Vol Apartheid*" [South-Africa Subsidizes Dutch Associations: A House Full of Apartheid]. *Amandla:* 7–8, March.

Fisher, Jeffrey D., and Reuben M. Baron. 1982. "An Equity Based Model of Vandalism." *Population and Environment* 5(3): 182–200.

Grundy, Kenneth W. 1974. "*We're against Apartheid, But. . . .*": Dutch Policy toward South Africa. *Studies in Race and Nations.* Denver, Colo.: University of Denver Press.

Grundy, Kenneth. 1991. *South Africa: Domestic Crisis and Global Challenge.* Boulder, Colo.: Westview Press.

Hainsworth, Paul. 1992. "Introduction. The Cutting Edge: The Extreme Right in Post-War Western Europe and the USA." In *The Extreme Right in Europe and the USA*, ed. Paul Hainsworth. New York: St. Martin's Press, 1–28.

Harris, Geoffrey. 1990. *The Dark Side of Europe: The Extreme Right Today.* Edinburgh: Edinburgh University Press.

Heldring, J. L. 1984. "*Gebaren Hebben Een Kort Leven*" [Gestures Have a Short Life]. *NRC*, 3 April.

Husbands, Christopher T. 1992. "The Netherlands: Irritants on the Body Politic." In *The Extreme Right in Europe and the USA*, ed. Paul Hainsworth. New York: St. Martin's Press, 95–125.

Jansen, Ena. 1984. "*Vandale tjank oor Nazi-klap: Gereformeerde tot Kommunistiese Koerante Le Lat In Oor boeke*" [Vandals Upset about Nazi Blow: Anger Expressed about Books from the Reformed to the Communist Newspaper]. *Beeld*, 24 January.

Jennett, Christine. 1989. "Signals to South Africa: The Australian Anti-Apartheid Movement." In *Politics of the Future: The Role of Social Movements*, eds. Christine Jennett and Randal G. Stewart. South Melbourne, Australia: Macmillan, 98–155.

Jennett, Christine, and Randal G. Stewart. 1989. "Introduction." In *Politics of the Future: The Role of Social Movements*, eds. Christine Jennett and Randal G. Stewart. South Melbourne, Australia: Macmillan, 1–28.

Katsiaficas, George. 1997. *The Subversion of Politics: European Autonomous Social Movements and the Decolonization of Everyday Life*. Atlantic Highlands, N.J.: Humanities Press.

Kennan, George F. 1971. "Hazardous Courses in Southern Africa." *Foreign Affairs* 49 (2):218–236.

Lane, David. 1990. "Your Pamphlet File Supports Apartheid." *Library Journal* 115 (4):174–177.

Lapchick, Richard Edward. 1975. *The Politics of Race and International Sport*. Westport, Conn.: Greenwood Press.

Laurence, John. C. 1987. "The Basic Historical Deception." In *The Anti-Apartheid Reader: The Struggle against White Racist Rule in South Africa*, ed. David Mermelstein. New York: Grove Press, 155–159.

Malan, D. F. 1987. "Apartheid: Divine Calling." In *The Anti-Apartheid Reader: The Struggle against White Racist Rule in South Africa*, ed. David Mermelstein. New York: Grove Press, 94–98. Letter written February 12, 1954.

Manning, C.A.W. 1972. "South Africa's Racial Policies—A Threat to Peace?" In *South African Dialogue: Contrasts in South African Thinking on Basic Race Issues*, ed. N. J. Rhoodie. Philadelphia: Westminster Press, 590–611.

Melucci, Alberto. 1985. "The Symbolic Challenge of Contemporary Movements." *Social Research* 52 (4):789–816.

"Mogelijke Legitimatieplicht Bij Bezoek Aan Bibliotheek: Schadeherstel Bij NZAV Kan Lang Duren" [Restoring the Damage at the NAZV Could Take a Long Time: Possible Compulsory Identification for Library Visits]. 1984. *Nederlands Dagblad*, 2 February.

Mudde, Cas, and Joop Van Holsteyn. 2000. "The Netherlands: Explaining the Limited Success of the Extreme Right." In *The Politics of the Extreme Right: From the Margins to the Mainstream*, ed. Paul Hainsworth. London: Pinter, 144–171.

Nederlands-Zuidafrikaanse Vereniging [Dutch-South African Association]. 1984. Statement Sent by the Executive Committee to ANP and National Newspapers (January 21, 1984).

O'Brien, Conor Cruise. 1987. "What Can Become of South Africa." In *The Anti-Apartheid Reader: The Struggle against White Racist Rule in South Africa*, ed. David Mermelstein. New York: Grove Press, 430–473.

"Pres. Steyn se kierie sou gepraat het" [President Steyn's Statue Would Have Spoken]. 1984. *Beeld*, 26 January.

Priemus, Hugo. 1983. "Squatters in Amsterdam: Urban Social Movement, Urban Managers or Something Else?" *International Journal of Urban and Regional Research* 7 (3):417–425.

Rhoodie, Eschel. 1969. *The Paper Curtain*. Johannesburg: Voortrekerpers.

"SA skatte in grag gegooi: Deel van SA geskiedenis dalk verlore" [SA Treasure Thrown into Canal: Part of South African History Completely Gone]. 1984. *Die Burger*, 21 January.

"*SA skatte verniel in aanval*" [SA Treasures Destroyed in Attack]. 1984. *Die Burger,* 20 January.

Schlesinger, Arthur M. Jr. 1989. "The Opening of the American Mind." *New York Times,* 23 July.

Shepherd, George W. Jr. 1977. *Anti-apartheid: Transnational Conflict and Western Policy in the Liberation of South Africa.* Westport, Conn.: Greenwood Press.

"*Soektog na boeke in grag*" [Search for Books in the Canal]. 1984. *Die Burger,* 21 January.

South African Embassy. 1984. Telexed Statement from The Hague Concerning an Announcement by the African-Dutch Cooperative in Pretoria. TO: All Interested Parties and Friends of South Africa. (January 26, 1984).

Touraine, Alain. 1985. "An Introduction to the Study of Social Movements." *Social Research* 52 (4):749–787.

Van Der Graaf, L. 1984. Letter to the Editor. *Bibliotheek* 5 [Library 5]. *Trouw,* 27 January.

Van Dis, Adriaan. 1984a. "*De Hond Mag Blijven, Pamfletten En Boeken Moeten Weg: Geen Kans Voor Kruger Aan De Keizersgracht*" ("The Dog Can Stay, Pamphlets and Books Must Go: No Chance for Kruger at the Keizersgracht"). *Folia,* 28 January.

Van Dis, Adriaan. 1984b. "*Faits Divers: Met weerzin geschreven*" [Reluctantly Written]. *NRC,* 30 January.

Van Seeters, Piet. 1984a. "*Actievoerders Gekrenkt Door Kritiek: 'Geweld Tegen Fascisten Mag.'*" [Activists Hurt by Criticism: 'Violence against Fascists Is Allowed'] *De Volkskrant,* 21 January.

Van Seeters, Piet. 1984b. "*Na Vernielingsactie in Bibliotheek: Zuid-Afrikaanse lobby wordt ongeduldig*" [After Destructive Action in Library: South African Lobby Is Becoming Impatient]. *De Volkskrant,* 16 April.

Van Seeters, Piet. 1984c. "*Vernielde Bibliotheek voorlopig dicht: Veel Schade Na Actie Bij Zuidafrikaanse Vereniging*" [Destroyed Library Closed for the Meantime: Much Damage after Action at South African Association]. *De Volkskrant,* 28 January.

"*Vandalisme in Amsterdam*" [Vandalism in Amsterdam]. 1984a. *Die Burger,* 23 January.

"*Vandalisme in Amsterdam*" [Vandalism in Amsterdam]. 1984b. *Die Transvaler,* 27 January.

Vandenbosch, Amry. 1970. *South Africa and the World: The Foreign Policy of Apartheid.* Lexington: University Press of Kentucky.

With, Julian S. 1984a. "*Aanpassing is al aardig op gang bij mij, niet?*" [Doing Pretty Well at Adapting So Far, Aren't I?]. *Utrechts Nieuws,* 7 February.

With, Julian S. 1984b. "*Actie*" [Action]. Letter to the Editor. *De Volkskrant,* 28 January.

Worrall, Denis. 1972. "South Africa's Reactions to External Criticism." In *South African Dialogue: Contrasts in South African Thinking on Basic Race Issues,* ed. N. J. Rhoodie. Philadelphia: Westminster Press, 562–589.

CHAPTER 4

Ethnic Biblioclasm, 1980–2005

> Soon kindling animosities
> Surmount the old civilities
> And start the first brutalities.
>
> Then come the cold extremities
> The justified enormities,
> The unrestrained ferocities.
>
> —F. R. Scott, "Degeneration"

The last chapter recounted the case of a radical Dutch group that took "action" against a library that was believed to be supporting a rogue regime. Slightly vindictive, but largely tactical and ideological, the attack had definite parameters: no one was hurt, not even the library's dog. This grassroots political protest was a low-affect, isolated event in a tense but reasonably stable sociopolitical atmosphere. In other, more turbulent environments, such as postcolonial India, Kashmir, and Sri Lanka, biblioclasm has tended to be more personal in nature, more passionate, and more violent, the product of social flashpoint as well as political calculation. Like the AARD, the perpetrators in these three Asian events had been thrown off balance by rapid secularization and urbanization, but their plight was further aggravated by extreme poverty and a dearth of economic and social safety nets. Polarization occurred along ethnic and religious rather than political lines, and achieving economic and political advantage was viewed as key to physical and cultural survival. Rival groups lashed out at each other in violent protests, ethnic riots, pogroms, and civil wars, and biblioclasm was a high-stakes, high-affect tactic in battles over clashing belief systems.

Alienated by modern economies in which they had no stake and victimized by deteriorating social circumstances, disaffiliated groups in Western democracies (such as the AARD) have turned to newly evolved social networks and found unity in political causes. In poorer countries—at the periphery of world systems—where the anomie and frustration were tenfold and democracy was a residue of colonialism, beleaguered groups have turned to tribal allegiances and millennial visions to stake out identity, mark territory, and justify claims to scarce resources. They define themselves ethnically according to race and cultural traits. Of course, according to sociologist Peter Worsely (1984, 249), cultural traits are not absolutes nor are they simply intellectual categories: they are markers that are embraced in certain situations to invoke identities that legitimize claims to rights and that serve as weapons in competitions over scarce resources. Ethnicity can be a useful way to define one's own group and, in contrast, the enemy. Where democracy has shallow roots, aggression against a rival is not only expedient, but it may be the *only* outlet for frustration. Committing acts of malicious and vindictive vandalism allows members of marginalized groups to feel powerful in their rage and to experience a sense of control over circumstances (Baron and Fisher 1984, 64). Especially for those on the edge, manufactured excitement is not only cathartic; it provides a momentary solution to the monotony of hardship (Cohen 1973, 51). Tactical and ideological motivations are more apparent in extreme groups (such as religious nationalists) whose ethnic and religious beliefs are catalysts leading to action. For others (such as splinter guerilla units), shared beliefs merely provide "an institutional framework in which to be destructive and to express far more personal conflicts with the world" (Canter 1984, 349).

Biblioclasm that results from ethnic conflict often takes the form of vandalism that is both "'directed' (in the sense that the identity and ownership of the target [are] not entirely incidental) and 'responsive' (in the sense that it responds to particular situations or needs)" (Cohen 1973, 48). Although perpetrators may be motivated by hatred or resentment, they also seem to seek pleasure from property destruction, and it becomes a hedonistic and even aesthetic experience (Greenberger and Allen 1980, 479). Ethnic vandalism usually involves hostility and the rage of impotence combined with a joy in destructiveness, and it is perhaps the most difficult type of vandalism to make sense of (Cohen 1984, 57). Participation in riots may be especially appealing to local toughs, who are attracted to bullying, and to ordinary people whose release of inhibitions is a break from a hard and overcontrolled life (Horowitz 2001). In ethnic race riots, a preferred target is the property of successful members of the community, suggesting that jealousy may also be a factor. Far from being the unstructured melee it seems, a riot is a highly patterned and purposeful attack on symbolic or economically significant targets. A recent book by Donald Horowitz (2001, 1) has defined a deadly ethnic race riot as "an intense, sudden, though not necessarily wholly unplanned, lethal attack by civilian members of one ethnic group on civilian members of another ethnic group." Horowitz (2001, 13) characterizes the ethnic race riot as an "amalgam of apparently rational-purposive behavior and irrational-brutal behavior"—a mix of calculation and passion. The attacks may be over religion or interpretations of history, but inevitably they involve entitlement to such things as land and influence. Economic considerations may come into play with riots designed to eliminate competition or clear desirable areas for subsequent development by the perpetrators' group. The division between the groups is usually caused by cultural differences of some kind (race, religion, language), and when resources are scarce, it becomes a social fault line. Groups with nothing to lose and little respect for authority choose violence as a well-trod path to assuaging their frustration at being outmaneuvered and victimized by a heretical group that they believe has grabbed more than its share of goods and influence. With their own community sanctioning their actions, perpetrators of ethnic violence operate with relative impunity.

There is a "widely accepted truism" that all religions have the potential to inspire violence (Fox 2002, 78). Religion invokes intense feelings and allows followers to pose their actions as divinely driven. It also provides a rationalization of violence as necessary to defending or advancing faith. To ethnic groups whose social cohesion and group identity is keyed to a particular religion, symbols and stories give substance to religious frameworks, provide vicarious experiences, and cement worldviews (Greeley 1982). A perceived attack on these "stories" is an offense of the first order.

In India, religious violence is so much a part of life that the Hindus have a special word for it: *dharmiklarai*, "religious fight" (Haught 1995, 58). Riots and protests have become commonplace there as Hindus and Muslims engage in conflicts over history and entitlements. The number of Muslim casualties has been disproportionately high, particularly in the 1980s. In organized massacres, hundreds, even thousands, of Muslims (including women and babies, the old and handicapped) were killed and maimed; railroad passengers were pulled from their trains and lynched; and people were burned alive (Pandey 1992, 34). The riots persist because they have become a customary activity. The police do not interfere and sometimes participate out of sympathy with the Hindu cause. "The maintenance of communal tensions, accompanied from time to time by lethal rioting at specific sites, is essential for the maintenance of militant Hindu nationalism" (Brass 2003, 9).

The Hindu majority (they outnumber other groups four to one) chafes against India's liberal, secular, democratic form of government, which it feels has not delivered on its promises. The Hindus want to return to the mythical era of Ram Rajya in which, according to collective memory, there was peace, happiness, and prosperity. *Hindutva*, "the rising ideal of an all-embracing, monolithic 'Hindu community,'" is a relatively recent development, a revived, militant form of "an openly fundamentalistic Hinduism" that began in the Punjab in 1907 (Frykenberg 1993, 239–240). It draws inspiration from the belief that the sacred blood of the Hindus, the original indigenous people, entitled them to possess the holy land of India (Frykenberg 1993, 240). The drive to "Hinduize" India is facilitated by school textbooks that are full of Hindu mythology and politics (Kumar 1992).

With the help of corrupt politicians who fan ethnic rivalry to attain political advantage, Hindu activists have begun to take action against art, journalistic pieces, literature, and commentary that offends them. Their "hypersensitivity" against what they perceive as "persistent slights on their faith" has taken various forms, including, in the 1990s, the repeated storming of the offices of *Mahanagar,* a Bombay daily that had criticized their party (Triparthi 1997, 84). Books have frequently entered the conflict. In 1956, the "symbolic pretext" for rioting was the local publication of *Living Biographies of Religious Leaders,* which was written by an American and contained references to the Prophet Muhammad that the Muslims considered blasphemous (Brass 2003, 76). Muslim processions protesting the book (and in some cases, ritual burnings of the Hindu religious text, the *Baghavad Gita*) were followed by Hindu counterdemonstrations that ended in arson and violence. In 2001, right-wing Hindus protested the Taliban's destruction of ancient Buddhist statues in Afghanistan by burning copies of the Koran in New Delhi and elsewhere. The *Hindutva* movement could be labeled fascist in light of its tactics (street violence, symbolic demonstrations, demagoguery, unabashed discrimination, and grappling for political power through militancy).

In January 2004, a Hindu mob destroyed most of the collections of the renowned 87-year-old Bhandarkar Oriental Research Institute (BORI), illustrating the volatility of conflicts over modernity and scholarship in India. The destruction was in retaliation for the publication, by Oxford University Press, of a book about Hindu king Shivaji. In *Shivaji: Hindu King in Islamic India,* author James Laine had presented a new picture of Hindu-Muslim relations from the seventeenth century to the present that included allegedly objectionable observations. Despite Laine's apologies and his publisher's withdrawal of the book from the market, violence erupted on January 5 when 250 protestors, members of a Hindu nationalist group called the Sambhaji Brigade, attacked the BORI. They cut telephone lines and smashed exhibit cases, computers, and furniture. They tore or otherwise damaged books, ancient texts that were inscripted on palm leaves, statues, and old photographs, and carried away rare materials. Lost were texts and digital files that supported the institute's combined mission of preservation, research, teaching, and publication. The most important loss was of 30,000 manuscripts, including 2,000 entrusted to the institute by the government of Bombay when the institute was founded in 1917 (Chapalgaonkar 2004). Many BORI scholars lost their life's work ("Mob Ransacks" 2004).

Michael Witzel's (2004) thoughtful article in the *Hindu* points out the ramifications of these and other attacks on intellectual freedom, objective research, and the field of Indology. The fact that even a few quotes in a scholarly book can set off a vandalistic rampage could have a chilling effect on historical research and printing in India. According to Witzel (2004): "Such a public climate simply runs counter to the growing worldwide exchange of ideas.

Vigorous exploration of each other's view, and keen, even contentious debate is the need of the hour, not book burning." But Hindu extremists not only soundly reject the basic tenets of international scholarly research; they either misunderstand the motives of Indologists, who engage in the comprehensive study of India based on its texts, or intentionally malign them for political purposes (Witzel 2004).

As with many of the communal riots that have plagued India, the incident at the BORI was staged by religious leaders, and "the high pitch of manic enthusiasm" masked its purposive, concerted nature (Horowitz 2001,13). At stake, literally, was the recorded history of India and the political purposes that history serves in cementing ethnic identity. "[H]istory," writes Eric Hobsbawm (1993, 62–63), "is the raw material for nationalist or ethnic or fundamentalist ideologies, as poppies are the raw material for heroin addiction." The *Hindutva* movement used the attack as a means of eradicating primary and secondary documents that contradicted its versions of history. In 1996, well-known scholar Gyanendra Pandey argued that a "new Hindu history" was being devised in order to reinforce and magnify ethnic stereotypes. Riddled with factual inconsistencies, fallacious logic, fraudulent use of sources, and fabrications of historic events, this history was based in myth rather than fact. By posing India's history as centuries of perennial Hindu-Muslim conflict, Hindu extremists can thwart the government's attempts to maintain a multicultural, democratic nation (a secular state that accords privilege to no religious group) and foster communal hatred. The *Hindutva* movement portrays the Muslim as an evil foreign invader and irreligious being, the innately scheming, greedy, and bigoted enemy of the Hindu who is, on the other hand, tolerant, peaceful, and part of the divine. This portrayal legitimizes Hindu aggression against the Muslims as both a necessary defensive tactic and a path to fulfillment of a divine destiny.

Such manipulated versions of history have been actively disseminated by politicians who have posed the *Hindutva* movement as the solution to chronic social problems. Hindu nationalism emerged in India as a result of eroding democratic institutions and failed economic development (Kothari 1998, 8). The fascist element of *Hindutva* feeds off the notion that the Hindu majority has remained illiterate and impoverished while minorities such as the Muslims have been given special treatment and prospered. Born out of despair, disillusionment, and socioeconomic disintegration, *Hindutva* is usually viewed as a form of Communalism, which, as the term is applied in India, refers to an attachment to one's own community combined with active hostility to other communities that share the same space. Communalism involves not only "identification with a religious community but also with its political, economic, social and cultural interests and aspirations"—and the belief that these interests are in conflict with those of other communities (Kakar 1996, 13). However, according to Dipesh Chakrabarty (1996, 209), what Indians do to one another is variously described as "communalism" and "regionalism" but never as the racism it is. Hindu nationalism, which theoretically exists independently of the Hindu-Muslim antagonism, in practice has flourished only when that opposition is present (Brass 2003, 7). Its goal, of course, is to make its extreme form of Hinduism the central belief system of India and reconstitute the nation's institutions and culture according to its mandates.

An authentic, localized, spiritually based way of life is the platform that Hindu politicians are riding to power. They reject secularism and multiculturalism as the basis for the state, posing them as foreign ideologies and remnants of colonialism. According to Indian scholars committed to humanism and mainstream academic scholarship, the Hindu nationalists' view of India's history is ethnocentric and designed primarily to substantiate Hindu claims to preeminence. There is no pretense of objectivity. According to Pandey (1996, 143), the *Hindutva* movement rejects modern, scientific, objective "ways of seeing," distinctions between religion and either history or politics, the diminishment of spiritual matters in daily life, and time as linear. Indeed, *Hindutva* activists claim that their form of history is superior because it speaks in the language and voice of the people about their most deeply rooted beliefs and long-suppressed desires. It is "authentic" as opposed to the "slavish imitation[s] of Western histories produced by *déraciné* scholars ensconced in privileged positions in the universities and research institutions" who write for their English-speaking peers (Pandey 1996, 143). There were also indicators that the attack on the institute was part of the politics of an ongoing "caste feud" in the area; the Maratha Seva Sangh group, which claimed responsibility for the attack, is known to be anti-Brahman, the scholarly class (Katakam 2004). A journalist for *Frontline*, a national magazine in India, believes that the Sangh group's leader, Purushottam Khedakar, accrued political advantage from publicity surrounding the incident and his group gained an identity (Katakam 2004)

The attackers sent a message that affirmed tribal over secular values and rejected Western civilization as the center of the universe. By and large, it passed under the radar of a global audience and, like other communal incidents in India, it was largely ignored by the national government. Khedakar was reputed to be well connected to several government ministers and unlikely to be held accountable (Katakam 2004). It is particularly unfortunate that no consequences were levied for the institute's destruction, because biblioclasts who frame their attacks as protests are almost always testing the authorities' commitment to defending humanistic values. In the face of little or no response, similar incidents are likely to occur. Extremists who participate in local incidents of book and library destruction are indicating a predisposition that, left unchecked, may lead to ethnic cleansing.

In India, Hindu nationalists, when indulging their habit of communal violence, committed their acts with reasonable assurance that local and national officials would not exact consequences. They perverted the legitimacy of government but nevertheless acknowledged the ultimate authority of a national government. Their biblioclastic protests were directed not only at

Muslims but at the secular, multicultural values upon which the nation was based. *Hindutva* members worked hard to win elections at both the local and national level and capture the center from within. Though flawed, democracy still functioned. In Kashmir, politics were murkier and the authority of the state of India even more compromised. In this case, the roles were reversed: the Muslims were destroying Hindu books and seeking to expunge the Hindu Pandits, who were seen as having a lock on employment and educational opportunities.

When the British left India in 1947, they hoped to forestall religious conflict by setting up two nations: Pakistan for the Muslims and India for Hindus. As the people rushed to their respective homelands, bloody clashes left as many as one million people dead. Gandhi tried to rise above the factionalism but was assassinated by a militant Hindu who thought he favored the Muslims (Haught 1995). The Himalayan state of Jammu and Kashmir (generally known as Kashmir) became part of India and served as buffer between that nation and Pakistan. In 1948, 1965, and 1971, the two nations fought border wars over the territory; today, each administers a segment, separated by a cease-fire line. Kashmir was the only Muslim-majority state in India, but the distribution of population was inconsistent: the Kashmir part was 95 percent Muslim, while the Jammu side was two-thirds Hindu. In the 1980s, a series of local political blunders and the Indian government's manipulation of political power led to widespread disillusionment with democracy and Kashmiri politics. After 1989, Kashmir was plagued by separatist violence as Muslim groups divided into those who wanted to secede and become part of Pakistan, those who wanted Kashmir to remain part of India, and those who wanted an independent state. Some Muslims claimed to be ready for holy war, but others wanted to live in peace with their neighbors. This was not to be. More than 30,000 people were killed in ethnic conflicts set off by Muslim militants. In the 1990s, the Indian government moved 700,000 troops into Kashmir, enforced a police state, and launched ruthless campaigns to weed out Muslim militants. By the end of the century, the scope of militantism had been curtailed, but conflict and tensions persist still. Cultural symbols retain their power to trigger protests, counter-protests, and passionate riots. According to James Haught (1995): "Hindu-Muslim hatred in Kashmir often defies its own rather bizarre logic: During the 1989 wave of Muslim riots over Salman Rushdie's novel *The Satanic Verses*, Kashmiri Muslims attacked a Hindu temple—even though the author came from a Muslim family!"

The Kashmiri Pandits were a small Hindu minority, 15 percent of Kashmir's population at one point. They were known for their 100 percent literacy rate and cultural and intellectual achievements. Since the late 1980s, Muslim militants have tried to rid Kashmir of the Pandit presence. Their ethnic cleansing campaigns were also an attempt to eliminate Kashmir's recognized status as a distinguished center of Sanskrit scholarship and to erase all traces of a 5,000-year-old Hindu cultural history (Kaul 1999). Pandit Professer Mohan Lai Kaul (1999) describes the cleansing as inspired by the same psychopathic, "theo-fascist" proclivities that had motivated Muslims during other periods of power in Kashmir. He identifies the Sayyid ruler, Sikander (1389–1413), as a Muslim icon who commanded that Sanskrit books be used as fuel for kitchen and bathroom fires. When the terrorized Pandits took their books and fled to the mountains, Sikander's troops went after them and threw their books into the lakes, wells, and ditches. Kaul (1999) believes that this early attempt to destroy Hindu culture is being replicated in modern Kashmir.

Sikander's twentieth-century heirs were young Muslim militants who were supplied by Pakistan with military training and automatic rifles. They were incited by a constant stream of anti-Hindu propaganda that posed the Indian state as an oppressive interloper and Pandits as elitists who had cornered the market on business, government jobs, educational opportunities, and land, while the majority (Muslims) suffered in poverty and illiteracy. The Pandits' secular orientation, physical presence, and status as a minority with rights were in opposition to Muslim activists' theocratic aspirations and their desire for an exclusive and homogeneous culture. The vitality of Pandit culture, its 5,000-year traditions and intellectual achievements (*pandit* literally means "scholar" or "Brahman") not only aroused envy but supported pluralism and a role for Kashmir as a vibrant multicultural society (Shivpuri 1998). However, Kashmir's Muslims take inspiration from an exclusive pan-Islamic culture rather than from the *Kashmiriat*, a common indigenous culture (Jaisingh 1996). The Pandits' secularism and Hindu ethnicity identified them with the hated government of India and raised suspicions that they were spies and agents of the regime. A Muslim pamphlet urged militants to throw off slavery and victimization by "atheism and godless philosophies," warning that "Your enemies are bent upon destroying your identity and faith. You are facing a ruthless imperialist power [India] whose Brahmanical psyche is bringing new troubles for you everyday" (Ray 1997, 4–5).

The Muslim-controlled local government did little to curtail the militants. The fundamentalist Muslim force, the *Jammaat-I-Islami*, censored books and institutions that violated its worldview. Two thousand books (including books by John Milton, George Bernard Shaw, and William Shakespeare) were removed from Kashmir University. Handwritten Sanskrit manuscripts in Srinagar's Research Library were dumped into gunny sacks and left to molder. Bookshops and the Government of India's Information Center library were looted and set on fire. Hindu temples and historical sites were blown up, burned, or desecrated. In 1989, attacks on the Pandits escalated, and Muslim paramilitaries selectively tortured, murdered, and raped Pandits, using particularly gruesome techniques to underscore their demands that Pandits leave Kashmir forever. The Pandits fled *en masse*, carrying only a few articles of clothing. Thereupon, the militants plundered and set fire to Pandit properties and temples and destroyed their artworks and sculptures. Images of living beings were offensive to fundamentalist Muslims. Books were favored targets, perhaps standing in for their owners. Sometimes militants piled books up and set them on fire, chanting "death to the Pandits" (Kaul 1999). Other books were torn up, scattered through the abandoned houses, or sold by weight for use in the market or to urban book dealers as far away as New Delhi.

Professor Kaul, concerned that book destruction was perpetrated to rob the Pandits of their distinctive heritage, contacted 93 Pandit exiles and recorded their book losses in a chapter in his book, *Kashmir: Wail of a Valley*. In each case, the owner is profiled, his losses quantified, and specific titles listed. The profiles reveal how integral the books were to the Pandits' professional and personal identities. Trilok Kaul, an artist who lost 150 paintings and thousands of books, said that it was "as if I was not born at all. As if I had done nothing in my life. I have not lived and struggled. I was not educated at all and I never painted. I have no family and no background" (Kaul 1999, 327). Scholar Dr. Kashi Nath Pandita lost 2,500 books, including 120 Persian manuscripts and 60 manuscripts inherited from his ancestors; his house was destroyed and turned into a public latrine. A retired secondary school principal, C. L. Changroo, was devastated to hear that all of his carefully acquired books on world history, philosophy, economics, and sociology were thrown out of a window, doused with kerosene, and set on fire. Physician K. L. Chowdhary left behind his reference materials and 5,000 books that had been collected by his family for nearly a century; he has heard that the collection is slowly dissolving. The loss makes him feel "intellectually crippled. The books call me to my homeland as much as the roots and the history of 5,000 years" (Kaul 1999, 348). The Indian government did very little to help the Pandits, many of whom still languish in refugee camps and consider themselves "the Tutsis of Rwanda and Jews of Germany" (Kaul 1999, vi) and, as victims of ethnic cleansing, kin to Bosnians (Newberg 1995). Young Pandits are increasingly calling for a homeland of their own.

Psychological theory pertaining to anger points out that the enabling state of mind in the shift from frustrated impotence to scapegoating and aggression is hatred, "an amalgam containing an emotion, a paranoid ideation, and an obsessive extended relationship to a perceived enemy" (Gaylin 2003, 62). The projection of one's internal conflicts onto another is a "paranoid shift" that is central to a culture of hatred. The hater is sure that his or her misery is the fault of the object of his or her animosity. Unlike anger, which is more spontaneous and transitory, hatred becomes an enduring, organized, aggressive, and obsessive attachment (Gaylin 2003, 36). In both India and Kashmir, the hatred felt by cultural groups was held together by ancestral bonds and common beliefs, and it sought outlet in attacks on neighbors that leaders had cast as enemies and rivals. Hatred fed by paranoia and sanctified by religious beliefs provided impetus for violent aggression.

In both Kashmir and India, books and libraries were held hostage during times of uneasy peace and endangered during conflict because religious violence had become routine political behavior that the government was unwilling or unable to control. Now we shall see what happens when an ethnic group takes over the government and has free reign to implement ethnic nationalism as national policy. In Sri Lanka, the flagrant destruction of the Tamil minority's primary cultural institution led to full-scale civil war.

In 1981, Sri Lanka was a country posed on the edge of political implosion. Since gaining independence from the British in 1948, the government had institutionalized the dominance of Sinhalese ethnic identity and adopted Buddhism as the state religion (Obeyesekere 1984, 157). Buddhist extremists enlisted the support of politicians and the Sinhalese people (70% of Sri Lanka's population) and began campaigns to marginalize their chief competitors, the Hindu Tamils. Their campaigns were driven by a deep-seated sense of grievance rising from the belief that Buddhism was under attack by the Tamils, who dominated the northern part of the country and the city of Jaffna. The threat ostensibly posed by the Sri Lankan Tamils was magnified by the existence of millions of Tamils in nearby India. Ignoring centuries of ethnic interchange in which Tamils and Sinhalese had "exchanged words, deities, cultures, and rulers," popular history among the Sinhalese now posed the Sri Lankan Tamils as long-standing enemies and the Sinhalese as chronically having to fend off Tamil invasions (Obeyesekere 1984, 155). Under the pretext of protecting Buddhism, the Sinhalese targeted Hindu Tamils in violent riots in 1956, 1958, and 1977. Three days of riots in 1981 and the burning of a famous Tamil institution, the Jaffna Public Library, marked a turning point in the conflict: the loss of the library, egregious to a group that treasured its literary heritage, shattered Tamil adults and radicalized Tamil youth. Sri Lanka was soon immersed in civil war. How the loss of a library could set a country on the path to bloody civil war is a question of great importance.

When the British took over control of the region they called Ceylon from the Portuguese and Dutch in 1796, they administered the Tamil areas as a separate entity. By 1815, they had conquered the whole island and set up a centralized government in Colombo. The British paid little attention to either the Tamil language and Hinduism or the Sinhala language and Buddhism, and instead enforced supremacy for the English language and Christianity. In the late nineteenth century, Sinhala-Buddhist nationalism was revived in the south, and in the north the Tamils maintained group consciousness by retaining their own language, culture, territory, and Hindu faith (Wilson 2000, 1). Linguistic consciousness became an integral part of the Tamil worldview during this time (Wilson 2000, 27, 29). During the 1920s and 1930s, regular conferences on the Tamil language marked a literary revival from which a vibrant Tamil cultural movement emerged. The distinctiveness of Sri Lankan Tamil literature was maintained with congresses and conventions that affirmed a separate Tamil identity (Wilson 2000, 105).

The Jaffna Public Library served as a storehouse of materials that validated this identity. It began as the private collection of the scholar K. M. Chellapha, who began lending books from his home in 1933. In 1934, a committee set up a formal library, with Chellapha as secretary. Initially, 1,000 books, newspapers, and journals were kept in a single room, but soon the collection was shifted into a building on Jaffna's main street and was opened to subscribers. From the beginning, "the library had evolved as a part of the Jaffna psyche and the desire of its people to attain higher levels of education" (Sambandan

2003). The library was so popular that a cross-section of prominent members of the community began raising funds to build a permanent, modern building. A noted architect designed the new building, and prominent Indian librarian S. R. Ranganathan served as an advisor to ensure that the library was held to international standards. Christian priests and educated members of the community donated books, and all known literary source materials of the Tamil people were gathered together (Sivathamby 2004). The main building opened in 1959; the children's section and an auditorium were added later.

The collection became well known internationally and was popular with both Sinhalese and Tamil intellectuals, as well as the general public. By 1981, it had become the major repository for almost 100,000 Tamil books and rare, old manuscripts and documents, some written on dried palm leaves and stored in fragrant sandalwood boxes. Some books were literally irreplaceable: the *Yalpanam Vaipavama*, a history of Jaffna, was the only existing copy (Peris 2001). The library held miniature editions of the Ramayana epic, yellowing collections of extinct Tamil-language newspapers (Dugger 2001), and microfilms of important documents and records of the *Morning Star*, a journal published by missionaries in the early twentieth century ("Civilization and Culture" 2003). It held historical scrolls, works on herbal medicine, and the manuscripts of prominent intellectuals, writers, and dramatists, including the acclaimed philosopher, artist, and author Ananda Kumaraswamy. Altogether, these materials sustained and advanced Tamil culture ("Heart and Soul" 2004). Indeed, one could think of the Jaffna Library as a national library even though a Tamil nation had not yet come into being.

With a high value for education and privileged-minority status assured by the British, the Tamils, although only one-fifth of the population, were well represented in the government until independence in 1948. Before leaving Ceylon, the British established both Sinhalese and Tamil as national languages. But the postcolonial government was increasingly dominated by Sinhalese Buddhists who operated on the premise that Sri Lanka was "inherently and rightfully" a purely Sinhalese state: this was posed as a fact, not a debatable issue (Nissan 1984, 176). The government actively suppressed dissent and controlled the media. There was intense competition between the two ethnic groups for resources including land, water, credit, employment, education, urban space, housing, and political power and representation (Senaratne 1997, 21). Sinhalese officials saw their role as rectifying perceived inequities by directing resources away from the Tamils and toward their own ethnic group. Religious leaders added impetus by appealing directly to the people for a "convergence of nation, religion, and ethnicity"—Sri Lankan, Buddhist, and Sinhalese (De Silva 1986, 175).

With the British gone, the Sinhalese majority claimed sovereignty and linguistic hegemony over the entire country, which was renamed Sri Lanka without Tamil input in 1972. Language policy became a vehicle for cementing the preeminence of its ethnic group. *Swabasha*, a movement whose initial mission, to eradicate English as the official language, was embraced by both

Tamils and Sinhalese, continued its campaigns against Christian and secular influences, but also began to eliminate Tamil privileges and rights (Horowitz 2001, 144–145). Language, "a symbol of group status and a gateway to career opportunities," became the focus of ethnic violence (Horowitz 2001, 282) as the government's Sinhalese-only policies undermined the Tamils' ability to secure and retain government and professional positions. The objective of Sinhalese lawmakers was to expunge all traces of Tamil influence, the last obstacle to the Sinhalese-Buddhist hegemony that they considered a birthright. The Sinhalese were redressing grievances, perceived loss of status, and the "presumed parlous plight of the Buddhist religion" after foreign rule and neglect (De Silva 1986, 174). A Buddhist cultural renaissance and corresponding decline of Tamil influences seemed the only sure route to national regeneration (De Silva 1986, 178). Politicians diverged from this path at their peril: In the late 1950s, the Buddhist prime minister declared Sinhalese to be the only official language; upon vacillating in the face of Hindu protests, he was assassinated by a Buddhist monk who considered him to be a traitor to the faith (Haught 1995, 108).

The Sinhalese claimed power in Sri Lanka on both demographic and ideological grounds. Their destiny as an ethnic group was inseparable from their religious beliefs (Obeyesekere 1984, 155). Though Buddhists are generally perceived as pacifists, the Sinhalese believed that their charge of preserving the "true" Theravada Buddhism justified violent measures (Fox 2002, 78). Anti-Westernization sentiments in the twentieth century fueled Buddhist nationalist claims that the Sinhalese *jatiya* (race or nation) had been weakened by the influence of Christianity, Western lifestyles, and foreign commerce (Roberts 1994, 191). In the 1950s in particular, there was a populist groundswell that targeted the Western-educated upper classes, imperialism, and all things foreign. A renewed sense of national pride grew alongside of an opposition to pluralism (Roberts 1989, 70). For poor and uneducated Sinhalese, the belief that Sinhalese identity was inextricable from the Buddhist faith gained strength from frustration with economic conditions (Obeyesekere 1984, 158). Buddhist nationalism was constructed in direct opposition to the Tamils who were viewed as "*parayo*"—foreign inferiors who had to be ruled, controlled, or cast out if catastrophic disorder was to be avoided (Roberts 1989, 70).

Throughout the 1970s, ethnic conflict arose from the breakdown of traditional norms and the population's frustration with inflation and economic problems. Sinhalese politicians used authoritarian measures in response and their attempts to maintain control pitted the government against the Tamils but also against civil society, liberalism, and moderation in general. United National Party (UNP) politicians and merchants hired gangs of "thugs" (a term that was common parlance in Sri Lanka) and used state-owned buses to transport them to sites where they broke up political meetings and protests and harassed opposition parties, trade unions, workers, and public employees. They attacked peaceful pickets at the Maharagama Teacher Training College and serious injury resulted (Senaratne 1997, 37). The thugs threatened judges, artists, and writers, and assaulted Ediriweera Sarachchandra, Sri Lanka's best-known dramatist whose satirical book highlighted the decay of cultural values brought on by the government's policies (Obeyesekere 1984, 163). No one was ever prosecuted or arrested for these attacks. Rather, paramilitaries and the police were empowered by draconian legislation that outlawed "terrorism," which was the word used to describe dissent in any form. The government had created a "many-headed monster" that threatened to destroy the entire fabric of Sri Lanka democracy (Obeyesekere 1984, 174).

Sinhalese rationalizations for violence were disseminated by propaganda that justified violence against the Tamils by inverting their prejudice and posing the Tamils as plotting against the Sinhalese. A pamphlet published in 1980 and entitled "The Diabolical Conspiracy" accused Tamil teachers of inflating the grades of Tamil students so that they might receive preference over Sinhalese students in university admissions. Another document denounced Tamil plantation workers as a dangerous threat to Sinhala culture, Buddhism, and up-country villagers (Peris 2001). The violence that erupted was cyclical: when the Tamils balked at Sinhalese-only and other discriminatory policies, whether through peaceful protests or isolated terrorism, the Sinhalese government and people responded in a "mood of savage paranoia" (Spencer 1984, 193). Captives of a "Sinhala-Buddhist-Chauvinist" ethos (Das 1990, 6), this people had come to believe that all Tamils were allied in a conspiracy against them. Mobs periodically turned on Tamils: "Anyone who saw them at work would have sensed the operation of something like a mass of visceral antagonisms, a frightening force fed on a diet of rumors, tensions, fears and paranoia, and a fearsome rage directed against the Tamils" (De Silva 1986, 339). The Sinhalese riots that targeted Tamils have been called pogroms by scholar Michael Roberts (1994). According to the *Oxford English Dictionary*, a *pogrom* is an organized massacre, persecution, or extermination of an ethnic group. The term has been applied to attacks on Jews in pre–World War II Eastern Europe, but, as a result of events in the 1990s, it has increasingly been applied to "all contexts in which a dominant section of a population systematically assails another segment in their midst" (Roberts 1994,185). Roberts used the term as a loaded epithet for behavior that stops short of genocide but, like genocide, is conducted with cool calculation by agents of the state or passionately by frenzied crowds. Sinhalese riots, like most pogroms, displayed some level of organization (i.e., they were not completely spontaneous) and were instigated as a frenzied response to atrocity stories and rumors that spread quickly and elicited first horror and then retributory vengeance (Roberts 1994, 323).

Systematic discrimination plus mob violence radicalized the Tamils and transformed Tamil consciousness into a reactionary, defensive nationalism (Wilson 2000, 5). During the first half of the 1970s, cultural vitality became linked to a budding culture of resistance that was expressed through literature and preservation efforts. In 1973, at its twelfth convention, the major Tamil political party, the Federal Party, invoked the recognized principle of the right to self-determination and resolved that the Tamils were "fully qualified to be regarded as a separate Nation by virtue of their language, culture, history, territory and the[ir] innate and intense desire to live as a separate nation" (Wilson 2000, 105). A shift occurred in the second half of the 1970s, when many Tamils moved away from liberalism and cultural activities and toward civil disobedience and violence. As in Chapter 3, extremism gave rise to extremism. Youth groups embraced terrorism as a method of self-defense and viewed themselves as engaging in a holy war against the Sinhalese state (Wilson 2000, 125). They confronted the government with guerilla tactics and through "carefully orchestrated symbolic acts of violence against persons and state property . . . violence, murder, robbery" (De Silva 1986, 327). They were not well organized, as Tamil militancy was in its formative years ("Civilization and Culture" 2003). But the desire for a separate state had moved "from the wild imagination of the lunatic fringes in Tamil politics into the center of Tamil political calculations" and events were building to a showdown (Arasaratnam 1979, 516). A crisis in 1979 was skirted by government officials at the national level, who promised to increase Tamil representation on District Development Councils and elections. But in Jaffna, when the elections were finally held in 1981, the Sinhalese UNP party was determined to control the results and sent a contingent of police, paramilitaries, and thugs to intimidate Tamil voters. An atmosphere of repression and violent provocation prevailed (Peris 2001).

On Sunday, May 31, the major Tamil political party, the Tamil United Liberation Front (TULF), held a rally at which three Sinhalese policeman were shot, two fatally. That night the Sinhalese police and paramilitaries began a pogrom that lasted three days. The TULF headquarters was burned, as were the offices and press of the Tamil-language newspaper *Ealanadu*. Statues of Tamil cultural and religious figures were defaced and demolished (Peris 2001). A Hindu temple and more than 100 Tamil-owned shops and homes were looted and torched. Four Tamils were taken from their homes and killed. Late on the first night, eyewitnesses saw uniformed police and Sinhalese gang members set fire to the Jaffna Public Library (Peris 2001). Two Sinhalese Cabinet members who watched it burn from the verandah of the nearby Jaffna Rest House claimed that it was "an 'unfortunate incident,' where a 'few' policeman 'got drunk' and went on a 'looting spree,' all on their own" ("Remembering the Jaffna" 2001). National newspapers did not cover the event or the pogrom that accompanied it. Sinhalese politicians expressed no regrets and used subsequent parliamentary discussion to drive home the message sent by the library's destruction: if the Tamils were unhappy, they should leave Sri Lanka and return to their homeland, India, where there was no discrimination: "There are your *kovils* and Gods. There you have your culture, education, universities, etc. There you are masters of your own fate" ("Destruction of Jaffna" 2004). The word spread slowly to the outer world. Reverend Long, who had helped raise money for the original building, died of a heart attack [in Australia] when told of the library's destruction ("Remembering the Jaffna" 2001).

The Tamils reacted to the loss of the building and collection with intense grief. Journalist Francis Wheen (1981, 13) visited the library soon after the destruction: "Today its rooms are thickly carpeted with half-burnt pages, fluttering in the breeze which comes through the broken windows. Inspecting the charred remains, I met a heartbroken lecturer from the local teacher training college . . . [who said] 'The Sinhalese were jealous of the library.'" Twenty years later, the mayor of Jaffna, Nadarajah Raviraj, still grieved at the recollection of the flames he saw as a college student (Dugger 2001). For the Tamils, the devastated library was burned into their consciousness as "an iconic marker of the physical and imaginative violence" of Sinhalese extremists (Nesiah 2003). Education and culture had been one mode of progress for the Tamil people who lacked physical resources ("Heart and Soul" 2004). For Tamils who had come from the "arid, hardscrabble north" and risen to prominence in the professions and civil service through a devotion to education, the attack was an assault on their aspirations (Dugger 2001), value for learning, and traditions of academic achievement (Nesiah 2003). The attack convinced many of the reality of Sinhalese goals, the extinction of the Tamil culture and race in Sri Lanka (Dugger 2001). Group loyalty solidified, and the budding secessionist militancy of Tamil radicals was affirmed (Wilson 2000).

After the attack on the Jaffna Library, the Sinhalese government accelerated its long-standing pattern of muzzling those who favored compromise with intimidation and assassination. For discerning moderates within both groups, the burning of the library brought home the horrors of ethnic conflict, with its renunciation of liberal traditions in the face of concerted efforts to maintain violent emotional reactivity (Nesiah 2003; Sivathamby 2004). The attack on the library ultimately benefited all those, Tamil and Sinhalese alike, who wished to foreclose a robust civil society, arrest public debate, and free leaders from accountability (Nesiah 2003). The Jaffna Library was an important symbol of the liberal tradition, and its demise in 1981 facilitated a power shift among the Tamils. Radicals gained power and attacked not only the Sinhalese majority but also Tamil liberals, who until that point had maintained at least some influence. In an increasingly polarized atmosphere, both Sinhalese and Tamil extremists seemed bent on negating any definition of Tamil identity that centered on a pluralistic culture of learning.

Moderate Tamils liberals, as a result, were forced into exile. Some of those who remained and witnessed the ensuing civil war would become profoundly despairing. In 1990, a Jaffna poet, Sivaramani (2001), made a bonfire of her poetry and then committed suicide. Her poem, "A War-Torn Night," mourns the brutalization of Tamil culture and renunciation of a culture of critical thinking:

> Our children
> grow
> in the oppression
> of a war-torn night . . .

To not ask
to be silent
when questions remain
unanswered,
they learn
to be mute,
to pluck the wings
Of dragon flies . . .

The pogrom of 1981 was followed by violent outbreaks in 1983. Hindu guerillas ambushed an army patrol and triggered another anti-Tamil riot in which
Buddhists massacred hundreds of Hindus. Then, in turn, the fanatical Tamil
Liberation Tigers launched terror campaigns with bombings and executions.
Armed Hindu groups attacked Buddhist holy sites and shot Buddhist monks
in line-ups. In one incident, 173 people were killed (Haught 1995). Counter-
executions and retaliatory cycles of violence led to full-scale civil war in which
an estimated 65,000 people died and 1.6 million were displaced (Aryaratnam
2003). Jaffna, the cultural heart of the Tamil people, was controlled by the
Tamil Tigers from 1990–1995. It was captured by the Sinhalese government
in 1996, whereupon Norway brokered an uneasy cease-fire.

For more than two decades, the shattered and derelict library has served
as a symbol of violation and violence. In May 1982, a year after the library's
initial destruction, the community sponsored Jaffna Public Library Week and
worked together to collect thousands of books. Repairs on parts of the building were near completion when war broke out in June 1983, and the library
building was damaged by bullets, shells, and bombs (Thuriarajah 1996). After
a partial restoration, rooms were reopened in 1984, only to be caught in the
crossfire yet again in 1985. When Tamil rebels attacked a police station near
the library, a librarian was able to negotiate safe passage for the staff and students. But that night Sinhalese soldiers entered the lending room and set off
bombs that shredded thousands of books. The library was finally abandoned,
and its grounds became a battlefield. Its shell- and bullet-pocked walls, blackened with the smoke of burnt books, haunted the city. In 1998, the government began renovating the library in response to international demands for
a negotiated end to the war. It was an effort to win back the confidence of
the Tamil people (Francis 2003). The media minister publicly lamented the
destruction of the library as an "evil act," the product of hatred and misguided
politics on the part of the previous government (Peris 2001). One million
dollars was spent, and 25,000 books in the Tamil and English languages were
collected. By 2001, a replacement building was finally built. The opening
was to serve as a step for healing the wounds of two decades of warfare, but
political conflict over its opening highlighted the mistrust that lingered (Beck
2003). The opening ceremony in 2003 was postponed after 23 members of
Jaffna's town council resigned in the face of threats by Tamil Tiger insurgents
(Aryaratnam 2003). The immediate fate of the library, of course, depends on
the longevity of the tenuous brokered peace. Its long-term survival is linked

to whether the government can manage tolerance and intellectual freedom and whether the Sinhalese and Tamil peoples can learn to live together in peace.

Destroying a library is a satisfactory way to lash out at a despised group and express contempt for its purpose and goals. The violence contributes to a repressive environment in which the perpetrator's exclusivist goals can be profitably pursued. The Jaffna attack was a malicious, vindictive act that was interpreted by Tamils as having tactical and ideological components. It demonstrated to the Tamils that the government's autocratic and discriminatory policies would not stop short of ethnocide. It was, however, a dangerous strategy for Sinhalese extremists who miscalculated the Tamils' capacity for resistance and the parallel strength of their ethnic nationalism. The ensuing civil war was disastrous for both sides.

The case is different when a powerful regime can crush a rebellious ethnic group without prolonged civil war. Then, as we shall see in Iraq, biblioclasm becomes part of a broad tactical initiative to extinguish a rival group permanently.

Leaders whose legitimacy is based on ethnic identity walk a tightrope in countries with sizable minorities. To get elected, they may play the race card and foster polarization. Once in office, they must deliver on promises to make their group supreme and fend off challenges by rivals seeking to regain political influence or promote their own ethnic nationalism and independence. To pursue their own interests and to please their constituencies, leaders such as those in Sri Lanka may use pogroms to cut the enemy down to size. To eliminate an intractable problem altogether, ethnic regimes may adopt ethnocidal policies. These tactics express the far reaches of ethnic party politics. Because they are taboo by international standards, extremists usually commit large-scale ethnocide or ethnic cleansing under cover of war and insurrection. Cultural destruction is justified as a defensive response to egregious aggression or explained away as the accidental byproduct of combat.

When an authoritarian regime lashes out at a troublesome minority, the danger to books and libraries in such initiatives becomes acute. In 1999, when the Timor people campaigned for independence from Indonesia, the Indonesian government's response was to allow a militia group, with some assistance from regular troops, to massacre and rape East Timor's inhabitants and destroy the region's infrastructure—including homes, businesses, and cultural institutions. The United Nations estimated that Timor-Manatuto, previously home to 16,000 people, was completely destroyed and depopulated; much of the damage accrued by fires, set in a "slash and burn" approach (Taft 1999). The population was stampeded out of other areas that also sustained heavy damage. Because students had been very active in the independence movement, schools and libraries were a preferred target. Ninety-five percent of all school buildings and libraries were destroyed. Students at the *Universitas Timor Timur* (UNTIM), the only university in East Timor, barricaded themselves into a small room and saved 45 boxes of books along with some sports trophies and graduation gowns ("*History of the Tertiary*" 2004). Seventy percent of the university, including its library, was burnt around them ("Australian Librarians" 2000). The building that later became the new university library was used as a killing site ("After the Burning" 2002). All government records, including land titles, were burnt or carried off; intercommunal land conflict was, and remains, a particular problem in East Timor because of the country's history of displacement and migration (Fitzpatrick 2001).

Peace returned to the region only in 1999 when, after international outcry, United Nations troops were left in control as Indonesian security forces pulled out. The intractable issue of Timorese entitlement to possession of East Timor that had plagued the Indonesian government was resolved, not in favor of the regime, but through the granting of independence to the Timor people. Refugees returned to burned homes and the ashes of their books. One survivor addressed the question of whether rebellion had been worth it: "I guess it's zero hour. Our boats have been burned behind us. Literally. . . Now we have not only to rebuild the buildings, but also our lives, our language, our culture. Everything is gone—but at least we are free" (Cristalis 2002, 257).

When totalitarian regimes have institutionalized racism, ethnic repulsion and rivalry become channeled into genocide. The Nazis achieved iconic status as genocidal murderers and book burners. The Serbs took up their legacy and used racism and religious fanaticism to justify ethnic cleansing and—though some argue the fact—genocide. When Bosnia-Herzegovina declared sovereignty and withdrew from the federation of Yugoslavia, the Serbs, who controlled the government and army, used the cover of civil war to seize lands for Greater Serbia. Homogeneity was achieved by killing or expelling Muslims and cleansing the land of the Muslim culture. Mosques, schools, museums, and libraries were systematically eradicated (Knuth 2003).

Ethnocide also occurs as a result of internecine, sectoral rivalry. This was the case in Iraq in 1991. The Shiites, followers of the Shi'a sect of Islam who comprised 55 percent of Iraq's population, had long chafed at the hands of Saddam's secular Ba'thist government. In 1991, they seized upon Iraq's defeat in the Gulf War as an opportunity for armed insurrection. The goal was to overturn the secular regime, break the dominance of Sunni Muslims like Saddam, and install a Shi'a-oriented theocratic government in Baghdad. Conditions were chaotic. In Basra, local rebels were joined by groups of armed refugee Shiites who poured in from Iran, stormed the Sheraton Hotel, burned the bars and casinos of the city, and proclaimed the establishment of a Shi'a Islamic Republic. The "idea of apostasy, *kufr*, the enemy within" was widespread, and the whole Ba'thist regime was declared *kafir*, apostate, traitors to Islam (Makiya 1993, 90). According to Islamic law, the penalty for apostasy is death, and as "revolution" broke out in Shiite cities, Ba'thist officials and sympathizers were summarily executed. Official records were destroyed, and looting became widespread. Some of the worst excesses were in Kerbala and Basra, where according to one housewife, "the pattern for every government building was the same: kill every official you could get your hands on, loot everything inside, spread some kerosene around the building, light a match, and get the hell out of the place fast" (Makiya 1993, 91). According to expatriate scholar Kanan Makiya (1993), in the complete vacuum of authority, a basic nihilistic impulse came into play: some of the rebels seemed genuinely to think that looting was what the revolution was all about.

Again we see extremism begetting extreme reactions. To put down the insurrection, Saddam's troops first fired ground-to-ground missiles and helicopter-launched rockets at the Shiite cities, and then sent in ground troops. The troops conducted house-to-house searches and publicly executed suspected rebels. In the holy city of Kerbala, where the rebellion had begun and where rebels had killed dozens of security officials and high-ranking members of the Ba'ath party, troops killed thousands of Shiites (including doctors, nurses, and patients) and damaged some of the city's most revered shrines. In al-Najaf, rebels set up a base in their beloved pilgrimage site, the Tomb of Imam Ali. They believed, perhaps, that the loyalist forces would not dare to attack it, but it was targeted by mortar fire and stormed. Troops wrecked and plundered other Shiite holy sites also, and the government subsequently blamed the damage on the Shiite rebels, "saboteurs" who had turned their own shrines into murder centers (Middle East Watch 1992, 54).

Saddam used repression of the uprising as an excuse for ethnocidal attacks on Shiite leaders and cultural identity (Middle East Watch 1992, 50). He sought to neutralize his rivals, "the greatest potential popular threat to his rule," by attacking the foundations of their ethnic identity (Middle East Watch 1992, 26). Roundups of prominent Shiite clerical families, religious scholars, and students began immediately. Government authorities arrested the 95-year-old Grand Ayatollah Sayyid abu al-Qassem al-Khoei and 105 of his associates and family members (Middle East Watch 1992, 8). According to witnesses, "every turbaned person" that had not fled the area was killed or arrested—5,000 scholars and students were arrested from al-Najaf alone (Makiya 1993, 100). A United Nations Special Rapporteur later put the elimination of al-Najaf's Shiite leaders into historical context: the clergy had been reduced in the last 20 years from 8,000 or 9,000 to 2,000, and then to 800 before the 1991 uprising, then, by the end of the year to zero (Middle East Watch. 1992, 27). The Rapporteur posited that this was a final push to destroy Shi'a culture by wiping out its traditional leaders, the *ulema* [learned] class (Middle East Watch 1992, 27–28).

Shiite holy sites, mosques, seminaries, and libraries were destroyed by Saddam's troops (Thurgood 1991). As part of the cultural offensive, an assault against an ancient tradition of religious scholarship and learning, the 1,000-year-old Houza, the Shi'a university, was closed, along with private and religious schools (Makiya 1993). The libraries of the religious schools and seminaries of al-Najaf, Kufa, and Kerbala were ransacked and burned. Losses included a public library run by the Hakim family (60,000 books and 20,000 manuscripts) and the library of the late Ayatollah Khoei (38,000 books and 7,500 manuscripts). The cultural implications of such losses were compounded by the fact that many of the ancient texts had never been studied or catalogued by modern methods, and those with knowledge of their contents and ability to reconstruct inventories were murdered or arrested. Ancient treasures were looted and taken to Baghdad. The jewels, gold, and manuscripts in the Shrine of Ali in al-Najaf—"gifts made over a thousand years ago by princes and kings"—were among those objects that disappeared (Makiya 1993, 101).

Exiled scholar Kanan Makiya (1993, 100) believed that "[e]verything that set the Shi'a apart, and that gave them their identity," was targeted. Although some of the damage to Shiite holy cities occurred during the fighting, much was a function of an ongoing campaign to exact revenge (Middle East Watch 1992, 26). After the uprising was put down, the government began programs of demolition. In al-Najaf, the Imam Ali, Baqee'a, Morad, Sami Kirmasha, Imam Sadiq, and Kuwait mosques were demolished along with other religious buildings. Government bulldozers flattened the city's vast cemeteries and monumental family tombs, and a highway was built over graves in which Shi'a pilgrims had been buried for more than 1,000 years (Makiya 1993, 100). In Kerbala, palm groves and many of its shrines were leveled in what a Ba'thist spokesman characterized as the first stage of a "massive urban renewal program" (Makiya 1993, 101). Concrete soon surrounded the two central shrines of the Shi'a faith, the shrines of Hussein and Abbas (Middle East Watch 1992, 26). An *El Pais* correspondent asked an official whether the damage had occurred during the uprising, and the official replied, "No, this zone was dynamited by the government in order to renovate it" (Middle East Watch 1992, 26). The evident goal of campaigns that targeted Shiite leaders and the group's heritage, landscapes, and institutions was nothing less than destruction of the very fabric of Shi'a society (Makiya 1993).

After invading Kuwait in 1990, Saddam's troops and bureaucrats had moved quickly to confiscate or destroy the cultural artifacts of Kuwait as part of plans to turn the nation into the 19th province of Iraq. The Iraqis rationalized their pillage by condemning Kuwaitis as greedy minions of the West, who needed to be brought back into the fold of Pan-Arabism, a belief system that posed the true Arab nation as transcending the boundaries of individual states. Saddam's subsequent destruction of Shi'a books and libraries was also about enforcing the dominance of his regime, the secular Pan-Arabic ideology of Ba'thism, and his tribe and sect, the Sunnis. Throughout his reign, Saddam had elevated Sunnis to positions of power and wealth, while emasculating both Kurds and Shiites. His repression of the Kurds had involved displacement of whole towns and mass murder, but while the Shiites had experienced discrimination and their share of violent repression because of their theocratic aspirations and doctrinal differences, they had never borne the full brunt of his wrath. Their opportunistic post–Gulf War rebellion provided Saddam with a cover behind which to settle old scores and permanently remove his rivals. After the debacle of the Gulf War, it was also, no doubt, satisfying to vent his rage on the Shiites. Saddam's attacks on institutions central to the Shi'a culture demonstrate the power of biblioclasm as both malicious vandalism and a tactical weapon of ethnic negation.

Ethnic and internecine conflicts such as those in India, Kashmir, Sri Lanka, Timor, and Iraq are unfortunately common in a world in which there are 200 sovereign states and 8,000 ethnic and cultural groups competing for recognition as "nations" (Boylan 1993, 3). In a stable nation with a strong civil society, the government and public opinion can mediate peaceful negotiation and channel rivalries into political initiatives and protests. In poor countries with unstable regimes—especially in the developing world, where physical survival is tenuous and multiculturalism and democratic traditions have not taken root—rivalries often lead to violent attacks on books and people as well. Social polarization and competitiveness can become extreme when one group believes that a rival group is manipulating the system to gain unjust economic advantage and advance its social agenda. Pogroms, race riots, and hate acts are signs of polarization, and they are often accompanied by biblioclasm. Ethnic rivalry also may lead to antagonistic political behavior (insurgency, separatism) that produces general chaos and regime change, and again, books and libraries may be destroyed collaterally or targeted directly.

Ethnically defined regimes that systematically destroy books are often ones possessed by a millennial vision of the way their society *must* be. Exclusivist language policy and the violent destruction of culture may be a strategy by which they impose hegemony or cleanse disputed territory. The African country of West Cameroon was a product of years of divided rule (as a United Nations trust territory) in which the British controlled one-fifth and the French controlled four-fifths of the country. After a United Nations plebiscite in late 1959, the country was reunited into a bilingual federal union of equal partners. The French-speaking majority in the east, however, soon attempted to subjugate the south by neglecting, looting, and destroying anglophone cultural institutions, including the Buea Archives and Museum and the Bamenda Archives and Museum (Mbunwe-Samba 2001, 31). Bamenda's francophone governor publicly burnt all the English records in his office. When civil war broke out, the destruction of English-language collections escalated, and in March and April 1997, the French-speaking army bombed and burnt down historic and cultural sites in Oku. According to scholar-preservationist Patrick Mbunwe-Samba (2001, 33), the destruction was cultural genocide, a well-calculated policy aimed at erasing anglophone identity.

Twentieth-century ethnic biblioclasm was often committed in postcolonial nations. The century inherited a lot of unfinished business in terms of nation-building, and in many regions, religious and tribal entities were making halting progress on the road to identifying with a larger, secular community. As we saw in Sri Lanka, exclusivist language policy can become a high-stakes game over control of the state. The destruction of the Jaffna Public Library was, among other things, an escalation of an ongoing conflict over language and privilege. The selection of an official national language is often an area of tension. As linguist and activist Noam Chomsky (1998, 191) has written: "questions of language are basically questions of *power.*" The language that is adopted by a new nation becomes the core around which it organizes itself (Anderson 1991, 34–35). The elite class inevitably will be those with the necessary language skills. In attacks on libraries that involve language policies, distinctions as to whether an attack is primarily political, class-based, or directed against a particular ethnic group can become blurry. In Dang, Nepal, in 2002, guerillas set fire to the Mahendra Sanskrit University, the only Hindu university in the country, and destroyed 50,000 historic Sanskrit textbooks. Nepalese officials identified the perpetrators as the revolutionary All Nepal Independent Students' Union, a Maoist group that opposed Sanskrit education on the grounds that it gave unfair advantage to the Brahman caste, the only people allowed to study at the university ("Sanskrit Books" 2002). The issue of whether or not Nepal was a "Hindi nation," as specified in the constitution, was a chronic source of irritation to the non-Hindu minorities and secular communists. In a press release, the Nepal National Committee of the World Hindu Federation stated that "the attack on the only university established to uplift the Sanskrit language, the originating point of Hindu civilisation, has revealed the character of the Maoists"—that is, that they were racist ("Attack on Sanskrit" 2002). The committee warned the Maoists that they were prepared to defend the Hindu religion and culture.

The animosity of ethnic extremists is often multilayered, directed at specific local targets and, simultaneously, at larger international systems. Ethnic extremists often appear riddled with cultural jealousy as they expunge objects and institutions that testify to an opposing group's scholarly and literary advancement and its place within the wider sphere of humanistic, international culture. We can see this clearly in Sri Lanka, India, Kashmir, and Iraq. The targets were a renowned library, an internationally important research institute, the books of the scholarly Pandits, and libraries that supported a 1,000-year Shiite tradition of learning. Extremists rationalize the destruction of libraries and denial of intellectual freedom as a healthy repudiation of pluralism and democracy as well as a forthright rejection of a rival group's worldview.

Democracy threatens any single group's perceived right to seize what its members believe they are entitled to or to direct their rage at an enemy that they define as being outside the parameters of social obligation. Democracy comes with the expectation that groups must share resources, accommodate each other's lifestyles and beliefs, and allow them voice. Biblioclasm occurs, in many cases, in the absence of democracy and a viable civil society and serves simultaneously as the means by which extreme groups *fend off* the development of democracy and the pluralism and diversity that threaten their dominance and totalistic worldviews. The ultimate prize for ethnic extremists is absolute control of their own state. The pursuit of this dream may so threaten other groups that they, in turn, embrace ethnic nationalism and link their group's survival to forming their own nation.

Extreme messages elicit extreme responses, and biblioclasm is no exception. Ethnic party systems are driven toward violent conflict, Horowitz (1985) claims, because of dynamics arising from the ethnic divisions. They are peripheral groups fighting for the center. Political parties typically have a centripetal movement toward each other's positions and a middle ground as they woo voters. But ethnic-based parties are essentially centrifugal: they become more extreme over time because they have only to protect and please their guaranteed constituency and prevent interethnic split (Horowitz 1985). As a means of achieving and maintaining power, the politicians whose constituency is an ethnic group legitimize themselves by promoting religious doctrines and associating themselves with their group's myths of greatness. They weave a web of tribalism and extremism and disseminate self-righteous rationalizations that elicit, among their own group, passionate loyalty and willingness to act against rivals. Horowitz's (1985) theory that ethnic parties become more violent as their leaders assume more and more antagonistic positions has been used to explain the events in Kashmir and also in Bosnia, where Serbian politicians manipulated ethnic hatred in quests for personal power and exclusive possession of contested lands (Maas 1996, 273).

At both national and local levels, political leaders are key figures in the context of cultural violence. Whether a regime responds to its citizens' biblioclasm with rejection, accepts it by default, or actively encourages it varies according to its stability and police powers, authoritarianism, and identification with the perpetrators' group. Its response also depends on its assessment of the threat posed by the group that is being attacked. India's secular government was not secure enough to effectively police the Hindu majority and rioters who, simultaneously, enacted ethnic hatreds and rebelled against the state's multicultural policies; local police often sympathized with the Hindus and turned a blind eye to communal violence. The Indian government's grip was even looser in Kashmir, where sympathetic local Muslim government officials refused to curtail Muslim militants. The government sent in troops only when conditions deteriorated to the point that they feared loss of Kashmir to Pakistan. Sinhalese government officials in Sri Lanka embraced ethnic violence out of group loyalty and because of political expediency; the incident in Jaffna was one of a series of pogroms. In both Timor and Iraq, highly authoritarian governments wreaked cultural devastation in campaigns to eviscerate long-standing political and ethnic enemies who dared to rebel. The government does not have to be directly involved in the destruction of culture to be complicit: politicians merely have to stand by and let it go unpunished. The government sets the tone for a nation. If the central belief system accommodates pluralism and if the government is not overly influenced by one ethnic group, then books and libraries are fairly secure. If, however, the central government is captured by an exclusionist group, then books and libraries really enter the danger zone. Inflamed by ideological entitlements and possessing far too much power, an extreme regime may conclude that ethnic cleansing is justifiable. A case can be made that ethnic cleansing is the logical end of ethnic conflicts that have been intensified exponentially by grievance, greed, and power.

There are many possible bases for ethnic identity: language, shared historical experiences or myths, religious beliefs, ethnicity, and region of residence. But the key element in group-identification is "the shared perception that the defining traits, whatever they are, set the group apart" (Gurr 1993, 3). Ethnicity is an intensely politicized basis for difference. Participation in a group that excludes and scapegoats leads to an "us against them" mindset that serves as a basis for violence. When rivalry fuels hatred and clashes over beliefs spawn extremism, violence visited upon the bodies of the enemy is also visited on its texts.

REFERENCES

"After the Burning of the Books . . . " 2002. *Lingua Franca, Radio National.* http://www.abc.net.au/m/arts/ling/stories/s563312.htm. May 25, 2002.

Anderson, Benedict. 1991. *Imagined Communities: Reflections on the Origin and Spread of Nationalism*, rev. ed. London: Verso.

Arasaratnam, S. 1979. "Nationalism in Sri Lanka and the Tamils." In *Collective Identities, Nationalisms and Protest in Modern Sri Lanka*, ed. Michael Roberts. Colombo: Marga, 500–519.

Aryaratnam, Joe. 2003. "Council Members in Tamil Town in Sri Lanka Resign to Protest Rebel Threats." *Asian Tribune*, February 2, 2003. http://www.asian.tribune.com/show_news.php?id = 2521.

"Attack on Sanskrit University Condemned." 2002. *Kathmandu Post*, May 15, 2002. http://www.nepalnews.com.np/contents/englishdaily/ktmpost/202/may/may15/local.htm.

"Australian Librarians in East Timor." 2000. *ALIA INCITE Website.* http://www.alia.org.au/publishing/incite/2000/11/east.timor.html, June 6, 2003.

Baron, Reuben M., and Jeffrey D. Fisher. 1984. "The Equity-Control Model of Vandalism: A Refinement." In *Vandalism: Behaviour and Motivations*, ed. Claude Lèvy-Leboyer. Amsterdam: Elsevier Science, 63–75.

Beck, Lindsay. 2003. "Rebel Pressure Halts Reopening of S. Lanka Library." Reuters *AlertNet*, February 13, 2003. http://www.alternet.org/thenewsnewsdesk/COL56970.

Boylan, Patrick. 1993. "Thinking the Unthinkable." *ICOM News* 48 (1):3–5.

Brass, Paul R. 2003. *The Production of Hindu-Muslim Violence in Contemporary India.* Seattle: University of Washington Press.

Canter, D. 1984. "Vandalism: Overview and Prospect." In *Vandalism: Behaviour and Motivations*, ed. Claude Lèvy-Leboyer. Amsterdam: Elsevier Science, 345–356.

Chakrabarty, Dipesh. 1996. "Modernity and Ethnicity in India." In *Politics of Violence: From Ayodhya to Behrampada*, eds. John McGuire, Peter Reeves, and Howard Brasted. New Delhi: Sage, 207–218.

Chapalgaonkar, Rupa. 2004. "Mob Ransacks Pune's Bhandarkar Institute." *Mid Day*, January 5, 2004. http://www.mid-day.com/news/city/2004/january/73054.htm.

Chomsky, Noam. 1998. *On Language: Chomsky's Classic Works 'Language and Responsibility' and 'Reflections on Language' in One Volume.* New York: New Press.

"Civilization and Culture Set on Fire." 2003. *Daily Mirror Online*, July 23, 2003. http://www.dailymirror/k/2003/7/23/opinion/2.htm.

Cohen, Stanley. 1973. "Property Destruction: Motives and Meanings." In *Vandalism*, ed. Colin Ward. London: Architectural Press, 23–53.

Cohen, Stanley. 1984. "Sociological Approaches to Vandalism." In *Vandalism: Behaviour and Motivations*, ed. Claude Lèvy-Leboyer. Amsterdam: Elsevier Science, 51–61.

Cristalis, Irena. 2002. *Bitter Dawn: East Timor, a People's Story.* London: Zed Books.

Das, Veena. 1990. "Introduction: Communities, Riots, Survivors—The South Asian Experience." In *Mirrors of Violence: Communities, Riots and Survivors in South Asia*, ed. Veena Das. Delhi: Oxford University Press, 1–36.

De Silva, K.M. 1986. *Managing Ethnic Tensions in Multi-Ethnic Societies: Sri Lanka 1880–1985.* Lanham, Md.: University Press of America.

"Destruction of Jaffna Public Library and Continued Attacks on Tamil Civilians, 1981." 2004. *TamilCanadian*, January 2, 2004. http://www.tamilcanadian.com/pageview.php?ID = 572&SID = 94&pr-v = yes.

Dugger, Celia W. 2001. "Rescuing Sri Lankan Heritage from War's Ashes." *New York Times*, August 19, 2001. http://www.nytimes.com/2001/08/19/international/asia/19LANK.

Fitzpatrick, Daniel. 2001. *Land Issues in a Newly Independent East Timor.* Research Paper 21 2000–01 by the Law and Bills Digest Group, the Parliamentary Library of Australia. http://www.aph.gov.au/library/pubs/rp/2000–01/01RP21.htm. February 6, 2001.

Fox, Jonathan. 2002. *Ethnoreligious Conflict in the Late Twentieth Century: A General Theory.* New York: Lexington Books.

Francis, Krishan. 2003. "Destroyed Tamil Library Raised from Ashes." *Asian Tribune*, February 14, 2003. http://www.asiatribune.com/shaw_news.php?id = 2303.

Frykenberg, Robert Eric. 1993. "Hindu Fundamentalism and the Structural Stability of India." In *Fundamentalisms and the State: Remaking Polities, Economies, and Militance*, eds. Martin E. Marty and R. Scott Appleby. Chicago: University of Chicago Press, 233–255.

Gaylin, Willard. 2003. *Hatred: The Psychological Descent into Violence.* New York: Public Affairs.

Greeley, Andrew M. 1982. *Religion: A Secular Theory.* New York: Free Press.

Greenberger, David. B., and Vernon L. Allen. 1980. "Destruction and Complexity: An Application of Aesthetic Theory." *Personality and Social Psychology Bulletin* 6 (3):479–483.

Gurr, Ted. Robert. 1993. *Minorities at Risk: A Global View of Ethnopolitical Conflicts.* Washington, D.C.: United States Institute of Peace.

Haught, James A. 1995. *Holy Hatred: Religious Conflicts of the '90s.* Amherst, N.Y.: Prometheus.

"Heart and Soul of Tamil Culture: The Jaffna Public Library." 2004. *Infoeelam: Gateway to Tamil Eelam*, January 2, 2004. http://www.infoeelam.com/culture.htm.

History of the Tertiary Education Sector in East Timor. 2004. National University of East Timor Library Project Report. http://www.untl.labor.new.au/print_version/history.html. March 19, 2004.

Hobsbawm, Eric. 1993. "The New Threat to History." *New York Review of Books* 1000 (21):62–64.

Horowitz, Donald L. 1985. *Ethnic Groups in Conflict.* Berkeley: University of California Press.

Horowitz, Donald L. 2001. *The Deadly Ethnic Race Riot.* Berkeley: University of California Press.

Jaisingh, Hari. 1996. *Kashmir: A Tale of Shame.* New Delhi: UBS Publishers' Distributors.

Kakar, Sudhir. 1996. *The Colors of Violence: Cultural Identities, Religion, and Conflict.* Chicago: University of Chicago Press.

Katakam, Anupama. 2004. "Politics of Vandalism." *Frontline*, January 17–30, 2004. http://www.flonnet.com/fl2102/stories/20040130003802800.htm.

Kaul, Mohan Lai. 1999. *Kashmir: Wail of a Valley.* New Delhi: Gyan Sagar.

Knuth, Rebecca. 2003. *Libricide: The Regime-Sponsored Destruction of Books and Libraries in the Twentieth Century.* Westport, Conn.: Praeger.

Kothari, Rajni. 1998. *Communalism in Indian Politics.* Delhi: Rainbow Publishers.

Kumar, Krishna. 1992. "Hindu Revivalism and Education in North Central India." In *Fundamentalisms and Society: Reclaiming the Sciences, the Family, and Education*, eds. Martin E. Marty and R. Scott Appleby. Chicago: University of Chicago Press, 536–557.

Maas, Peter. 1996. *Love Thy Neighbor: A Story of War.* New York: Alfred A. Knopf.

Makiya, Kanan. 1993. *Cruelty and Silence: War, Tyranny, Uprising, and the Arab World.* New York: W. W. Norton.

Mbunwe-Samba, Patrick. 2001. "Should Developing Countries Restore and Conserve?" In *Destruction and Conservation of Cultural Property*, eds. Robert Layton, Peter G. Stone, and Julian Thomas. New York: Routledge, 30–41.

Middle East Watch. 1992. *Endless Torment: The 1991 Uprising in Iraq and Its Aftermath.* New York: Human Rights Watch.

"Mob Ransacks Bhandarkar Institute." 2004. *Deccan Herald*, January 6, 2004. http://www.deccanherald.com/deccanherald/jan062004/n12.asp.

Nesiah, Vasuki. 2003. "Monumental History and the Politics of Memory: Public Space and the Jaffna Public Library." *Lines Magazine*, February 2003. http://www/lines-magazine.org/Art_Feb03/editorial_vasuki.htm.

Newberg, Paula R. 1995. *Double Betrayal: Repression and Insurgency in Kashmir.* Washington, D.C.: Carnegie Endowment for International Peace.

Nissan, Elizabeth. 1984. "Some Thoughts on Sinhalese Justifications for the Violence." In *Sri Lanka in Change and Crisis*, ed. James Manor. New York: St. Martin's Press, 175–186.

Obeyesekere, Gananath. 1984. "The Origins and Institutionalisation of Political Violence." In *Sri Lanka in Change and Crisis*, ed. James Manor. New York: St. Martin's Press, 153–174.

Pandey, Gyanendra. 1992. "In Defense of the Fragment: Writing about Hindu-Muslim Riots in India Today." *Representations* 37:27–55.

Pandey, Gyanendra. 1996. "The New Hindu History." In *Politics of Violence: From Ayodhya to Behrampada*, eds. John McGuire, Peter Reeves, and Howard Brasted. New Delhi: Sage, 143–157.

Peris, Vilani. 2001. "Two Decades after the Burning Down of the Jaffna Library in Sri Lanka." *World Wide Socialist Website*. http://www.wsws.org/articles/2001/may2001/sri-m30.shtml, May 30, 2001.

Ray, Arjun. 1997. *Kashmir Diary: Psychology of Militancy.* New Delhi: Manas Publications.

"Remembering the Jaffna Public Library." 2001. *Sangam Research Website*. http://www.sangam.org/ANALYSIS/Library-6–01, June 2001.

Roberts, Michael. 1989. "Apocalypse or Accommodation?: Two Contrasting Views of Sinhala-Tamil Relations in Sri Lanka." *South Asia* 12 (1):67–83.

Roberts, Michael. 1994. *Exploring Confrontation: Sri Lanka: Politics, Culture and History*. Chur, Switzerland: Harwood Academic Publishers

Sambandan, V. S. 2003. "The Story of the Jaffna Public Library." *Frontline*, March 28, 2003. http://www.frontlineonnet.com/f/2006/stories/20030328000505900.htm.

"Sanskrit Books Destroyed." 2002. *News India-Times*, May 24, 2003. http://www.newsindia-times.com/2002/05/24/24/sa-brief.html.

Scott, F. R. 1966. "Degeneration." *F. R. Scott: Selected Poems*. Toronto: Oxford University Press, 98. [Stanzas reprinted with the permission of William Toye, literary executor for the Estate of F. R. Scott]

Senaratne, Jagath P. 1997. *Political Violence in Sri Lanka 1977–1990: Riots, Insurrections, Counterinsurgencies, Foreign Intervention*. Amsterdam: VU University Press.

Shivpuri, B.L. 1998. "Regional Minority: Crisis and Alienation—A Case Study of Kashmiri Pandits." In *Jammu-Kashmir-Ladakh: Ringside Views*, eds. Shyam Kaul and Onkar Kachru. New Delhi: Khama Publishers, 212–222.

Sivaramani. 2001. "A War-Torn Night." In *Lutesong and Lament: Tamil Writing from Sri Lanka*, ed. Chelva Kanaganayakam. Toronto: TSAR Publications, 144–145. [Lines from the poem reprinted with the permission of TSAR Publications]

Sivathamby, Karthigesu. 2004. "Opening of the Jaffna Public Library." *Northeastern Herald*, January 2, 2004. http://www.sooriyan.com/library/library.asp.

Spencer, Jonathan.1984. "Popular Perceptions of the Violence: A Provincial View." In *Sri Lanka in Change and Crisis*, ed. James Manor. New York: St. Martin's Press, 187–195.

Taft, Julia V. 1999. *The Situation in East Timor and the Role of the U.S. Government:* Testimony by Assistant Secretary of State Taft before the Subcommittee on International Operations and Human Rights, House International Relations Committee, September 30, 1999, Washington, D.C., Foreign Policy Association.

Thurgood, Liz. 1991. "Iraq: President Saddam Initiates Drive on Shi'ite Holy Cities." *Guardian*, 23 July, p. 31.

Thuriarajah, V. S. 1996. Letter to the Sri Lanka Government. *Ceylon Daily News*, July 17, 1996. http://www.tamilcanadian.com/eelam/hrights/html/article/SU980516114546N30.html.

Triparthi, Salil. 1997. "The March of Vishnu." *Index on Censorship* 6: 84–89.

Wheen, Francis. 1981. "The Burning of Paradise." *New Statesman* 102 (2626):13.

Wilson, A. Jeyaratnam. 2000. *Sri Lankan Tamil Nationalism: Its Origins and Development in the Nineteenth and Twentieth Centuries*. London: Hurst.

Witzel, Michael. 2004. "Vandalism and Preservation." *Hindu*, December 1, 2004. http://www.thehindu.com/2004/01/12/stories/2004011201581000.htm.

Worsely, Peter. 1984. *The Three Worlds: Culture and World Development*. Chicago: University of Chicago Press.

Part II

Absolute Power and the Drive to Purify Society

Because the legitimacy of a regime is linked to public acceptance of the central value system it represents, a peripheral group that successfully overthrows the government must embed its value system into the institutional structure of the nation. In order to do this, libraries may be purged or, at times, eliminated. Extremists in power maintain mindsets developed when they were on the periphery—they feel threatened, surrounded by those who would destroy them. Maintaining ideological orthodoxy and political advantage is an ongoing, high-stakes life-or-death battle that may be used to justify the imposition of a police state. Ideologues will seek to purify and reform society and to extinguish alternatives and any peripheral groups or ideas that might threaten their hegemony, because controlling the central belief system is key to attaining and holding on to power. To retain legitimacy, the regime conflates its authority with the authority of the belief system and a challenge to one is perceived as a challenge to the other. Libraries become casualties of this embrace of totalitarianism.

CHAPTER 5

National Socialism and the Destruction of Berlin's Institute for Sexual Science, 1933

> The symbolism of fire and flame dates back to primitive times. Fire and torch were used to fight demons, and the power of the flame derived from the fact that it linked earth and heaven.
> —George L. Mosse, *The Nationalization of the Masses*

In 1933, the National Socialists gained control of Germany, marking the end of the Weimar Republic. The republic, a product of the 1918 revolution and the dissolution of the monarchy, had given Germans a new lease on life and allowed a brief experiment with modernity, liberalism, and individualism. But beneath the excitement and creativity was also "anxiety, fear, [and] a rising sense of doom" (Gay 2001, xiv). Revolutionary National Socialism and fascism, packaged as a conservative backlash and return to familiar values, spelled the end of the so-called Golden Twenties and the beginning of a period of severe repression for those whose lifestyle, beliefs, or race disqualified them for participation in the new order.

For homosexual men, an estimated two million or 2 percent of the population, it was the end of relative freedom and the beginning of a time when they "lived like animals in a wild game park, always sensing the hunters" (Burleigh and Wipperman 1991, 194). After Hitler's ascension to power, the Nazis, in suppression of corrupt modernity, quickly dismantled the gay-rights movement that had thrived during the Weimar Republic and closed down all organizations, clubs, periodicals, films, and institutions supporting this cause. An early target was the library of the Institute for Sexual Science, internationally known as a research and treatment center for all areas of sexual functioning—a product of Weimar democracy that was created by outsiders (homosexuals and sexologists), who, for a brief moment, gained access to the inside (institutionalized respectability) (Gay 2001). The institute was quick to become a target because of its status as a government agency that had legitimized alternate views of sexuality and because of its ties with founder and director Magnus Hirschfeld (1868–1935). Hirschfeld was a confirmed enemy of the Nazi Party because he embodied all that the Nazis despised and vilified. He was a Jew, a pacifist and leftist, a political activist and social reformer, and an independent scholar, and was presumed to be homosexual. While Hirschfeld survived in exile, his institute was vandalized and dismantled, and the institute's library and collections were burnt in the huge student bonfires of May 10, 1933. A bronze bust of Hirschfeld was also thrown into the flames.

Legal sanctions against homosexuals began in the Middle Ages, but in the nineteenth century, because of the impact of the French Revolution and the Enlightenment, four German states (Bayern, Hanover, Württemberg, and Braunschweig) decriminalized homosexuality. This leniency began to erode in 1871, when Prussia's harsh legislation was implemented throughout the reich in the form of Paragraph 175 of the Criminal Code: unnatural sex acts between persons of the male sex or between humans and animals were punishable by imprisonment and the loss of civil rights. On the average, 500 men a year were prosecuted for homosexual acts. This cast a pall over Germany, and blackmail and the threat of exposure led many to suicide. Legal consequences were reinforced by a climate of public intolerance. Homosexuality was met with disgust and perceived as a significant mental, moral, economic, and political problem (Taeger 1998, 23). It was perceived by many as evidence of anarchy that threatened the stability of the state. Homosexuality and, indeed, all forms of unbridled sensuality undermined the basic unit of civil order, traditional marriage—a controllable, clearly arranged social unit that, in its nineteenth-century form, reflected the hierarchical ruler-subject relationship and thus supported the development of a powerful modern nation (Taeger 1998, 20).

Nevertheless, by the end of the nineteenth century, a recognizable subculture existed, with 40 homosexual meeting places in Berlin alone (Burleigh and Wipperman 1991, 184). A gay-rights movement had surfaced and received support from the medical profession, most notably the neurologist Magnus Hirschfeld. In 1897, under Hirschfeld's leadership, doctors and jurists began to challenge the practice of prosecuting homosexuals and founded the Scientific-Humanitarian Committee (SHC). The SHC would lobby continuously for reform of Paragraph 175 until the Nazis took over the government. With the 1919 founding of the Institute for Sexual Science, also initiated by Hirschfeld, German intellectuals emerged as acknowledged leaders in an international movement for sexual reform and social equality for homosexuals. Indeed, Germany's gay movement was considered to be the world's most advanced (Guerin 1994, 14). With the relatively liberal interpretation of Paragraph 175 that followed World War I, momentum built within the homosexual community until at least 25 homosexual organizations existed and some 30 periodicals for homosexuals appeared regularly. The Weimar era represented a "high-water mark for tolerance toward homosexual men" (Lautmann 1998, 354).

Magnus Hirschfeld was a towering figure within this movement. Hirschfeld was profoundly influenced by his father, a prominent Jewish doctor and humanitarian whose memory was immortalized by a monument erected in his hometown in 1895 (this monument was demolished by the Nazis in 1933, the same year that Hirchfeld's bust and library were publicly burned). Like his father, Hirschfeld specialized in public health until the 1895 trial of Oscar Wilde and the nonrelated suicide of a homosexual patient triggered a "life-long devotion to sexology in general, and homosexuality in particular" (Garde 1964, 674). Under a pseudonym, Hirschfeld published *Sappho and Socrates*, in which he argued that the homosexual urge, like the heterosexual, is inborn, not an acquired vice, and influenced by glands. Hirschfeld would develop this theme over the rest of his life and use it to undermine rationales behind the criminalization of homosexuality. After 1897, Hirschfeld gained national recognition by mobilizing the SHC to petition the Reichstag for repeal of Paragraph 175, and over the next 20 years, he would lead campaigns to overturn this legislation. He achieved notoriety by serving as an expert witness in high-profile court cases against homosexuals, including the 1909 Moltke-Eulenberg Trial, which transfixed the nation with its revelations about sexual improprieties and intrigues in Kaiser Wilhelm II's court. International stature was assured after he cofounded the World League for Sexual Reform, which eventually grew to 130,000 members, sponsored high-profile conferences in Copenhagen, London, and Vienna, and promoted sexology and sexual reform worldwide.

Hirschfeld recognized the need for an objective and scientific approach to the question of human sexuality, and he collected empirical data through interviews, consultations, and ethnographic fieldwork. More than 6,000 of his meticulously prepared psychobiological questionnaires, the world's first survey of its kind, were administered to Berlin students and factory workers; 2.2 percent of the German male population admitted to being homosexual. The information he collected was the basis for both Hirschfeld's theories and the popular psychosexual instruction that he promoted so extensively. The collection and analysis of empirical data led to numerous publications as Hirschfeld developed into a prolific author and editor. He authored notable volumes on male and female homosexuality, transvestitism (in fact, he coined the term *transvestite*), racism, and psychopathology. His annual *Yearbook for Sexual Intermediaries*, published from 1899 to 1923, was a previously unavailable medium for the dissemination of cutting-edge articles by learned specialists: jurists, ethnologists, biologists, physicians, psychoanalysts, and activists. This series produced "the richest collection of homosexual studies of all time in the areas of history, literature, art, music and psychology" (Garde 1964, 675). Hirschfeld's influence was immense. According to his contemporary, historian Max Hodann (1937, 73), he was the man who made the right of homosexuals to live, love, and survive according to their nature "a discussible and mentionable problem."

In 1910, Hirschfeld moved to Berlin and became "Germany's first avowed specialist in the psychosexual [field]" (Garde 1964, 675). He was recognized as a sociological pioneer for his merging of social medicine with social science. Hirschfeld demonstrated a thoroughly modern commitment to inquiry— a "continuing process of trial and error, acceptance and rejection, discovery and rediscovery, refinement and re-definition, [through which] each new scientific breakthrough induces social changes that ramify throughout the entire culture" (Shera 1965, 4). He sought to further the scientific study of homosexuality and related manifestations as well as the whole range of human emotions, and he sought to use studies to advance the progress and welfare of humanity (Hodann 1937, 38). In his campaign to make homosexuality acceptable, or at least toler-able, Hirschfeld developed graphic and practical materials for doctors and the legal profession and was known as "a great populizer of knowledge" because of frequent public lectures in which he discussed sexual issues in an understand-able and nonsensational manner (Hodann 1937, 50). He took great risks: in 1919, he appeared as himself in a feature-length silent film, *Anders al die Andern*, the story of a homosexual victim of blackmail who turned to Hirschfeld for help (Steakley 1975, 88). It was an effort to influence public opinion and create sym-pathy for beleaguered homosexuals by humanizing their plight.

Hirschfeld was surrounded by adversaries. The doors of German universities were shut to him because of his efforts to make sexuality a respectable area of inquiry, to use science for purposes of political and social reform, and to popu-larize scientific knowledge. In addition, heterosexual academics asserted that his alleged homosexuality disqualified him from objectivity and credibility. As historian of homosexuality Noel Garde (1964, 677) wryly commented, "This seems rather like saying that a naval officer with long service on submarines is much less qualified to write about submarine warfare than a naval officer who has never been in a submarine." Because of his race and high profile as a homosexual activist, Hirschfeld was repeatedly the target of anti-Semitic and conservative right-wing interest groups who viewed homosexuality as a vice introduced and promoted by Jews intent on degrading the nation. In their eyes, sexology and related critical efforts, such as Freud's psychoanalysis, were degen-erate "Jewish science" (Haeberle 1989, 371). During the 1909 trials, leaflets were distributed in front of his house announcing: "Dr. Hirschfeld—A Public Danger. The Jews Are Our Undoing" (Wolff 1986, 74). *Anders al die Andern* was banned all over Germany and provoked widespread anti-Semitic demon-strations; it was attacked as "a piece of rampant obscenity" and as "a feast for degenerates which could ruin German youth" (Wolff 1986, 194). Hirschfeld was repeatedly criticized for causing or encouraging homosexuality, and he responded, "I do not encourage and propagate homosexuality: I only open the eyes of those who are homosexually inclined about themselves, and try to strug-gle against their social ostracization" (as quoted in Grau 1995a, 23).

As Hirschfeld explored sexual constitutions and proclivities that never before had been systematically studied or classified, his findings confirmed his belief in the inborn nature of homosexuality (Hodann 1937, 45–46). He concluded that homosexuality was a constitutional variant, a middle ground between the male-female opposition, which in both psychological and physical respects placed homosexuality in the large domain of intersexuality (Grau 1995a, 23). Of course, this was antithetical to religious and cultural mores concerning the binary nature of female and male identities. And in the 1920s, despite the fact that Germany was a democracy, his positions repeatedly evoked verbal and physical public attacks by right-wing conservatives, especially the National Socialists, who were struggling for political power and control of the nation's central belief system. Danger was ever present as journalists and editors called Hirschfeld names such as "the big boss of the perverts" (Burleigh and Wipperman 1991, 187) and urged their readers to disrupt the lectures of "the Jew Dr. Magnus Hirschfeld" (Wolff 1986, 197). He was physically assaulted in Munich in 1920—attacked from behind, beaten, and left with a fractured skull: his death was announced mistakenly, and he had the subsequent experience of reading his own obituary. His foes were disappointed by his survival, and one Nazi newspaper lamented: "Weeds never die. . . . We have no hesitation in saying that we regret that this shameless and horrible poisoner of our people has not found his well-deserved end" (Wolff 1986, 198). In Vienna in 1923, a troop of young Nazis threw stink-bombs at the stage where he was lecturing, fired shots, and randomly beat members of the audience. It was the paradoxical nature of the Weimar Republic that the regime's liberal approach to censorship made Hirschfeld's activities possible, while the government would not or could not protect him.

The outrage engendered by Hirschfeld's presumed (though never declared) homosexuality, his advocacy of sexual freedom, and his racial origins was compounded by his international stature as an intellectual. The growing fascist element in Germany was extremely nationalistic and appalled at the "rootlessness" of those intellectuals who functioned in the cross-national arena of global scholarship (Mosse 1970, 156). The fascists opposed ideas about the solidarity of all humankind (Buchheim 1968, 27) and believed that intellectuals lacked sufficient patriotism. In addition, they were worthless and effeminate, too often Jewish, and utterly unrepresentative of the ideal man: masculine, virile, athletic, decisive, and committed to a new order based on instinct rather than reason. In their reverence for the physical and for brutal action, the fascists particularly despised "'dekadenten Zivilisationsliteratentums,' decadent literary people with the values of Western liberal civilization" (Hill 2001, 20). Nazi leaders, like Joseph Goebbels, who would ultimately serve as the Third Reich's director of propaganda, spoke openly about the need to destroy the intellectual basis of the Weimar Republic as well as its political system (Frei 1993, 63). They hounded Hirschfeld because he epitomized the un-German spirit: "the rationalism, materialism, cosmopolitanism, egalitarianism, parliamentarism, pacifism, tolerance, assimilationism, ecumenism, and modernism [that] the Nazis detested" (Hill 2001, 11).

Early in 1919, Hirschfeld acquired an elegant mansion in Berlin and established the world's first institute for sexual science. He announced at the opening that it was, first, an institute for research, and second, a center for teaching and therapy (Wolff 1986, 79). Of particular interest to Hirschfeld was the study of endocrine glands and their involvement in sexual impulses. In general, the archives and library were crucial in supporting studies of the biology of sexuality. The fundamental disciplines of the institute were biology, pathology, sociology, and ethnology, and research and educational activities focused on psychological and social issues of sexuality and forensic medicine (Wolff 1986, 175). The treatment services were comprehensive, and consultation was available to those with sexual difficulties, including impotence. A state-of-the-art medical clinic provided treatment for venereal diseases and sex-related illnesses. Marriage and premarital counseling were available, as were family planning, abortion information, sex education, and treatment for transvestites, pedophiles, hermaphrodites, androynes, masochists, those with endocrine dysfunctions, and, of course, homosexuals. The legal department advised men accused of homosexuality and represented them in court (Isherwood 1976, 19). Specialists visited from all over the world, and thousands of foreign students, doctors, visiting specialists, jurists, and curious members of the public attended lectures and courses. Lectures on sexual sociology encompassed relations between sex and society, eugenics, overpopulation, problems of abstinence, marriage, free love, prostitution, laws, and sexual hygiene (Biale 1997, 273). The auditorium where these lectures were held bore this inscription: "Not for its own sake is Science, but for all Humanity" (Hirschfeld 1936, 319). It was generally packed on evenings when discussion centered on anonymous written questions that the general public could deposit in a box. The institute served as a "visible guarantee of his [Hirschfeld's] scientific respectability. . . . It was a place of education for the public, its lawmakers, and its police [especially pathologists]" (Isherwood 1976, 18).

The activities were supported by a library and archives that eventually included an estimated 20,000 volumes and a unique collection of about 35,000 pictures. There were medical theses written by students at the institute, journals, and informational materials in all formats. There were thousands of case studies and photographs of patients who were either borderline cases of sexual variants or people with psychosexual disorders; there were 3,000 microscopic slides of brain tissues, statistical tables, and a collection of fetishes (Wolff 1986, 189). Christopher Isherwood (1976, 16), the homosexual writer whose autobiographical works inspired the movie *Cabaret*, a compelling picture of sexually permissive post–World War I Berlin, described the institute's archive and museum, which was under the supervision of Karl Geiss, Hirschfeld's alleged longtime lover:

Here were whips and chains and torture instruments designed for the practitioners of pleasure-pain; high-heeled, intricately decorated boots for the fetishists; lacy female undies which had been worn by ferociously masculine Prussian officers beneath their uniforms. . . . Here were fantasy pictures, drawn and painted by Hirschfeld's patients. Scenes from the court of a priapic king who sprawled on a throne with his own phallus for a scepter and watched the grotesque matings of his courtiers. Strange sad bedroom scenes in which the faces of the copulators expressed only dismay and agony. And here was a gallery of photographs, ranging in subject matter from the sexual organs of quasi-hermaphrodites to famous homosexual couples. . . . Christopher [Isherwood referred to himself] giggled because he was embarrassed. He was embarrassed because, at last, he was being brought face to face with his tribe.

Isherwood (1976, 15) observed that, in contrast, the *public* rooms had an atmosphere of the former owner, a famous musician and aficionado of Brahms: "Their furniture was classic, pillared, garlanded, their marble massive, their curtains solemnly sculpted, their engravings grave. Lunch was a meal of decorum and gracious smiles, presided over by a sweetly dignified lady with silver hair: a living guarantee that sex, in this sanctuary, was being treated with seriousness." Over the door an inscription in Latin read: "Sacred to Love and to Sorrow." Isherwood (1976, 17) was at first repulsed by Hirschfeld but would come to honor the "silly solemn old professor with his doggy mustache, thick peering spectacles, and clumsy German-Jewish boots" as a heroic leader of his "tribe."

A German journalist who visited also expressed his surprise about the institute's intimate, as opposed to clinical or academic, atmosphere: "That—a scientific institute? No cold walls, no linoleum on the floors, no uncomfortable chairs and no smell of disinfectants. This is a private house: carpets, pictures on the walls, and nowhere a plate saying 'No entrance.' And it is full of life everywhere, with patients, doctors and other people who work here" (Wolff 1986, 177). The peacefulness found in spacious rooms with garden-view windows and comfortable sofas fostered an atmosphere of acceptance for homosexuals, a retreat from the harsh treatment they received in the outside world. Patients reported that Hirschfeld would often take them for a walk and treat them with respect and love. He fostered self-confidence, self-acceptance, a sense of biological normality, and the ability to take pleasure in oneself (Wolff 1986, 177). For many, the institute was an oasis of tolerance in an increasingly threatening world.

As the Nazis gained power, they found many ordinary citizens who shared their racist and homophobic attitudes and clamored for the institute's destruction. Tensions between the general public and urban homosexuals had been exacerbated by demographic concerns and by homosexuals' "blatant" flouting of norms. The depressive effect of homosexuality on the birth rate, acceptable during the nineteenth century, was less tolerable after the loss of two million men in World War I. By "choosing" not to reproduce, German homosexuals were lowering the birth rate and thus compromising the nation's ability to field armies and redress the disgraceful loss in World War I. To add insult to injury, recalcitrant homosexuals were flouting norms in which reproduction, not sensuality, was the dominant rationale for sexual contact. According to Hans Peter Bleuel (1973, 27),

Berlin was branded the sinful Gomorrah of a degenerate civilization. . . . All that was good, beautiful and true—the classical German heritage—was rejected, scorned and subverted . . . [into a] horrible panorama of moral decadence and cultural decline that accorded with the resentment harboured by a broad section of the public which still dwelt in the nineteenth-century world of ideas.

In the nineteenth century, bourgeois respectability had become linked with nationalism (Mosse 1985). In the 1920s and early 1930s, as old communities and religious and familial attachments were undermined by secularization, urbanization, and the influence of liberal thought, the nation became the "principal surviving factor in an individual's sense of identity" (Pfaff 1993, 44). The issue of homosexuality as a threat to the nation became incendiary and was used by the Nazis to build their following. The Nazis incorporated long-standing antihomosexual norms and proposed "solutions" into their platform. Economic and political unrest, fueled by the stock market crash of 1929 and the ineffectuality of the Weimar regime, caused many to turn to National Socialism. The Nazis increased calls for harsher penal sanctions, compulsory medical treatment of homosexuals, preventive detention, and court-ordered castration or sterilization (Grau 1995b, 2). They hammered home the need to wage war on eugenic inferiors. Head of the Gestapo Heinrich Himmler characterized homosexuals as "sociosexual propagation misfits" and "as use-less as hens which don't lay eggs" (Plant 1986, 102). The National Socialists capitalized on a conservative backlash against the cosmopolitanism and modernism of the 1920s. Indeed, modernization, according to historian James D. Steakley (1975), had come so quickly and had produced such glaring contradictions that the situation could only be brought under control by making a great leap forward—or back. The Nazis carried out a "conservative revolution which attempted to restore the discipline, the community, and the morality of a bygone era" (Steakley 1975, 119).

National Socialism was an amalgamation of linked ideas, whose combined impact fed virulent extremism. At its base were intense nationalism and a racism that was compatible with the German population's broader nationalistic yearnings. The Nazis would repeatedly demonstrate that attachment to country, group, or "fatherland" could cause people to disregard others' claims to justice and abandon reason or common morality (Pfaff 1993, 24). Borrowing freely from Darwinian notions of the survival of the fittest, the Nazis translated their belief in Aryan superiority into state policy. To achieve the final supremacy of the Nordic race and Germany's dominance, they believed it was necessary to create a conflict-free, homogeneous "community of the people" and to achieve what Hitler called a "moral purification of the body politic" (Gellately and Stoltzfus 2001, 3). In fact, the Nazis had no new morality to offer and, instead, contented themselves with furious attacks on prevailing immorality (Bleuel 1973, 34). As right-wing radicals on the periphery of German society, the Nazis claimed legitimacy by scoring off against values such as liberalism, individualism, equality, democracy, humanistic values, and internationalism (Curtis 1979, 92). They conflated politics and racism and rationalized their extremism by identifying certain groups as posing an acute and immediate danger to the rest of the population, in particular, homosexuals and Jews.

"Both popular anti-semitic culture and the dominant medical opinion of the fin de siècle considered Jews to be a neurologically diseased people whose pathology was inextricably linked to perversion and hypersexuality" (Biale 1997, 274). The Nazis held the Jews responsible for corrupting German culture by introducing homosexuality; indeed, they believed that "all the foul urges of the Jewish soul" had come together in homosexuality (Grau 1995b, 3). Fascist race eugenicists posited that Jews were the source of various nervous diseases, including homosexuality, and were thus responsible for the physical and mental degeneration of the human race (Taeger 1998, 29). This belief lent to the Nazi's prejudice the power of scientific legitimation (Biale 1997, 274). Sexologists sought to deconstruct such pseudoscience and defuse the myths they supported by establishing the innateness of sexual variety; but when they defended tolerance of variant sexual behavior, they were demonized as "pimps under scientific camouflage" (Heidtmann 1991b, 440). Indeed, independent intellectuals in general, as well as homosexuals and Jews, inspired condemnation, dread, admiration, and vulnerability, as one Nazi historian witnessed with this statement: "Hirschfeld . . . has upon his conscience a good deal of the outrage at Jewish frivolity which was building up in the German people and finally exploded in 1933" (Steakley 1975, 90).

A key concept of National Socialism was virility and masculinity as the essential life force behind a triumphant *volk*. A Nazi articulated this in 1928: "it is necessary that the German people live. And it can only live if it can fight, for life means fighting. And it can only fight if it maintains its masculinity. It can only maintain its masculinity if it exercises discipline, especially in matters of love. . . . Anyone who even thinks of homosexual love is our enemy. We reject anything which emasculates our people" (Steakley 1975, 84). With manliness a vital part of the National Socialist ethos, ideological opposition merged with a general cultural hostility toward the "immorality" of homosexuality and fed a movement to reshape and purify society (Giles 2001, 238). Homosexuality became one of the most serious morals offenses in Nazi Germany, and the Gestapo was dedicated to its extinction. To this end, homosexuals were watched, registered, arrested, prosecuted, and segregated; they were to be reeducated, castrated, or—if this was unsuccessful—exterminated (Grau 1995b, 2). And yet, in his 1937 *History of Modern Morals* (1937, 73), Hodann, a liberal, pointed out that it was irony as well as "tragedy of the deepest and most savage kind" that the Nazis should have so adamantly targeted Hirschfeld, his gay-rights movement, and homosexuals in general when the Nazi ranks were "honey-combed with homosexuality both in sentiment and active practice!"

Indeed, within the Nazi leadership there was ambivalence about the issue of homosexuality. A persuasive case can be made that Nazi policies were affected by division within the homosexual population in general. German homosexuals were almost totally lacking in feelings of solidarity; they had trouble organizing and indulged in a great deal of infighting and backbiting. The liberal reformers were at odds with an estimated 75 percent of male homosexuals in Germany who sympathized with parties of the right (Johansson and Percy 1990). As Hirschfeld's movement emphasized science and human rights, it became a "Femme approach" positing heterosexuality and homosexuality as equally legitimate forms of sexual love, and pederasty and sadomasochism as abusive and unacceptable. Hirschfeld's chief rival for control of the gay-rights movement was Adolf Brand. His followers were right-wing homosexuals who defined the true homosexual as virile and aggressive, a male in all respects. They characterized Hirschfeld's theories as laughable, false, and a "catastrophic danger for our whole movement" (Brand 1995, 35). They rejected theories of homosexuality as a third sex, instead touting homosexuality as a *superior* form of male sex (Biale 1997, 277). This approach was militantly prohomosexual, racist, nationalistic, and misogynistic. Brand's publication, *Der Eigene* ("the Special") promoted masculine homosexuals as *Ubermanner* (supermen) because of their intense masculinity and the esthetic superiority of pedophile relations. The Community of the Special sought to revive the pederastic military society of pre-Christian pagan cultures, and their ideal society was the *mannerbund*, "an all-male 'comradeship-in-arms' comprised of rugged men and boys" (Lively and Abrams 1996, 8). For them, masculine homosexuals were an ideal type, a master race, as opposed to effeminate homosexuals who were, in fact, freaks of nature and degenerated examples of this ideal. Effeminate homosexuals were viewed as self-indulgent, petty, scheming, and gossipy; they had warped self-images, acted like women, and, unlike "Butch" homosexuals, would not propagate (Lively and Abrams 1996, 23). In 1914, Hirschfeld dismissed Brand's group as fanatical and "exaggerated side-currents," but by 1920, that group had made great headway in wresting control of the movement (Oosterhuis 1991, 24). A case could be made that their beliefs dovetailed somewhat with the tenets of National Socialism.

A line of reasoning exists, championed by antigay authors Scott Lively and Kevin Abrams (1996), that the Nazi regime was riddled with masculine homosexuals. This type of homosexuality had been fostered in the Wandervogal movement, which had stressed male bonding, and in its successor, the Hitler Youth. Ultramasculine Nazi homosexuals realized in the Third Reich their dream of a revived Hellenic culture of virile militarism, and part of that dream was the extinguishing of those homosexuals who, like Hirschfeld, violated their prototype. Whether one accepts this feminine-masculine conundrum or views the Nazis as either bourgeois perpetrators of traditional antihomosexual values or genocidal homophobes, this ambivalence in the party's embrace of antihomosexual values and their selective and expedient implementation of discriminatory measures is noteworthy.

Within the Nazi elite, it seems that homosexuality was officially condemned but tolerated internally, especially in the early years (Heidtmann 1991b, 440). It appears that Hitler himself did not include homophobia among his major obsessions (Giles 2001, 233), and there was a tension behind his basic bohemianism and his public and politically expedient espousal of traditional values (Johnson 2000, 287). His public condemnation of homosexuality may have been a means to eliminate political opponents both within his party and without, while at the same time, proving his respectability to the German population. Many analysts believe that the famous 1934 murder of Ernst Rohm, a longtime ally and creator of the *Sturm Abteilung* or "Brown Shirts," and the subsequent purge of its ranks was actually a high-profile realignment of power and not the attack on homosexuality it was professed to be (Lively and Abrams 1996). After all, Hitler had known for 15 years that the ultramilitaristic Rohm was a homosexual. Evidence exists that Hitler despised effeminate homosexuals, but may not have had a major problem with the more masculine types that permeated the Nazi elite. Hitler declared privately: "I won't be a spoilsport to any of my men. If I demand the utmost of them, I must also permit them to let off steam as *they* please, not as it suits a lot of elderly church-hens. My lads are no angels, God knows, nor are they expected to be. I've no use for goody-goodies and League of Virtu-ites" (Bleuel 1973, 4). Rumors persist, perhaps fostered by antifascist propagandists, that certain high-level Nazis, such as Walther Funk, Reich Minister of Economics, and Rudolf Hess, Deputy Party Leader, were active homosexuals (Wolff 1986, 429). But Hitler maintained a public face as an enforcer of norms, and in this, he was ably assisted by the homophobic Himmler, who fought homosexuality as if it were a plague (Steakley 1975, 111). Himmler is noted for recounting to Secret Service generals the ancient mode of executing homosexuals (drowning in bogs) and for equating homosexuality and pederasty. "Raising the specter of homosexuals as likely predators on children was also a handy way to bring the general public around to embrace the . . . blanket marginalization [of homosexuals] as outsiders deserving of contempt" (Giles 2001, 236).

There are two different schools of thought concerning the apparent contradiction between the presence of sexual deviants in the Nazi leadership and persecution of homosexuals. One focuses on the leadership's ambivalence about homosexuality and latency and contends that this explains, in some measure, the perverse and sadistic treatment of male homosexuals during the Third Reich (Johnson 2000, 287). Lively and Abrams in *The Pink Swastika: Homosexuality in the Nazi Party* (1996) debunk the idea of a homosexual holocaust and openly oppose gay rights (indeed, they deny that homosexuality is innate). They characterize the Nazi Party as heavily homosexual, united under a "pink swastika," and primarily concerned with attacking feminized homosexuals only—those who were unwilling to reproduce and unwilling to conform to the prevailing conservative values and nationalism. Another tack (more acceptable to gay rights advocates) downplays this focus because ideological models more effectively substantiate their thesis that German homosexuals were victims of a genocidal campaign. They explain the persecution of homosexuals as clearly the product of National Socialism's incorporation of popular norms and the imperatives of eugenics. By studying Nazi records and archives, Günter Grau (1998) and others have found that the assumption the Nazis had a long-term social strategy for a final solution for homosexuals does not withstand the test of critical analysis, although their findings lend support to the idea of an ideological basis to the destruction of feminized homosexuals.

Within this complicated morass of political, ideological, and cultural motivation, one fact emerges as clearly indicating that thought had been translated into action, extremism into attack. In 1933, the Institute for Sexual Science became an early casualty in a Nazi purge of institutions and organizations that were active in sexual reform (Grau 1998, 341). With control of the government came the power to decide which institutions accurately reflected the values of the nation and which did not. An eyewitness account tells the story.

On the morning of May 6th, the *Berliner Lokalanzeiger* reported that the cleansing of Berlin libraries of books of un-German spirit would begin that morning, and that the students of the Gymnastic Academy would make a start with the Sexual Science Institute. . . . On the publication of the press notice referred to, an attempt was made to remove for safe-keeping some of the most valuable private books and manuscripts; but this proved to be impossible, as the person removing the books was arrested by a guard which had evidently been placed round the institute during the night. At 9:30 some lorries drew up in front of the Institute with about one hundred students and a brass band. They drew up in military formation in front of the Institute, and then marched into the building with their band playing . . . [and] broke open doors. . . . [T]hey emptied ink bottles over manuscripts and carpets and then made for the book-cases. They took away whatever they thought not completely unobjectionable, working for the most part on the basis of the so-called "black list." But they went beyond this, and took other books also, including for example a large work on Tutankhamen and a number of art journals which they found among the secretary's [Geiss's] private books. They then removed from the archives the large charts dealing with inter-sexual cases, which had been prepared for the International Medical Congress held at the Kensington Museum in London in 1913. They threw most of the charts through the windows to their comrades who were standing outside.

    They removed from the walls other drawings and photographs of special types and kicked them around the room, leaving it strewn with torn drawings and broken glass. When one of the students pointed out this was medical material, another replied that this was of no importance, that they were not concerned with the confiscation of a few books and pictures, but that they were there to destroy the Institute. A long speech was then made, and a life-size model showing the internal secretion process was thrown out of the window and smashed to pieces. In one of the consulting rooms they used a mop to smash a pantostat used in the treatment of patients. They also took away a bronze bust of Dr. Hirschfeld, and a number of other statues . . . [and] seized a few hundred books out of the library of the Institute. . . . [T]he band played throughout, so that a large crowd of inquisitive people gathered outside. At 12 o'clock the leader made a long speech, and then the gang left, singing a particularly vulgar song and also the *Horst-Wessel* [a popular Nazi] song.

The people in the institute assumed that this concluded the robbery proceedings, but at three o'clock in the afternoon a number of lorries filled with storm troopers appeared and explained that they would have to continue the work of confiscation, as the men who had been there in the morning had not had time to make a proper clearance. This second troop then proceeded to make a careful search through every room, taking down to the lorries basket after basket of valuable books and manuscripts—two lorry-loads in all. It was clear from the oaths used that the names of the authors whose books were in the special library were well known to the students. Siegmund Freud, whose photograph they took from the staircase and carried off, was called "that Jewish sow Freud"; and Havelock Ellis was called "that swine." Other English authors wanted by them were Oscar Wilde, Edward Carpenter, and Norman Hare; and also the work of Judge Lindsay, the American juvenile judge; Margaret Sanger and George Silvester Viereck; and of French writers, the works of Andre Gide, Marcel Proust, Peirre Loti, Zola, etc. The sight of the works of the Danish doctor Leunbach also make them break out into oaths. Many bound volumes of periodicals were also removed. They also wanted to take away several thousand questionnaires which were among the records, but desisted when they were assured that these were simply medical histories. On the other hand, it did not prove possible to dissuade them from removing the material belonging to the World League for Sexual Reform, the whole edition of the journal *Sexus*, and the card index. In addition, a great many manuscripts, including many unpublished ones, fell into their hands.

They repeatedly inquired when Dr. Hirschfeld would be returning; they wanted, as they expressed it, to be given the tip as to when he would be there. Even before this raid on the Institute storm troopers had visited it on several occasions and asked for Dr. Hirschfeld. When they were told he was abroad, owing to an attack of malaria, they replied: "Then let's hope he'll die without our aid: then we shan't have to hang him or beat him to death." (World Committee 1933, 158–161)

This account was published in 1933 in *The Brown Book of the Hitler Terror and the Burning of the Reichstag*, a volume prepared by the World Committee for the Victims of German Fascism (1933). The *Brown Book* also included a sample of German newspaper articles on the institute's destruction, one of which approved it as a "deed of culture" (p. 163). This is from Goebbels' weekly, *Der Angriff*, May 6, 1933:

Energetic Action Against a Poison Shop
German Students Fumigate the "Sexual Science Institute"

Detachment X of the German student organisation yesterday occupied the "Sexual Science Institute," which was controlled by the Jew Magnus Hirschfeld. This institute, which tried to shelter behind a scientific cloak and was always protected during the fourteen years of Marxist rule by the authorities of that period, was an unparalleled breeding-ground of dirt and filth, as the results of the search have proved beyond question. A whole lorry-load of pornographic pictures and writings as well as documents and registers have been confiscated. . . . The criminal police will have to deal with a part of the material found; another part of it will be publicly burnt. (World Committee 1933, 161–162)

These accounts illustrate the vandalistic nature of the attack and provide insight into the perpetrators' motivations. The ceremonial nature of the activities, complete with a band and speeches, the staging as a protest, indicates that the students' vandalism was malicious: they kicked artifacts, smashed glass cabinets and mirrors, and threw books around the institute and out the windows. They marched and sang Nazi songs and checked titles against a "black list." There was a vindictive subtext to the tactical and ideological elements, especially in the afternoon after storm troopers arrived in lorries and the confiscation of texts began in earnest. The storm troopers loudly cursed and denigrated specific authors, and lamented the absence of Magnus Hirschfeld, against whom they made threats of physical violence. The students and storm troopers clearly saw themselves as engaged in a cleansing operation. The institute was merely the first library in Berlin to be purged of un-German materials. Metaphors of toxins and disease were plentiful in newspaper reports. The German students "fumigated" the "poison shop" that was a "breeding-ground" of filth, and its materials would either be dealt with by the criminal police or burned.

Three days later, the students staged massive bonfires of books all over the country. As part of a public ceremony in Berlin's *Opernplatz* (Opera House Square), an estimated 12,000 to 20,000 books and a large part of the collection of 35,000 pictures confiscated from the institute were burned. The slogans of the participants declared "No to decadence and moral corruption!" and to a treasonous "intellectual underclass" (Heidtmann 1991a, 99). A contemporary described the burning of Hirschfeld's "unique testimony" as "a kind of psychic and mental *auto-da-fé* with the bronze portrait bust [of Hirschfeld] committed to the flames as a final gesture of hatred and contumely" (Hodann 1937, 73). The fires, which were captured on film and screened globally, became iconic images that irretrievably linked book burning with the Nazis. One week later, Hirschfeld, in self-imposed exile, watched a newsreel of the event in a Paris cinema and likened the experience to watching his own funeral (Steakley 1975, 105). Later, he described in a letter the loss of his institute and library as a violation similar to rape, saying the government had "taken by force the greatest part of our library and many other items, and willfully destroyed them. Most of the books . . . were removed with violence" (as quoted in Wolff 1986, 379). Making the analogy between rape and cultural destruction is appropriate, because in both cases, physical violence is aimed at the spirit.

The institute's demise signaled the beginning of the end for the German homosexual reform movement and sexology as objective inquiry. Symbolically, the event marked the end of independent private lives in post–Weimar Germany and the onset of "a policy of arbitrary measures designed to deter and to eradicate through terror, coercive measures to cure the 'scourge' of homosexuality" (Grau 1995c, 26). All homosexual periodicals and publications were confiscated and shut down. Public and subscription libraries were purged of all works that dealt with the theme of homosexuality and "the love without a name" (Grau 1995c, 26). Throughout the summer of 1933, as the Nazis "cleansed" schools, museums, and other cultural institutions, they eliminated all elements that had been active in the sexual reform movement. The party leaders were interested in ensuring political and aesthetic conformity by dismantling the institutes that had proliferated during the Weimar Republic and intellectual freedom in general.

In his Berlin-bonfires speech, Goebbels announced that hand in hand with the destruction of the political system of Weimar should go the elimination of the republic's intellectual basis (Frei 1993, 63). Under the Nazi regime, intellectual activity was only permitted if it served the state and validated the basic tenets of National Socialist ideology (Rothfeder 1963, 347). Hitler sought to counter "enervation and effeminization" by eliminating excessive intellectual activity; it was unsuitable to be studious in a period in which issues were decided by physical might (Bleuel 1973, 33). Indeed, the regime required that all institutions foster the creation of a "German man of strength," and every aspect of culture and social life had to further this end (Staub 1989, 96). Institutions became simply a means to an end, and their "moral purging [was] as thorough as its intended political purging" (Stieg 1992, 18). There could be no sphere—sexual, intellectual, or otherwise—that was not understood politically (Shils 1931, 68). By 1937, in an off-the-record speech, Hitler would claim supreme moral authority in the name of the party: "Today *we* claim leadership of the people, that is to say, we alone are entitled to lead the people as such—the individual man and woman. *We* determine the conditions under which the sexes live! *We* fashion the child!" (Bleuel 1973, 7). Under the Nazis, Germany became a totalitarian state and intellectual freedom a moot issue.

In retrospect, it is obvious that the institute and its library were doomed. But how was the destruction viewed at the time? Many right-wing German homosexuals saw it as an anti-Semitic act rather than as an expression of anti-homosexual sentiment (Steakley 1975, 105). This camp included Nazi sympathizers, and male supremacists such as Adolf Brand, who approved of the measure and welcomed the end of Hirschfeld's "pseudo-scientific activity" (Brand 1995, 35). Though Brand himself was never arrested or physically persecuted by the Nazis, his journal and publishing business were later shut down and his papers confiscated. Those promoting the theory that the Nazi Party harbored masculine homosexuals downplay ideological motivation and blame the attack on the Nazis' need to destroy evidence of their own sexual deviance

(Lively and Abrams 1996, 99). Ludwig L. Lenz, a gynecologist who worked at the institute at the time of the attack, argues this position in his memoir:

Why was it then, since we were completely non-party, that our purely scientific Institute was the first victim which fell to the new regime? . . . Whence this hatred, and, what was even more strange, this haste and thoroughness. The answer to this is simple and straightforward enough—we knew too much. . . . [N]ot ten percent of those men, who, in 1933, took the fate of Germany into their hands, were sexually normal. . . . [W]e saw the tragic results: . . . [to] a thirteen year old boy who suffered from a serious lesion of the anal muscle brought about by a senior party official in Breslau and to a youth from Berlin . . . with severe rectal gonorrhea, etc. etc. . . . Our knowledge of such intimate secrets regarding members of the Nazi party and our other documentary material—we possessed forty thousand confessions and biographical letters—was the cause of the complete and utter destruction of the Institute for Sexology. (Haeberle 1989, 369)

The attack on the institute ushered in a dark period in German and world history. If, as historian John Boswell (1980, 17) postulates, history indicates that public reactions to homosexuality are a measure of social tolerance generally, then the destruction of the institute was an indicator of the genocide that was to come. A society that lacks social tolerance and embraces extremism is dangerous to itself, to others, to scholarship, and to the printed word. Historian Peter Gay (2001, 1) writes of a prevalent Allied belief in "two Germanies: the Germany of military swagger, abject submission to authority, aggressive foreign adventure, and obsessive preoccupation with form, and the Germany of lyrical poetry, Humanist philosophy, and pacific cosmopolitanism." Weimar represented the latter; the Third Reich, the former. The institute and its library were victims of Germany's deadly espousal of a militaristic and brutally masculine ideology. The day after the raid on the institute, the fascist newspaper *Berliner Lokal-Anzeiger* announced, "We are not and do not want to be the land of Goethe and Einstein. Not on any account" (World Committee 1933, 163). Three days later, students burned thousands of books, including those of Johann Goethe, Albert Einstein, and Magnus Hirschfeld, in a demonstration against the "un-German" spirit. The regime went on in 1938 to persecute homosexuals, to destroy Jewish synagogues, schools, and texts during *Krystallnacht*, and ultimately, to commit genocide against Jews, Poles, and other groups deemed inferior.

The Nazis were masters of institutionalized vandalism. They knew that they could persuade students to perform acts of destruction and create circumstances in which they could get away with it, and they fostered comradery and high spirits in order to neutralize compunctions. Students were the perfect group to employ in ceremonies that link protest and playful and malicious vandalism. They tend to be rebellious and susceptible to extreme rationalizations, have a low sense of control, and are more likely to experience pleasure from destruction. The storm troopers who finished up the job were more thoroughly schooled in tactical and ideological vandalism, although an inclination toward violence and taking pleasure in malicious acts was also a defining characteristic of this self-selected group. Both groups were exhilarated by power. They were needed as tools of leaders anxious to use National Socialism as a catalyst to eliminating corruption and effecting social change.

Masters of symbolism, the Nazi leaders were building on a tradition in Germany of burning books as a means of protest that linked radical repudiation of retrogressive ideas with iconoclasm. They translated their ideology into ceremonies that elicited powerful affective, cognitive, and social responses, and effectively united Germans against their antitheses. The tactical and ideological advantages of destroying the Institute for Sexual Science were enhanced by the vengeful satisfaction of destroying objects so closely related to despised elements. In the burning of books, they were destroying the intellectual progeny of the enemy, and with the burning of the bust of Magnus Hirschfeld, they were attacking an archfiend. The Nazis had so thoroughly demonized opposing groups and beliefs that the physical and symbolic destruction of these elements had become rational and necessary. Indeed, what was perceived worldwide as deviant and socially problematic behavior was given official validation by the Nazi officials and professors whose bonfire speeches outlined the book burners' "vocabulary of motives." The students and paramilitaries were told that they were akin to Teutonic knights, "leading protagonists in a community of destiny," and engaged in a "titanic struggle against the forces of tradition and cultural intransigence" (Carlton 1990, 178). Book burning was an affirmative and celebratory act of purification, the cauterizing of a diseased society and necessary prelude to a new and triumphant order.

REFERENCES

Biale, David. 1997. "1906. The Discipline of *Sexualwissenschaft* Emerges in Germany, Creating Divergent Notions of the Sexuality of European Jewry." In *Yale Companion to Jewish Writing and Thought in German Culture 1096–1996*, eds. Sander L. Gilman and Jack Zipes. New Haven, Conn.: Yale University Press, 273–279.

Bleuel, Hans Peter. 1973. *Sex and Society in Nazi Germany*. Ed. Heinrich Fraenkel. Trans. J. Maxwell Brownjohn. Philadelphia: J. B. Lippincott.

Boswell, John. 1980. *Christianity, Social Tolerance, and Homosexuality: Gay People in Western Europe from the Beginning of the Christian Era to the Fourteenth Century*. Chicago: University of Chicago Press.

Brand, Adolf. 1995. "All That Was 'Aimed Only at the Ugly Excesses of the Movement': Letter from the Gay Publisher Adolf Brand, 29 November 1933." In *Hidden Holocaust?: Gay and Lesbian Persecution in Germany 1933–45*, ed. Günter Grau, trans. Patrick Camiller. London: Cassell, 34–36.

Buchheim, Hans. 1968. *Totalitarian Rule: Its Nature and Characteristics*. Trans. Ruth Hein. Middletown, Conn.: Wesleyan University Press.

Burleigh, Michael, and Wolfgang Wipperman. 1991. *The Racial State: Germany 1933–1945*. Cambridge: Cambridge University Press.

Carlton, Eric. 1990. *War and Ideology*. Savage, Md.: Barnes and Noble Books.

Curtis, Michael. 1979. *Totalitarianism*. New Brunswick, N.J.: Transaction Books.

Frei, Norbert. 1993. *National Socialist Rule in Germany: The Fuhrer State 1933–1945*. Trans. Simon B. Steyne. Oxford: Blackwell.

Garde, Noel I. 1964. *Jonathan to Gide: The Homosexual in History*. New York: Nosbooks.

Gay, Peter. 2001. *Weimar Culture: The Outsider as Insider*. New York: W. W. Norton.

Gellately, Robert, and Nathan Stoltzfus. 2001. "Social Outsiders and the Construction of the Community of the People." In *Social Outsiders in Nazi Germany*, eds. Robert Gellately and Nathan Stoltzfus. Princeton, N.J.: Princeton University Press, 3–19.

Giles, Geoffrey J. 2001. "The Institutionalization of Homosexual Panic in the Third Reich." In *Social Outsiders in Nazi Germany*, eds. Robert Gellately and Nathan Stoltzfus. Princeton, N.J.: Princeton University Press, 233–255.

Grau, Günter. 1995a. "Disputes about Whether Homosexuality Should Be a Criminal Offence." In *Hidden Holocaust?: Gay and Lesbian Persecution in Germany 1933–45*, ed. Günter Grau, trans. Patrick Camiller. London: Cassell, 18–23.

Grau, Günter. 1995b. "Persecution, 'Re-education' or 'Eradication' of Male Homosexuals between 1933 and 1945: Consequences of the Eugenic Concept of Assured Reproduction." In *Hidden Holocaust?: Gay and Lesbian Persecution in Germany 1933–45*, ed. Günter Grau, trans. Patrick Camiller. London: Cassell, 1–7.

Grau, Günter. 1995c. "Police Raids, Bans and Arrests: 1933 to 1935." In *Hidden Holocaust?: Gay and Lesbian Persecution in Germany 1933–45*, ed. Günter Grau, trans. Patrick Camiller. London: Cassell, 26–27.

Grau, Günter. 1998. "Final Solution of the Homosexual Question?: The Anti-homosexual Policies of the Nazis and the Social Consequences for Homosexual Men." In *The Holocaust and History: The Known, the Unknown, the Disputed, and the Reexamined*, eds. Michael Berenbaum and Abraham J. Peck. Bloomington: Indiana University Press, 338–344.

Guerin, Daniel. 1994. *The Brown Plague: Travels in Late Wiemar and Early Nazi Germany*. Trans. Robert Schwartzwald. London: Duke University Press.

Haeberle, Erwin. 1989. "Swastika, Pink Triangle, and Yellow Star: The Destruction of Sexology and the Persecution of Homosexuals in Nazi Germany." In *Hidden from History: Reclaiming the Gay and Lesbian Past*, eds. Martin Bauml Duberman, Martha Vicinus, and George Chauncey, Jr. New York: New American Library, 365–379.

Heidtmann, Horst. 1991a. "Book Burning." In *The Encyclopedia of the Third Reich*, eds. Christian Zentner and Friedemann Bedürftig, trans. Amy Hackett. New York: Macmillan, 99–100.

Heidtmann, Horst. 1991b. "Homosexuality." In *The Encyclopedia of the Third Reich*, eds. Christian Zentner and Friedemann Bedürftig, trans. Amy Hackett. New York: Macmillan, 440.

Hill, Leonidas E. 2001. "The Nazi Attack on 'Un-German' Literature, 1933–1945." In *The Holocaust and the Book*, ed. Jonathan Rose. Amherst: University of Massachusetts Press, 9–46.

Hirschfeld, Magnus. 1936. "Magnus Hirschfeld." In *Encyclopaedia Sexualis: A Comprehensive Encyclopaedia-Dictionary of the Sexual Sciences*, ed. Victor Robinson. New York: Dingwall-Rock, 317–321.

Hodann, Max. 1937. *History of Modern Morals*. Trans. Stella Browne. London: William Heinemann.

Isherwood, Christopher. 1976. *Christopher and His Kind 1929–1939*. New York: Farrar Straus and Giroux.

Johansson, Warren, and William A. Percy. 1990. "Homosexuals in Nazi Germany." In *Simon Wiesenthal Center Annual*, Vol. 7, ed. Henry Friedlander. New York: Allied Books, 225–363.

Johnson, Eric A. 2000. *Nazi Terror: The Gestapo, Jews, and Ordinary Germans.* New York: Basic Books.

Lautmann, Rüdiger. 1998. "The Pink Triangle: Homosexuals as 'Enemies of the State.'" In *The Holocaust and History: The Known, the Unknown, the Disputed, and the Reexamined*, eds. Michael Berenbaum and Abraham J. Peck. Bloomington: Indiana University Press, 345–357.

Lively, Scott, and Kevin Abrams. 1996. *The Pink Swastika: Homosexuality in the Nazi Party.* Keizer, Ore.: Founders Publishing.

Mosse, George L. 1970. *Germans and Jews: The Right, the Left, and the Search for a "Third Force" in Pre-Nazi Germany.* New York: Howard Fertig.

Mosse, George. L. 1975. *The Nationalization of the Masses: Political Symbolism and Mass Movements in Germany from the Napoleonic Wars through the Third Reich.* New York: Howard Fertig.

Mosse, George L. 1985. *Nationalism and Sexuality: Respectability and Abnormal Sexuality in Modern Europe.* New York: Howard Fertig.

Oosterhuis, Harry. 1991. "Homosexual Emancipation in Germany before 1933: Two Traditions." *Homosexuality and Male Bonding in Pre-Nazi Germany: The Youth Movement, the Gay Movement and Male Bonding before Hitler's Rise: Original Transcripts from* Der Eigene, *the First Gay Journal in the World*, ed. Harry Oosterhuis, trans. Hubert Kennedy. New York: Harrington Press.

Pfaff, William. 1993. *The Wrath of Nations: Civilization and the Furies of Nationalism.* New York: Simon and Schuster.

Plant, Richard. 1986. *The Pink Triangle: The Nazi War against Homosexuals.* New York: Henry Holt.

Rothfeder, Herbert. 1963. *A Study of Alfred Rosenberg's Organization for National Socialist Ideology.* PhD diss., University of Michigan.

Shera, Jesse. 1965. *Libraries and the Organization of Knowledge.* Ed. D. J. Foskett. Hamden, Conn.: Archon Books.

Shils, Edward. 1931. "The Concept and Function of Ideology." In *Encyclopaedia of the Social Sciences*, Vol. 7, ed. Edwin Seligman. New York: Macmillan, 66–74.

Staub, Ervin. 1989. *Roots of Evil: The Origins of Genocide and Other Group Violence.* Cambridge: Cambridge University Press.

Steakley, James D. 1975. *The Homosexual Emancipation Movement in Germany.* New York: Arno Press.

Stieg, Margaret F. 1992. *Public Libraries in Nazi Germany.* Tuscaloosa: University of Alabama Press.

Taeger, Angela. 1998. "Homosexual Love between 'Degeneration of Human Material' and 'Love of Mankind': Demographic Perspectives on Homosexuality in Nineteenth-Century Germany." In *Queering the Canon: Defying Sights in German Literature and Culture*, ed. Christoph Lorey and John L. Plews. Columbia, S.C.: Camden House, 20–35.

Wolff, Charlotte. 1986. *Magnus Hirschfeld: A Portrait of a Pioneer in Sexology.* London: Quartet Books.

World Committee for the Victims of German Fascism. 1933. *The Brown Book of the Hitler Terror and the Burning of the Reichstag.* New York: Alfred A. Knopf.

CHAPTER 6

Secular Fanaticism and the Auto-Genocide of Cambodia, 1975–1979

> The attempt to make heaven on earth invariably produces hell. It leads to intolerance . . . [and] the saving of souls through the inquisition.
> —Karl Popper, *The Open Society and Its Enemies*

A quarter of a century after the Nazi regime locked down Germany, the Khmer Rouge appeared and took Cambodian society to the brink of cultural annihilation in attempts to purify it. In five short years, 1975–1979, Pol Pot and his comrades operated a totalitarian regime that demonstrated Karl Popper's (1966, 237) hypothesis: the most dangerous of all political ideas, he proposed, is the wish to make people perfect. The Khmer Rouge launched a revolution without parameters, and with a momentum that carried it headlong into the tragedy of genocide, ethnocide, and libricide (Knuth 2003). Educated Cambodians were singled out and killed and cultural institutions were purged in the name of revolutionary progress. In a frontal assault on modern and traditional culture, books and religious texts were torn apart and burned, thrown into the canals and ponds of Cambodia, and destroyed by exposure to the elements. Ultimately, conditions were created in which the physical obliteration of texts became unnecessary: there was virtually no one left to read them.

Wrenching interviews and memoirs from survivors recount the details of their ordeal, serving as historical witness and tools of catharsis. Because of these accounts, we have some window into the motivation of the Khmer Rouge. The titles express the scale of loss and survivor's search for meaning in fables, proverbs, folktales, and musical metaphors from Cambodia's rich cultural heritage: *First They Killed My Father: A Daughter of Cambodia Remembers* (Ung 2000); *The Stones Cry Out: A Cambodian Childhood 1975–1980* (Szymusiak

1986); *When Elephants Fight: A Memoir* (Imam 2000); *When Broken Glass Floats: Growing Up under the Khmer Rouge* (Him 2000); and *Music through the Dark: A Tale of Survival in Cambodia* (Lafreniere 2000). Even children understood the connection between destroying books and expunging identity. One survivor, a child when forced out of Phnom Penh, remembers:

> Along the road to get out of the city, we passed by my school. The library was gone. All those beautiful, colorful books were gone. They were either burned or used for toilet paper. That's because the Khmer Rouge believed that the only way to change things was to erase everything. . . . Rumor was they wanted to start the society from scratch, age 12 and up. If they could have burned people's brains, they would have. But they couldn't. So they punished everyone who remembered. (Stephanie 2003)

Along with politicians, journalists, and others who have contemplated this period, scholars writing about the Pol Pot era have themselves turned to literature, poetry, and scripture to express their shock and horror, while attempting to balance objectivity with outrage and empathy. Statistician R. J. Rummel (1994, 202) returned to Milton's *Paradise Lost* to describe Cambodia as a "torture without end," "A dungeon horrible, on all sides round . . . / Regions of sorrow, doleful shades, where peace / And rest can never dwell, hope never comes." Ironically, witnesses found recourse in many things their persecutors had tried to extinguish, perhaps aware of the life-sustaining power of culture.

Cambodia was the ultimate case, in a very destructive century, of a society whose commitment to political and social cleansing metamorphosed into cultural suicide. Societal meltdown, aggravated by war, had produced conditions in which extreme solutions seemed to be mandated. Filled with ideological fervor, certain that Communism was the answer to their woes, and inflamed by xenophobic nationalism, the Khmer Rouge believed that Cambodia was a sick society whose health could only be restored by excising both traditional culture and contemporary influences. But instead, they demonstrated poignantly that diversity and heterogeneity are the foundations of a thriving society and that the line between cultural purification and the complete obliteration of a people is very thin indeed.

A case can be made that twentieth-century Cambodia was predisposed to xenophobic nationalism. A culture rich in memories of a glorious past, Cambodia had suffered centuries of humiliating invasions and occupations by neighboring Vietnam and Thailand (called Siam until 1939). These invasions came to a head in the nineteenth century with Thailand's repeated incursions in 1811, 1833, and 1840, punctuated by periods of Vietnamese occupation (1834–1847) and Thai occupation (1847–1863) (Chandler 1979, 411). In a last-ditch effort to preserve sovereignty, the king accepted the protection of France, and in 1863, Cambodia was transformed into a French protectorate. However, the French fueled the historical rivalry between the people of Cambodia (the Khmers) and the Vietnamese by publicly denigrating the former group, labeling them lazy and unreliable and importing

Vietnamese labor to fill key government positions. The French finally merged Vietnam and Cambodia (along with Laos) into a political unit called Indochina. This alliance with their enemy was a difficult pill for the Cambodians to swallow. Also hard to swallow were policies that accorded French interests primacy and promoted the economic and cultural underdevelopment that was the fate of most colonies (Ponchaud 1978, 145).

At the same time, French adventurers, intellectuals, and scholars interested in Cambodia's history brought the Khmers the gift of historical consciousness and pride in their history as a people. French explorers discovered a forgotten temple complex buried deep in the jungle and spread across 125 square miles. They identified it as the remains of the Angkar Empire. From the ninth to the twelfth centuries, the triumphant Angkar kings had built monuments, including archival depositories and libraries that witnessed the glory of their civilization. Hundreds of ancient stone inscriptions testified to the fact that Khmer people had "the longest actively flourishing written record of any South East Asian language" (Vickery 1990, 49). The wealth and reach of the empire were indications of military and administrative expertise, and remnants of extensive agricultural and hydraulic systems supplied proof of technical prowess and innovation. But with the empire's disintegration in the fourteenth century had come abandonment of the complex, and over the ensuing centuries, the Cambodians lost awareness of this "rich and often tragic heritage" except as recounted in fables and traditions (Criddle and Mam 1987, xv). The rediscovery of this glorious heritage conferred distinction on the Khmer people and showed that they had much to offer to the world, but the knowledge of this past from their contemporary situation of subservience and poverty kindled feelings of victimization and injustice—which in turn fed nationalistic sentiments.

By the twentieth century, the grandeur and achievements of the Angkar era had faded from the consciousness of many Cambodians, while, for others, it kept alive a sense of pride in their country. However, according to Western scholars, its sociocultural patterns still influenced Cambodian society: master-slave relationships, a hierarchy led by an absolute and divine king, and a wealth-based system of merit (Chandler 1979, 414). Class divisions were still thoroughly entrenched in twentieth-century Cambodia, and commonplace people were labeled "stinking brutes" and "dogs" by the aristocracy (Staub 1989, 196). Peasants, whose skin was darkened by long hours in the sun, were called "the big, black people," whereas the sheltered rich were "white as jade" (Becker 1998, 68). There were traditions of slavery (though it was legally outlawed), passive submission to authority, and extreme violence toward enemies during times of war and peace.

The spark of Cambodian nationalism was fanned in 1945, when occupying Japanese troops allowed the formation of a Khmer government. When the French regained possession at the end of World War II, they hoped to be able to work through the young and seemingly compliant Prince Sihanouk, whom they installed as king. However, Sihanouk proved to be an astute politician, and he capitalized on international consensus regarding the need for decolonialization and led Cambodia to independence in 1953. With sovereignty, Cambodia's future seemed bright. The 1950s were, in retrospect, years of peace and relative prosperity. Though the country remained isolated, economically stagnant, and politically and educationally backward, it was a fertile land that regularly supplied its people with more rice than any other Southeast Asian country (Becker 1998, 5). Sihanouk ruled over a relatively homogeneous country in which 90 percent of the people were Khmer and Buddhist and most Cambodians were owner-cultivators living in small villages of less than 300 people (Chalk and Jonassohn 1990, 398). At first, Sihanouk ruled with a "light authoritarian hand" (Rummel 1994, 162). He fostered racial and national pride by emphasizing the ancestry of the Angkar Empire: he built schools, and he was progressive enough to give women the right to vote.

But in the 1960s, social conditions deteriorated and cracks in the system began to appear. There was a population explosion, food shortages, a decline in the living standards of those at the lower end of the social scale, and persistent strife. The disaffected middle classes and intellectuals (particularly the monks and teachers) lost respect for Sihanouk and attempted to organize against him. They suffered the consequences: Sihanouk ordered 40 teachers, suspected of subversive activity, to be thrown from the cliffs at Bakar and left to die (Rummel 1994, 164). Some intellectuals with a French education and exposure to Marxism fled the cities and organized disaffected, poverty-stricken and illiterate peasants into small and isolated guerilla units. Sihanouk dubbed them the Khmer Rouge ("Red Khmers"). They led a brutal and primitive life on the run. Early military training was provided to these groups by North Vietnamese Communists, but the leaders ultimately rejected this alliance for reasons racial and historical. Also a factor was their desire for a singularly Khmer form of Communism. Nationalism was a strong component in their commitment to socialist ideals. Even though proselytizing was difficult in the early days, the rural poor became increasingly resentful of the rich. When village protests began to occur, the government responded by sending troops in to quell dissent, and in late 1967, official repression took the form of massacres and escalating atrocities. The severed heads of protestors were collected to document the army's diligence in weeding out protest. Such events turned many peasants against the government, and soon the ranks of the Khmer Rouge were swelling. From 1968 to 1970, Khmer Rouge guerillas engaged Sihanouk's army on a regular basis. In March 1970, civil unrest, deteriorating economic conditions, and political instability generated by the Vietnam War culminated in a reactionary coup. While Sihanouk was vacationing in France, his minister of defense Lon Nol seized power, declared Cambodia a republic, and attempted to offer alternatives to the authoritarianism of Sihanouk and the primal Communism of the Khmer Rouge.

The coup was welcomed by those who hoped Lon Nol would restore Cambodia's ancient glory and create a new era of justice. This hope soon withered as civil war laid waste to the countryside. Guerillas and army troops battled for territory and supremacy, driving more and more peasants from the land. To complicate matters, the South Vietnamese made incursions into Cambodia to attack Viet Cong supply lines. In further attempts to cut these lines, the United States launched bombing campaigns from 1969 to 1973. In 1973 alone, more than 250,000 tons of explosives were dropped on Cambodia, more than one and a half times the tonnage dropped on Japan in all of World War II (Stuart-Fox 1985, 30). The bombs caused an estimated 150,000 civilian casualties (Kiernan 1990a, 22), one-fourth of an estimated 600,000 people killed during the Lon Nol years, 1970–1975 (Rummel 1994, 178). So much land was taken out of cultivation (a drop from six million to one million acres cultivated in rice) that starvation became prevalent (Becker 1998, 17). Urban populations increased exponentially as the peasants fled into the cities. The peasants, who found urban life marked by a conspicuous consumption that contrasted starkly with the rural poverty and squalor they had left behind, lived a precarious life on the streets of Phnom Penh. The middle classes were disgusted as the rich squandered millions of dollars of American military aid on luxury goods, alcohol, and gambling, and official corruption under Lon Nol quickly surpassed that of Sihanouk's regime. The humiliation was particularly galling to nationalists who contrasted current conditions with the glorious past.

The chaotic conditions were helpful to the Khmer Rouge leaders, who saw their role in the struggles as fulfillment of an apocalyptic destiny. In their hands, stories of government atrocities and devastating U.S. bombing campaigns became recruitment propaganda, allowing them to tighten their grip on the peasants' loyalties. The Khmer Rouge leadership gained legitimacy by living simply, advocating social reform, and eventually forging an expedient alliance with their old enemy, the deposed Sihanouk, who still commanded devotion from many peasants. By spring 1975, the Khmer Rouge controlled most of the countryside and was poised to take over the capital city and overthrow Lon Nol's government. The United States retracted its support of his regime, and it collapsed. The fall of Phnom Penh to the Khmer Rouge on April 17, 1975, set the stage for revolution—a full-scale campaign to capture the soul of Cambodia.

Saloth Sar, a French-educated intellectual renamed as Pol Pot, had emerged as leader of the Khmer Rouge. He and his comrades were inspired by the theories of Karl Marx, Vladimir Lenin, Joseph Stalin, and, especially, Mao Tsetung. Mao had been waging the Cultural Revolution in China since 1966. His Jacobean approach to revolution, as a war against traditional culture and the past that allowed history to begin anew, appealed to the Khmer Rouge leaders. Nationalistic to excess, they sought to surpass the achievements of Russian and Chinese pioneers of socialist extremism through a revival of the Angkar Empire and the creation of the first truly pure Communist state. They envisioned a racially homogeneous, classless, culturally unified, economically self-sufficient, and strictly egalitarian nation: an "agrarian utopia" from which all undesirable elements (including non-Khmer minorities, capitalists, those with ties to the West, and the previous elite) had been purged (Keyes 1990, 60).

Pol Pot believed that the great Angkar Empire could be reconstituted and a purified and revitalized new Khmer race created by force of will (Chandler 1990, 18). He was instrumental in developing the four operating principles that were key to the regime's agenda of purification: independence-sovereignty (a phrase that encapsulated the rejection of all foreign influences), self-reliance, defending and constructing the country, and taking destiny into one's own hands (Ponchaud 1978, 73). His cohorts mixed ultranationalism, radical Communist principles, and terror techniques to fashion a stark, totalitarian universe. A battlefield mentality, forged during the harsh years of guerillas and civil war, was applied to the revolution. The instruments of revolution were illiterate young peasants, who were hardened by guerilla warfare and abysmal living conditions and thoroughly indoctrinated by Communist cadres. There were taught to despise those who lived in the cities.

According to Martin Stuart-Fox (1985, 167–168), Khmer Rouge leaders felt that victory over Lon Nol's troops (and by extension, defeat of the United States) had been achieved without the help of urban dwellers who were considered "spoiled" by modernity and as having "lost their intuitive identity with the Khmer soul." In the interests of the collective, they had to be "physically eliminated from the brotherhood of the pure" (Ponchaud 1978, 50). The migration of peasants fleeing the countryside during the civil war had swelled Phnom Penh's population from 600,000 to between two to three million people. Many refugees lived in the streets with their pigs and chickens. Their failure to fight with the Khmer Rouge placed them in the camp of the enemy. Like the rest of the urban population, they were considered too influenced by capitalism and imperialistic culture, and their lack of dedication to socialist principles presented a threat to the revolution that was to follow the takeover. The leaders concluded that their desired semimystical renewal of the race required abandonment of cities, which were viewed as "artificial creations of colonialism" (Taylor 1993, 43). Those who survived initial execution were to be given the chance of redeeming themselves through labor in the fields.

The inhabitants of Cambodia's capital were caught off guard by the Khmer Rouge's plans. Even those in reasonably secure circumstances were sick of war and corruption and desperate for change. Despite some negative reports about the Khmer Rouge from refugees, many were willing to accept the regime as "nationalists above all, fighting for a more just, less corrupt social order" (Stuart-Fox 1985, 3–4). Thus, they watched in dismay as Khmer Rouge troops, "sullen-faced, openly hostile child-soldiers" clad in black uniforms and checkered scarves, swarmed into the city and ignored both their cheers and the "courteous if careful welcome" (Griffith 2000, 198). This was the first intimation that their fate was in the hands of pitiless adolescents from the countryside who had been taught that Phnom Phen was the "great whore on the Mekong" (Griffith 2000, 217) and a breeding ground for capitalists and foreigners, such as the Chinese and Vietnamese, who controlled commerce (Lafreniere 2000, 38).

The Khmer Rouge leadership's plan for purifying society by evacuating the cities was pursued by means of a ruse: soldiers went door to door warning that the Americans were going to bomb the city and ordered the people to evacuate the city immediately. The residents were not to take much (everything would be provided), and they would be allowed to return in three days. Those who refused to leave were shot on the spot. Hospital patients were pushed through the streets on gurneys. Pregnant women gave birth by the side of the road. The elderly collapsed in exhaustion. No one was allowed to backtrack to find missing family members. Soldiers set up checkpoints and confiscated weapons, medicines, gold, precious stones, radios, watches, eyeglasses, pens, and other personal objects. Money, however, they tossed into the air because Angkar, they said, had put an end to currency as a means of exchange (Ponchaud 1978, 25). *Angkar* was the omniscient "revolutionary organization" that was to function as mother and father (Chandler 1999, 1). It was a code word for the leadership, a secretive group of French-trained intellectuals led by Pol Pot. Evacuees watched helplessly as books, photographs, identification papers, and diplomas were thrown into heaps and trampled into the mud (Stuart-Fox 1985, 15): "No more capitalist books now!" they shouted. "Capitalist books are Lon-Nol style, and Lon Nol betrayed the nation! Why do you have foreign books! Are you CIA? No more foreign books under Angka[r]!" (Ngor 1987, 130). According to one memoir:

They went through every single thing, and took all our pens and notebooks away. My bags contained nothing but books. As these fell out, one Khmer Rouge exclaimed, "What are these books about? Whose are they?" His face had hardened. One of the soldiers picked up *The Wooden Horse* and went through it, page by page, upside down, pretending to read it. I turned to my father and realized he was stuck for words. "They belong to me, comrades," I replied. "I picked them up along the road because I thought they would be good for rolling cigarettes." "Well," said the soldier reading Erick Williams, "there are plenty of banana leaves where you're going. You don't need this rubbish." And he threw *The Wooden Horse* into a corner of the room, onto a huge pile of photographs and money. (May 1986, 113)

The methods of intimidation that included confiscation and destruction of personal property seemed designed "to bewilder, to create debilitating anxiety" (Criddle and Mam 1987, 42).

Shot dead on the spot were not only those who resisted the soldiers but also the handicapped, mentally ill, overtly effete or recalcitrant people, who were deemed unable to participate in the revolution. A new standard of usefulness—the potential for laboring long hours in the fields—was put into effect. An observer told of a man killed because of his appearance: "Long hair symbolized all the Khmer Rouge hated most, the corruption of American imperialist culture and the aimless and unproductive leisure of an exploitative class of urban parasites" (Stuart-Fox 1985, 12). Young male evacuees quickly cut their hair and tried to be inconspicuous. Spontaneous executions, however, merely supplemented uniform procedures that separated out those marked for arrest. At the checkpoints, the soldiers asked for members of the establishment—army officers, politicians, government officials, professors, students, teachers, and bureaucrats—to step forward and volunteer to rebuild the country. Most were taken away and executed. There was a disturbing simplicity to the Khmer Rouge's plan of purification. Scheduled for systematic eradication were capitalists (i.e., businesspeople), professionals, and all those who were capable of leadership, creativity, and critical thinking—anyone "who embodied or perpetrated the notion of individualism" (Quinn 1989, 193).

Under the Khmer Rouge, everything became the property of a state that rejected the notion of private ownership and commerce. The Khmer Rouge left in possession of the cities doggedly smashed in the doors of shops and hurled television sets, tin cans, and refrigerators "pell-mell" into the street (Ponchaud 1978, 10). Later, mountains of air conditioners, refrigerators, and other appliances were piled up, left to rust, burned, or cannibalized for parts. Automobiles, the "gadget[s] of Western consumer society and symbol[s] of inequality among the classes," were left where abandoned (Ponchaud 1978, 36). Stores were turned into warehouses as houses and buildings were cleared of their furnishings. Furniture—another representation of class—was left in the street (Ponchaud 1978, 45).

Implementing a four-year plan "to abolish, uproot and disperse the cultural, literary and artistic remnants of the imperialists, colonialists, and all of the other oppressor classes" (Mehta 1997, 142–143), the new regime shut down all businesses and institutions, including libraries, schools, courts, and hospitals. Those who staffed them were killed. Of 527 graduates of the medical school in Phnom Penh, about 40 survived the regime (Ngor 1987, 406–407). Damned as foreign and forbidden were ethnic minorities such as the Chams, Vietnamese, and Chinese, religious faiths, and cultural objects epitomizing cosmopolitan or high culture. During and immediately after the evacuation, French priest François Ponchaud (1978) observed trucks filled with books heading north, and the Catholic library burning on the lawn. The cathedral was blown up, and Buddhist and Islamic temples, too, were destroyed, along with religious texts and statues. The library of the French Far-Eastern School was burned; other libraries were ransacked or padlocked and abandoned. French books in particular were targeted, because French was the language of the educated and "the language that made contact with the outside world possible" (Criddle and Mam 1987, 31).

But Cambodian books were also destroyed, and bookstores, newsstands, and stationary shops torched. During the course of the Communist regime, an estimated 80 percent of written works in the Khmer language were lost (Ledgerwood 1990). The fate of books followed that of the condemned people, whose corpses the Khmer Rouge threw down wells or into ponds and rivers, or left to the elements. One evacuee remembers seeing, during the evacuation of Phnom Penh, "a buzzing, black cloud of flies [that] lifted from bloated bodies as we approached, then settled once more when we passed. Looking down into the Bossac River, I saw books and magazines by the hundreds floating in lazy eddies; the river was awash with soggy French literature" (Criddle and Mam 1987, 32).

For the most part, exiled former residents never witnessed the ghost town that Phnom Penh became during the era. However, one former student, in transit between work sites, passed through the city by his old university and later recorded: "Now the street was empty and littered with torn books. Just for a moment I could see down the length of it with paper blowing everywhere" (May 1986, 143). Phnom Penh was effectively cut off from the outside world: it was without regular telephone, telegram, cable, mail, air, or train service. Publishing and the normal media outlets had ceased to exist; in all of Cambodia, the Khmer Rouge allowed only two newspapers, one rudimentary magazine for the cadres, and one radio station that broadcast political propaganda. Printing presses were destroyed, and all but about 5 percent of Cambodian journalists would die under the regime (Mehta 1997, 127). For the duration of the Khmer Rouge regime, the city's population never exceeded 50,000. Its sole residents were party cadres and their families, soldiers, trusted workers, and a few advisors sent by Communist China. The Cambodians, although the new elite, led a spartan existence and worked long hours growing their own food, running the government, staffing a few rudimentary factories, and "cleaning" the city. The initial purging of books was replaced by policies of pragmatism and neglect. Books were used for fuel, wrapping, waste paper, and cigarette wrappers. Rural residents had no access to books; those in the city had neither the time nor energy to read, even if reading had not become a forbidden activity.

The people driven out of the city, the urbanites and the refugees alike, were labeled "the new people" because they had not "joined" the revolution until the fall of Phnom Penn (Chandler 1999, 1). Considered incorrigible enemies, still committed to the old order and capable of sabotaging the revolution, they were accorded the status of prisoners of war and slaves. Any small rebellion, any hint of "Western capitalist culture and its selfish, individualistic norms" made them superfluous to the new Communist society and worthy only of death (Stuart-Fox 1985, 44). The new people had to prove by flawless behavior and extraordinarily hard labor that they were worth more alive than dead. The old people were allowed more food, less work, better homes, some family life, and power over the new people. All new people over the age of six worked 17 or 18 hours a day and were fed thin rice gruel. Their life boiled down to "just the sun that rose and set, the stars at night and the rain that fell from the sky. And work. Everything was work in the empty, primitive countryside" (Ngor 1987, 199). The "old" people—illiterate peasants who had lived in the village before and during the civil war and thus had never been exposed to corrupting influences—became their "teachers" and judges and transformed their villages into penal camps. Local chiefs ruled over village work units of 10 to 15 families, and unquestioning obedience was enforced by Khmer Rouge soldiers who served as policemen and executioners. Recruited from the poorest strata of village youth, the soldiers had been trained to kill by watching torture and death and trained to believe that the new people deserved execution "without pity, as one would kill a lizard or a rat" (Stuart-Fox 1985, 145). Implementing cadre policy, the chief, the old people, and the soldiers approached the pursuit of revolution as a series of military campaigns to be conducted with discipline and combat-level intensity. Those who did not work (even the sick) did not eat. The mildest opposition, even a lack of enthusiasm, was not tolerated: "To question anything . . . meant that you were an enemy to your new 'parent.' That was Angka[r]'s rule. To disobey means the *kang prawattasas*, the wheel of history, would run over you" (Him 2000, 14). Their keepers often told them that there was nothing to gain by keeping them alive, nothing to lose by doing away with them.

Members of the original guerilla movement had been named the "Khmer Rouge," or the "Red Khmers," because of an association, by Sihanouk, of the color red with Communism. But after their takeover of Cambodia, the label acquired symbolic overtones, with redness expressing the propensity for violence that characterized the regime, its cadres, and soldiers. A fascination with blood as a revolutionary agent was reflected in the national anthem of Democratic Kampuchea, the country's name under the Khmer Rouge regime:

> Bright red blood which covers towns and plains
> Of Kampuchea, our Motherland,
> Sublime Blood of workers and peasants,
> Sublime Blood of revolutionary men and women fighters!
>
> The Blood changing into unrelenting hatred
> And resolute struggle
> On April 17th, under the Flag of the Revolution,
> Free from slavery! (Stuart-Fox 1985, 168)

Under the Khmer Rouge, purity was a cruel, "angry," and binary concept of purity versus corruption (Becker 1998, 107). Local village people demanded that the new people rid themselves of the "corrupt Western creation of vanity" by wearing black clothes and cutting their hair in the same style; colored clothes were destroyed because they corrupted the mind (Ung 2000, 58). *Purity* was defined as a homogeneous, austere state of being in which no private identities or allegiances (including familial) were allowed. "Neither private property, knowledge, nor pleasures were to differentiate people or separate the individual from the community" (Staub 1989, 194). There were no holidays or religious festivals. Recreation and reading and all forms of intellectual development were forbidden. "Cultural ties, community and family obligations, blood bonds and security were obliterated" (Imam 2000, 301). The Khmer Rouge leadership outlawed flirting, punished premarital sex with death, controlled marriages, and restricted conjugal sex, and punished even simple gestures of affection between relatives. They broke up families through forced relocations. Making food preparation and consumption communal triggered a concerted effort to gather up all remaining private belongings, including knives and spoons. The Khmer Rouge leadership was reacting in a Romantic, Luddite way to the encroachments of a modern world; at the village level, fear and resentment of things urban was visceral (Marston 2002, 47). The new people soon realized that their survival depended on blending in and defusing jealousy and suspicion. In Chanrithy Him's (2000, 228) memoirs, she recounts an incident involving her older sister, Chea, who was suddenly confronted by a Khmer Rouge informant:

[His] piercing, sinister eyes look accusing. "Angka needs to look for books," he declares. . . . I'm baffled, disbelieving . . . as he carries away a package, our once-hidden past, Chea's personal belongings . . . a leather briefcase and a handbag. They are *Pa* and *Mak*'s gifts to her for her academic success. The briefcase contains memories of her school years: a spiral math notebook; two Cambodian novels . . . , written by Chea's friend in college. Primly secured in their slots opposite the books are fancy pens and pencils, souvenirs from her friends. Their pictures, and pictures of her with them, are in a picture album. Beside each wallet-sized photo is a brief friendship note. . . . In the handbag are documents of our births and the titles to our houses. . . . In the informant's hands is the tangible evidence of our former lives. *How did he suspect us of having books?*

Chea saved herself and the family by shaving her head, scratching herself so as to look ugly and crazy and thus pure. She claimed that she had found the books on a road during the evacuation from Phnom Penh: "I didn't get to study much because of the fighting," she told the informant. "I know how to read a little. Why? Does comrade want those books? You may have them. I just keep them for wiping myself after I poop."

To ensure conformity in the rice that was consumed, differences in strains and taste between the rice from different regions, which the Cambodians took great pride in, were bred out (Becker 1998, 255). Because the desired citizen was an illiterate Khmer peasant or soldier, a blank tablet upon which the new Communist culture could be imprinted, survival of a new person depended on feigning illiteracy and ignorance and modeling compliance. According to a survivor, "If the Khmer Rouge say rain falls from the earth to the sky, you have to say it too; otherwise, it means you think and thus you're an intellectual" and that was punishable by death (Martin 1994, 179). "Year Zero was the dawn of an age in which, *in extremis*, there would be no families, no sentiment, no expression of love or grief, . . . no books, no learning, no holidays, no music: only work and death" (Him 2000, 226). Thousands of the new people died of exhaustion; starvation; insufficient or bad food; diseases such as malaria, poor sanitation, marginal medical treatment; and, of course, execution.

A key tactic in the imposition of ideological purity was the elimination of religion, no small task in a country where 90 percent of the people were Buddhist and Buddhism had been a central pillar of Cambodian social systems for 600 years. The 65,000 Buddhist monks were labeled enemies of Angkar, counterforces to Communism whose moral authority had to be broken (Keyes 1990, 60). The Khmer Rouge killed the most influential monks immediately and then killed any monks who refused to disrobe, work in the fields, or stop practicing Buddhism. By 1979, fewer than 1,000 monks survived to return to what was left of their temples (Rummel 1994, 187). The nation's 3,000 pagodas were either destroyed or vandalized and used as stables, prisons, and execution sites. The ancient texts that these Buddhist temples had sheltered, many of which had been tenuously preserved on palm or mulberry leaves, were burned or shredded (Jarvis 1995, 394). Statues of the Buddha were decapitated or thrown in ponds and rivers. In 1978, the regime's minister of culture told a Yugoslav journalist, "Buddhism is dead, and the ground has been cleared for the foundation of a new revolutionary culture" (Keyes 1990, 60). Some of the regime's antipathy toward Buddhism may have stemmed from the fact that the Khmers had always been "great borrowers," and few aspects of their culture and traditions were untouched by outside forces (Etcheson 1984, 28). They believed that Buddhism, and other religions, had been brought in by imperialists and had contaminated the pure Khmer race (Ponchaud 1978).

The Khmer Rouge members were racist and their cleansing of "inferior" Catholic and Muslim minorities reached genocidal proportions. After the Khmer Rouge captured Phnom Penh, one of their first acts, as mentioned above, was to blow up the Roman Catholic cathedral, which they called "the Vietnamese church" (Chandler 1990, 17). The Vietnamese, many of whom were Catholic, were almost entirely eradicated (Kiernan 1990b, 64). Cambodia's largest indigenous minority, the Muslim Chams, were subjected to internecine policies and prohibited from speaking their language (Kiernan 1990b). Entire families were killed and villages dispersed. Mosques were destroyed or turned into pigpens, and sacred books were torn apart. The Chams had been a target of the Khmer Rouge even during the civil war. In 1973, after Chams from the large village of Koh Phol resisted the Khmer Rouge's attempts to collect all copies of the Koran, the guerillas massacred the population and razed the village. An estimated 90,000 Chams lost their lives under the Khmer Rouge regime: only 20 of 113 *hakkem* (community leaders) survived, and only 25 of their 226 deputies were still living in 1978. Of 300 religious teachers at Koranic schools, all but 38 perished (Kiernan 1990b, 65).

Ethnic cleansing and the extinction of religion occurred simultaneously with the dismantling of public education. Many of the nation's children had been educated in religious settings, in particular Buddhist pagodas. Since Angkorean times, literacy in Cambodia (which had reached 86% in the 1960s [Imam 2000, 345]) had been linked with the study and promulgation of religious texts; indeed, in the colonial era, literacy in Khmer was almost entirely in the hands of the Buddhist monkhood (Chandler 1999, 159). Sihanouk encouraged literacy, and in 1970, he devoted 25 percent of the national budget to education: three-quarters of the primary school–aged children went to school; there were 28,000 teachers, 118,000 students in the high schools, and 7,000 university students (Becker 1998, 6). The schools were crowded; they relied on memorization and, for the most part, lacked laboratories, libraries, textbooks, and audiovisual equipment, but they provided children with some form of education (Chhim 1989, 32). In addition to destroying Buddhist, Catholic, and Muslim schools, deemed tainted by religion, the Khmer Rouge demolished the entire secular educational system, because it was contaminated by Western influences. Schools were shut down, instructors were killed, and "students in higher grades were condemned to die along with their teachers" (Chhim 1989, 33). Ninety-six percent of Cambodia's college students became casualties (Chepesiuk 1992, 32). Tuol Seng, the "central interrogation, torture and death chamber," was set up inside a complex that had once housed a primary and secondary school (Becker 1998, 260); an estimated 2,000 children were killed along with their parents at this site.

In the countryside, the program of eradication that had first been put into effect in Phnom Penh had to be applied to those who had survived the urban evacuation and were hiding their past by posing as illiterates in the fields. These "Western-educated enemies" were disposable because the workers and peasants were considered the real source of all knowledge—pure, Kampuchean, practical knowledge that was far superior to foreign findings and anything to be found in books (Stuart-Fox 1985, 132). "The only wise man is the one who knows how to grow rice," said the cadres (Ngor 1987, 199). Khmer Rouge educational programs were rudimentary and ideological: In between chores, some of the younger children were gathered into makeshift structures where they were taught basic arithmetic and songs about love for Angkor and the joy of sacrificing their lives for the revolution (Y 2000, 80): programming was aimed at building a new mentality in which life centered around work. "The young people don't even have to go to school!" declared one disingenuous cadre. "Under Angk[ar], the 'school' is the farm. The 'fountain pen' is the plow. The 'paper' is the land. You can 'write' all you want. Anytime" (Ngor 1987, 198–199).

Biblioclasm is often driven by fear. Pol Pot and the other leaders may have realized that they, as scholars and teachers, were themselves living proof of the power of intellectuals to overturn a previous order. If education could produce the leaders of the revolution, "it could also produce a new dissident group to overthrow them" (Quinn 1989, 188). Unlike China, where literacy was promoted (though access to texts was controlled) and the people were exposed to Marxist-Leninist texts, in postrevolutionary Cambodia, there were no materials available for political study or discussion: "The decisions of its own leaders alone constituted a suitable guide for the nation" (Stuart-Fox 1985, 45). The new people were told, "The rice field is your university" and "Your hoe is your pen" (Lafreniere 2000, 80). In one sense, the nation was being reverted to a state of orality; but even the cultural roots of orality were severed. "Administration of the country as if it were a battlefield erased the rural traditions—the folk and formal arts, the village crafts, the dance, the music, and storytelling" (Becker 1998, 255). The transmission of culture through folktales—"stories rich with ribald, often black humor, with a taste for sensuality and for great food"—came to a halt: communication was constrained to the transmission of commands and political slogans (Becker 1998, 66). Democratic Kampuchea, composed of villages sealed off from the outer world and each other, was a "society of silence" (Ponchaud 1989, 158). Surveillance and spies extinguished private conversation (Van Lee 1988, 257–258). Only illiterate cadres were allowed some measure of freedom of speech, and they had to monitor their comments for fear of being purged (Ponchaud 1989, 158). After working long hours in the fields, the new people had to endure group meetings in which there was no discussion, no questions—only the endless repetition of Khmer Rouge doctrines.

The fanatical nature of Khmer Rouge Communism was intensified by the leadership's concurrent allegiance to Communism's antithesis—nationalism. Like many supranationalists, Pol Pot and his colleagues simultaneously claimed race as the basis for asserting supremacy while acting out a group mentality of inferiority and vulnerability (Staub 1989, 199). They saw themselves as engaged in both revolution and a defensive struggle against racial and national extinction; they perceived threats all around, from expansionist neighbors to foreign imperialists, effete urbanites, and cunning racial minorities. Given their propensity for revolutionary bloodletting (i.e., purification through physical violence) and an ideological commitment so absolute that setbacks could only be explained as the product of human failure and insufficient rigor, the leadership began consuming itself. Whenever the revolution faltered, they blamed it on internal enemies, and their "fratricidal search for ideological purity and internal security" resulted in extensive purges within the leadership itself (Jackson 1989, 3). Wives and children often shared the fate of targeted cadres. The auto-genocide that was consuming the Cambodian people as well as the Khmer Rouge regime was finally halted by the Vietnamese. When Pol Pot sought to secure disputed lands through attacks and incursions along the Vietnamese border, that country responded by invading for the purpose of bringing down what it saw as a rogue genocidal regime. The Khmer Rouge was driven back into the jungles, and a dangerous and unstable peace prevailed.

Survivors slowly made their way back to the cities and were confronted with infrastructures devastated by policy and neglect. An estimated one to two million Cambodians died under the Khmer Rouge out of a population of approximately seven million, and cultural losses were of a scale parallel in magnitude and nearly as difficult to quantify. Libraries and archival institutions suffered to varying degrees. The archives of the *Commission des Moeurs et Coutumes Cambodgiennes*, an institute dedicated to the preservation of ethnographic data, disappeared along with its manuscripts dealing with prerevolutionary Cambodian customs, culture, history, and religion (Chandler 1982, 26). The entire library of the Royal Palace, which contained historical manuscripts, was lost (Chandler 1982, 26). Fortunately, most of the small collection in the National Museum survived, though in complete disarray (Jarvis 1989, 389). In a ruined pagoda, thousands of valuable and rare handwritten, palm-leaf prayer books were recovered from an underground room (Jarvis 1995, 403). But perhaps two-thirds of the manuscripts from the sacked Buddhist Institute, founded in 1930 as a center for Buddhist intellectuals and clearinghouse/ repository for Cambodian religious and literary texts, were lost (Chandler

1999, 16; Chandler 1982, 25). Some had been 500 years old, their letters incised into palm or mulberry leaves and rubbed with black ink, the leaves folded concertina style and strung on cords between wooden covers (Jarvis 1989, 388).

Although early reports claimed that all or the vast majority of the nation's books had been destroyed (and the figure of an 80% loss of written works in Khmer is still given credence), significant numbers of books did survive, though neglected and misappropriated. After the regime fell, some of these books found their way into private hands and began to appear for sale in the resuscitated markets. Old Khmer, Chinese, French, and English dictionaries and novels could be bought with several kilograms of rice (Ung 2000, 213). People returning to Phnom Penh often picked up books and palm-leaf manuscripts from the streets (Jarvis 1991, 16) or carted away books from the National Library for personal use or to sell as artifacts or paper (Jarvis 1995, 406). Others collected books from the streets and markets and brought them to the National Library, where they were piled in large mounds. After the library's premises had been secured, Do Huu Dun, a librarian from the National Library of Vietnam, arrived to assist in reconstruction and collected books from along the streets, from the ruins of bookshops and stores, and from abandoned houses.

In 1979, the National Library was reported to have retained only a minimal amount of its collections. As time went by, various portions of the collection emerged as having survived, including archival holdings from the colonial era and the 1950s (Jarvis 1995, 405). Exact figures do not exist. Reconstruction of the library advanced slowly as Do Huu supervised students who, despite "sallow skins and thin bodies with patched clothes," seemed happy to be engaged in the endeavor (Jarvis 1995, 403). Workers in the institution were highly motivated and perhaps mindful of the library's original motto, written in French with large graceful letters and positioned over the entrance: "Force binds for a moment, ideas link forever." Another phrase was added to a doorway in the 1980s: "Culture is the soul of a nation. Without the culture there is no nation" (Sam 1990, 44). Of the National Library's staff of 40 in 1975, only Mao Kin, the night watchman, and two librarians returned in 1979. Six to eight others survived, but never returned to work; this leaves 30 unaccounted for and presumed dead. Conditions in the library were chaotic: the building had been used to store food for the kitchen of a nearby lodging for Chinese advisors. Bookshelves held pots, pans, and supplies. Its gardens housed a pig farm, and the National Archives Building behind the library was bloodstained; it had apparently been used as a barracks for those who tended and butchered the pigs (Jarvis 1991, 16). The pre-1975 catalog was in total disarray; cards that had not been destroyed were strewn throughout the building.

On a national level, cultural losses were daunting and the progress slow. The tasks were the same: grieving, taking stock, and reconstructing. Survivors mourned the loss of family members, possessions, homes, and fields. "Whole categories of people, buildings, arts, and books had disappeared, along with the knowledge they carried" (Mortland 2002, 164). The loss of culture-bearers such as teachers, artists, and craftsmen was particularly devastating (Mortland 2002, 164). Lost were monks who knew how to chant certain religious texts correctly; storytellers and their memorized folktales; craftsmen who knew how to construct distinct kinds of ox carts, traditional musical instruments, masks, and Buddhist images; and women who knew how to weave unique designs (Gargan 2002, 210). Only 300 of the approximately 3,000 members of the Khmer Association of Artists in 1975 remained alive or in country after 1979. They were faced with, among other things, restoring the artworks that had been vandalized by the Khmer Rouge: of 6,465 sculptures from the Angkar period, only four or five remained intact (Young 1990, 11). The famous royal ballet was destroyed; its instruments were smashed, books and costumes burnt, and musicians and dancers (including relatives of Pol Pot) murdered (Griffith 2000, 227). When the Khmer Rouge lost power, a few dance and music masters, the "walking dictionaries," emerged and painstakingly revived the institution (Sam 1990, 43). A University of Fine Arts was founded by the Vietnamese-sponsored government and undertook to make audio and visual recordings of demonstrations by surviving artisans and performances of traditional music, to write down poems, and to build a publishing house and bookstore (Sam 1990, 44). Television and radio programming, restaurants, entertainment venues, a telephone system, and production and distribution networks for books and newspapers were slowly restored. Into the 1980s, all textbook printing had to be done in Vietnam because there were literally no functioning presses in Cambodia (Vickery 1990, 52). The educational system had to be reconstructed almost from scratch—a task complicated by the low survival rate of teachers. Public motivation, however, often outpaced necessary resources for these efforts. Political instability, the persistence of Khmer Rouge guerillas in the jungles, and the lack of a meaningful official vision for the reconstruction of Khmer culture and identity further complicated reconstruction initiatives, as did the unwillingness of the Vietnamese to open up the country to Western aid and influences.

In a travel book on the Mekong, Edward Gargan (2002, 184–185) mused that societies

invariably create edifices that bit by bit and in their collectivity provide a description of who they are, why they are, what they think and imagine and what, in some cases, they hope to be. These edifices are the museums, theaters and libraries that display a society's art, its crafts, its written words, the panoply of its cultural expressions; these edifices also document the choices societies make about how they define who their people are.

The destruction of Cambodia's libraries and culture was designed to extinguish independent intellectual functioning and to transform the Cambodian people into blank tablets upon which the Khmer Rouge would stamp their imprint. They succeeded so well that the recovery of a balanced and healthy society in Cambodia has been tentative. Hope remains the primary impulse behind ongoing reconstruction efforts, but it yet requires a vision that reaches beyond extremism, utopian solutions, and the substitution of politics for culture.

Of course, the successful creation, incubation, production, and propagation of new visions take time and thoughtful attention. In an interview in May 1989, Chheng Phon, an artist who had survived the Khmer Rouge regime to become Cambodia's Minister of Information and Culture, struggled with the question of how a people's culture could help "the moral intellect of the world" (Young 1990, 12). He turned his back on the Khmer Rouge as having separated intellect and morality and conceived of Cambodia as a whole universe. For Chheng, a healthy system must integrate intellect, ideology, and morality, and locate the nation meaningfully within a larger civilization. Cambodia can come into its own, culturally, by serving the interests of "a universal, regional, and national aesthetic" (Young 1990, 12). As a government spokesperson, Chheng Phon has a universal aesthetic, based in global norms that value multiculturalism and pluralism rather than an exclusive form of Communism, and a national aesthetic, based on pride and inclusion rather than hubris and hateful exclusivity. His statements gave hope to those who wanted Cambodia's government to place the country on a sustainable path toward modernity and cultural recovery.

The Khmer Rouge movement was a response to socioeconomic breakdown, political oppression, and despair. Pol Pot and his cohort sought relief in the Enlightenment notion that man could, through his own efforts, transform his universe. They were soon caught up in the most dangerous of post-Enlightenment impulses—the desire to achieve utopia. In thrall to extreme ideals and to purification processes that promised triumph over chaos, the extinction of cultural practices that had betrayed them, and social perfection, they tried to realize a heaven on earth. Such attempts, Karl Popper (1966, 237) has hypothesized, ultimately produce not heaven, but hell, and Cambodia was no exception. Cambodia testifies to the terrifying potential for annihilation, rationalized as purification, that resides in ideological extremism. When ideas are backed by absolute power, revolutionary fervor may transmute into violent nihilistic impulses that then consume society. It is the same potential that was first realized during the Reign of Terror, when Jacobins steered France into a similar situation. The Khmer Rouge chose an exclusive, violent, and absolutist path toward the future. Surviving Cambodians and their children are choosing a more moderate path. They are reconstituting their shattered cultural institutions and traditions for themselves, for Cambodia, and to participate in a common global culture. This bodes well for the preservation and expansion of Cambodia's surviving books and libraries.

REFERENCES

Becker, Elizabeth. 1998. *When the War Was Over: Cambodia and the Khmer Rouge Revolution.* New York: Public Affairs.

Chalk, Frank, and Kurt Jonassohn. 1990. *The History and Sociology of Genocide: Analyses and Case Studies.* New Haven, Conn.: Yale University Press.

Chandler, David P. 1979. "The Tragedy of Cambodian History." *Pacific Affairs* 53 (3):410–419.

Chandler, David P. 1982. "Monash Scholars Go to Phnom Penh." *International Association of Orientalist Librarians Bulletin* 20:25–28.

Chandler, David P. 1990. "Reflections on Cambodian History." *Cultural Survival Quarterly* 14 (3):16–19.

Chandler, David P. 1999. *Brother Number One: A Political Biography of Pol Pot.* Revised Edition. Boulder, Colo.: Westview Press.

Chepesiuk, Ron. 1992. "Cambodian Libraries in Crisis: The Cornell University Library Preserves a Heritage." *Wilson Library Bulletin* 66 (5):30–33.

Chhim, Sun-Him. 1989. *Introduction to Cambodian Culture.* San Diego, Calif.: San Diego State University.

Criddle, Joan D., and Teeda Butt Mam. 1987. *To Destroy You Is No Loss: The Odyssey of a Cambodian Family.* New York: Doubleday.

Etcheson, Craig. 1984. *The Rise and Demise of Democratic Kampuchea.* Boulder, Colo.: Westview Press.

Gargan, Edward. 2002. *The River's Tale: A Year on the Mekong.* New York: Alfred A. Knopf.

Griffith, Clare. 2000. *Insight Guide: Laos and Cambodia.* Singapore: APA Publications.

Him, Chanrithy. 2000. *When Broken Glass Floats: Growing Up under the Khmer Rouge.* New York: W. W. Norton.

Imam, Vannery. 2000. *When Elephants Fight: A Memoir.* St Leonards, New South Wales: Allen and Unwin.

Jackson, Karl D. 1989. "Introduction. The Khmer Rouge in Context." In *Cambodia 1975–1978: Rendezvous with Death,* ed. Karl D. Jackson. Princeton, N.J.: Princeton University Press, 3–11.

Jarvis, Helen. 1989. "Report on a Visit to Kampuchea in 1987." *International Library Review* 21 (3):387–393.

Jarvis, Helen. 1991. "Libraries in Cambodia: Starting Anew." *Asian Libraries* 1 (1):15–18.

Jarvis, Helen. 1995. "The National Library of Cambodia: Surviving for Seventy Years." *Libraries and Culture* 30 (4):391–408.

Keyes, Charles. 1990. "Buddhism and Revolution in Cambodia." *Cultural Survival Quarterly* 14 (3):60–63.

Kiernan, Ben. 1990a. "Roots of Genocide: New Evidence on the US Bombardment of Cambodia." *Cultural Survival Quarterly* 14 (3):20–22.

Kiernan, Ben. 1990b. "The Survival of Cambodia's Ethnic Minorities." *Cultural Survival Quarterly* 14 (3):64–66.

Knuth, Rebecca. 2003. *Libricide: The Regime-Sponsored Destruction of Books and Libraries in the Twentieth Century.* Westport, Conn.: Praeger.

Lafreniere, Bree. 2000. *Music through the Dark: A Tale of Survival in Cambodia.* Honolulu: University of Hawaii Press.

Ledgerwood, Judy. 1990. "A Building Full of Books." *Cultural Survival Quarterly* 14 (3):53–55.

Marston, John. 2002. "Democratic Kampuchea and the Idea of Modernity." In *Cambodia Emerges from the Past: Eight Essays,* ed. Judy Ledgerwood. DeKalb: Northern Illinois University, Southeast Asia Publications.

Martin, Marie Alexandrine. 1994. *Cambodia: A Shattered Society*. Trans. Mark W. McLeod. Berkeley: University of California Press.

May, Someth. 1986. *Cambodian Witness: The Autobiography of Someth May*. Ed. James Fenton. New York: Random House.

Mehta, Harish C. 1997. *Cambodia Silenced: The Press under Six Regimes*. Bangkok: White Lotus Press.

Mortland, Carol A. 2002. "Legacies of Genocide for Cambodians in the United States." In *Cambodia Emerges from the Past: Eight Essays*, ed. Judy Ledgerwood. DeKalb: Northern Illinois University, Southeast Asia Publications, 151–175.

Ngor, Haing, with Roger Warner. 1987. *Haing Ngor: A Cambodian Odyssey*. New York: Macmillan.

Ponchaud, François. 1978. *Cambodia: Year Zero*. Trans. Nancy Amphoux. New York: Holt, Rinehart, and Winston.

Ponchaud, François. 1989. "Social Change in the Vortex of Revolution." In *Cambodia 1975–1978: Rendezvous with Death*, ed. Karl D. Jackson. Princeton, N.J.: Princeton University Press, 151–177.

Popper, Karl. 1966. *The Open Society and Its Enemies: The High Tide of Prophecy: Hegel, Marx, and the Aftermath*. Vol. 2. Princeton, N.J.: Princeton University Press.

Quinn, Kenneth M. 1989. "The Pattern and Scope of Violence." In *Cambodia 1975–1978: Rendezvous with Death*, ed. Karl D. Jackson. Princeton, N.J.: Princeton University Press, 179–208.

Rummel, R. J. 1994. *Death by Government*. New Brunswick, N.J.: Transaction Books.

Sam, Sam-Ang. 1990. "Preserving a Cultural Tradition: Ten Years after the Khmer Rouge." *Cultural Survival Quarterly* 14 (3):43–45.

Staub, Ervin. 1989. *Roots of Evil: The Origins of Genocide and Other Group Violence*. Cambridge: Cambridge University Press.

Stephanie. 2003. "The Cambodian Holocaust; A Survivor Speaks Out." [Interview with Thida Mam]. http://www.ustrek.org/odyssey/semester2/0401/040401stephcambodia.html. June 20, 2003.

Stuart-Fox, Martin. 1985. *The Murderous Revolution: Life and Death in Pol Pot's Kampuchea*. Chippendale, Australia: Alternative Publishing Cooperative.

Szymusiak, Molyda. 1986. *The Stones Cry Out: A Cambodian Childhood 1975–1980*. New York: Hill and Wang.

Taylor, Jay. 1993. *The Rise and Fall of Totalitarianism in the Twentieth Century*. New York: Paragon House.

Ung, Loung. 2000. *First They Killed My Father: A Daughter of Cambodia Remembers*. New York: HarperCollins.

Van Lee, Erik. 1988. "The Quest for Purity in Communism." In *The Quest for Purity: Dynamics of Puritan Movements*, ed. Walter E. A. van Beek. Berlin: Mouton De Gruyter, 247–261.

Vickery, Michael. 1990. "Cultural Survival in Cambodian Language and Literature." *Cultural Survival Quarterly* 14 (3):49–52.

Y, Ly. 2000. *Heaven Becomes Hell: A Survivor's Story of Life under the Khmer Rouge*. Ed. John S. Driscoll. New Haven, Conn.: Yale University South East Asia Studies.

Young, Evans. 1990. "Flowers in the Forest: A Talk with Chheng Phon, Minister of Information and Culture." *Cultural Survival Quarterly* 14 (3):11–12.

CHAPTER 7

Fundamentalism and the Destruction of Afghanistan's Cultural Heritage, 1994–2001

And thus I clothe my naked villainy
With old odd ends, stol'n forth of holy writ;
And seem a saint, when most I play the devil.
—William Shakespeare, *Richard III*

Two dangers constantly threaten the world: order and disorder.
—Paul Valéry, French poet, 1871–1945

For more than two decades, images from Afghanistan of Soviet tanks, freedom fighters, burkha-clad women, and the rubble of giant Buddhas have disturbed global consciousness. After the fall of the Taliban in 2001, these iconic images were joined by the photographs of bullet-ridden books and bombed-out libraries that accompanied accounts by forlorn Afghani librarians and scholars who lamented the loss of Afghanistan's books because of civil war and the purging of a fundamentalist regime. The imposition of Communism, followed by rebellion and guerilla warfare, civil war, and finally revolution, had laid waste to much of Afghanistan's rich written and archeological heritage. The nation and its heritage were casualties of the power struggle over the form its society should take and, as happened under the totalitarianism of the Nazis and Khmer Rouge regimes, the society that emerged was one in which books and libraries were either purged and fettered or eliminated.

Afghanistan was plagued by violent political conflict that began in 1979 when the Soviet Union invaded Afghanistan to prop up a floundering Marxist regime. The Soviets merely succeeded in uniting the diverse and independent clans into *mujahideen* (Arabic for "freedom fighter") units that waged a violent

guerilla war subsidized by Pakistan and the United States. For 10 years, the
Soviets poured resources and soldiers into the war to try to quell the rebellion. Large regions of Afghanistan were turned into wasteland, and libraries
joined the list of casualties as the conflict accelerated. When the Communists
withdrew in 1989, *mujahideen* alliances fell apart as ethnic and familial groups
fought a civil war under the leadership of warlords who sought territory and
power. The different factions shelled with abandon, claiming libraries among
their victims, but their destructive frenzy was laced with pragmatism. When
they could, they looted books and antiquities and sold them for guns and
supplies. Attrition among the various rival groups and public disgust at their
tactics eventually created an opening into which the Taliban stepped. Taliban
members were primarily from the Pashtun ethnic group, which comprised
about 44 percent of the Afghan population. They promised to rid Afghanistan
of corrupt leaders and build a purified fundamentalist and ultraconservative
Islamic nation, a plan linked in their minds with Pashtun dominance and
renunciation of Western influences. As the regime extinguished its rivals,
the people of Afghanistan and their cultural heritage were often caught in
the crossfire. The Taliban were powerful and proud. They held international
opinion in disdain, and they were fanatically committed to a life bounded by
their idiosyncratic interpretation of the Koran. It was, once again, a recipe for
righteous iconoclasm, a dangerous scenario for books and libraries.

Afghanistan's geographical location has granted it unique status as a cultural
crossroads where "Greek thought met Chinese philosophy, Indian gardens
inspired Persian poetry, and four major religions—Zoroastrianism, Buddhism,
Hinduism, and Islam—were either born or transformed" (Lawler 2002a,
1195). During ancient times, the Silk Road, a trade route that stretched from
Italy to Japan and ran through Afghanistan, facilitated cultural exchanges
between European and Asia civilizations. One has only to picture the Silk
Road merchants praying before the giant Buddhas of Bamiyan to get a fla-
vor of the cosmopolitanism of the area. The invading armies of great military leaders such as Alexander the Great (356–323 B.C.) and Genghis Khan
(1162–1227 A.D.) swept through the area and left in their wake new cultural
influences. As a result, the country amassed a "a richer past than almost any
place on earth" (Lawler 2002b, 1196–1197). In 645 A.D., armies introduced
Islam and contributed a new element to the ethnic, cultural, and religious mix
(Rashid 2000). In the centuries since, there were golden eras in which religious freedom prevailed, and the various Islamic sects lived in peace with each
other and with followers of different religions. In fifteenth-century Herat,
artist-librarians, men and women of letters, and researchers prepared beautiful calligraphic manuscripts that now rest in art museums throughout the
world (Vogelsang 2002). They compared, corrected, and copied historic texts.
Indeed, one team used 500 different copies to prepare a definitive collection
of the works of Hafiz, a Persian poet of the fourteenth century (Amirkhani
2001). But the diversity that was a residual function of repeated invasions

brought chronic ethnic and religious conflicts and devastation. By the latter quarter of the twentieth century, the remnants of cultural greatness lingered in ancient cities that combined Buddhist, Persian, and Turkish arts and architecture, and in archeological sites (Rashid 2000). Ancient manuscripts and texts had been gathered into museums and libraries that also housed contemporary books, documents, and archeological reports.

Twentieth-century Afghanistan was a conservative, patriarchal, traditional society run by a feudal government. Islamic revivalist movements had occurred periodically since the sixteenth century but never elicited consensus within the various ethnic groups (Marsden 1998). The same geographical position that led to its rich culture and common borders with China, Pakistan, Iran, and Soviet-dominated Turkmenistan, Uzbekistan, and Tajikistan resulted in volatile relations and external interference with internal affairs. Nation-building had proven difficult because of the complex ethnic, cultural, political, and religious mix. The population of from 14 to 20 million people comprised two major religious sects (Sunni Muslims at approximately 85% and Shi'a Muslims at 15%) and many different ethnic groups—the Pashtun (44%), Tajik (25%), Hazara (10%), Uzbec (8%), and others—that were often rooted in local and tribal rather than national identity ("Afghanistan" 1999). They spoke different dialects and languages, although Pashtu (35%) and Afghan Persian/Dari (50%) were dominant. Islam was the primary common ground, but the Sunnis and Shiites made unity impossible (Marsden 1998).

Throughout the century, leaders had tried to impose modernity from the top down, and this did not sit well with the fiercely independent population. The Marxist regime that had taken control in 1973 soon faced intense resistance, and, in 1979, after a bloody coup, the Soviets sent tanks into the country to preserve Marxist rule. In the name of socialism, the government enforced secularization and repression, banned bourgeois and capitalist books, and burned some religious books. Indeed, people burned their own books in the face of house-to-house searches and violent retribution against those with forbidden content. As the Soviets removed recalcitrant librarians and archivists and replaced them with those who were willing to encourage or enforce socialism, the literate began to realize that books as well as their intellectual freedom were potentially endangered. Twenty years later, an Afghani scholar would exclaim: "You know, every time a regime would change we would ask ourselves which books we should hide!" (Loving 2002, 72). During the Soviet occupation, many educated Afghans were killed or forced into exile.

The Afghani people were stunned and incensed at the Soviet invasion. *Mujahideen* from all the ethnic groups united in guerilla warfare against Soviet troops and Afghani Communists. The Soviets bombed populated areas and blanketed the country with mines. Millions of refugees (perhaps as many as six million) poured into neighboring nations. At the same time, the freedom forces killed and wounded so many Soviet troops that in 1989, the Soviet Union had to pull out. A civil war ensued. The residual Soviet-backed government was toppled in 1992, and seven political parties formed a *mujahideen* coalition government to rule the newly designated "Islamic State of Afghanistan." However, no effective central regime emerged: the various groups could not agree on the division of power and were soon fighting for supremacy. Much of Afghanistan was divided into warlord fiefdoms controlled by commanders who "fought, switched sides and fought again in a bewildering array of alliances, betrayals, and bloodshed" (Rashid 2000, 21). The *mujahideen* were very brutal and subjected the Afghani population to regular violence that included murder and rape.

Although Islam had strengthened the people's resistance to the Soviet presence by providing a measure of consensus, especially in defining a stance toward socialist and Western influences, religion proved an inadequate base for post-Soviet unity (Marsden 1998). Regional and ethnic fragmentation of *mujahideen* forces was made worse by sectarian and political disagreements, such as division over the appropriate role of Islam in state-building. The Islamic parties were led by intellectuals who sought to build a modern Islamic state by borrowing from Western political concepts and creating a new political philosophy that rested on reinterpretation of the Koran and Hadith (scholastic commentaries). These leaders were opposed by "traditionalists" who looked to the *ulema* (religious scholars), the *mullahs* (religious teachers, often illiterate), and tribal leaders for guidance; they interpreted the Koran literally and rejected any hint of secularism or modernity (Marsden 1998, 82). As the *mujahideen* struggled for power, people fled the country, and there were tremendous cultural losses as the different groups used the weaponry supplied by outside parties (including Pakistan and the United States) to wage civil war. Libraries, museums, archeological sites, and cultural institutions of all types were shelled, bombed, and ransacked. The contents of public libraries and the Academy of Science were sold by weight in the city's book markets and in Pakistan (Rahin 1998, 69). Rare books and manuscripts became part of an illicit-antiquities trade that was second only to opium smuggling in economic rewards (Lawler 2002a, 1195). Thousands of Hellenistic, Iranian, and Indian artifacts were smuggled out to feed a voracious Western art market (Hughes 2001). What could not be sold was vandalized or put to pragmatic uses. Books were burned as fuel or used for wrapping paper.

From 1992 to 1996, rival militias fought for Kabul and, in the process, killed 30,000 civilians. Kabul was divided, Beirut-style, into sections controlled by different factions, and law and order broke down completely. Street fighting and rocket attacks reduced more than half of the city and many of its cultural institutions to rubble. Kabul University sustained significant damage to its physical structures and tragic losses to its learning community. In 1994, a rocket attack took the lives of 10 faculty members, and three students were killed a few days later (Lloyd 1999). The National Museum, which had been well protected under the Soviets, was devastated during the civil war. In spring 1993, rockets exploded on the roof and gutted its upper floors. In the fall, another rocket destroyed the basement. The museum had amassed a world-class collection of Central Asian Art, artifacts, and research documents while serving as the chief repository for 60 years of excavations (Lawler 2002c, 1202). The collection included Neolithic female figurines, stone Hindu goddesses, intricate ivories, coins, early Islamic art, an extensive library, and tens of thousands of ancient pottery shards (Lawler 2002c, 1202). As different factions gained control of the immediate area, their soldiers and leaders took turns stealing portable items, including about 40,000 ancient coins. The division of Kabul into militia-controlled enclaves represented the division of Afghanistan into rival fiefdoms, in which local commanders struggled to establish rudimentary control in the midst of anarchy.

Civil war had been wreaking havoc for two years when the Taliban surfaced in 1994. Its members were young (many between the ages of 14 and 24) and very enthusiastic. Many had grown up in refugee camps along the Afghan–Pakistani border and had received rudimentary training in orphanages and *madrassas* (small religious schools) run by barely literate conservative mullahs. Their name came from the Arab word for student, *talib*, but their schooling was very basic: they were taught almost no math, science, geography, or history, and instruction focused on Islamic texts that supplied the dogma for an austere messianic Islam. In the *madrassas*, "a religious and peda-gogical hierarchy had replaced their familial and tribal connection" (Roy 1998, 209). Indeed, these boys had "no memories of their tribes, their elders, their neighbors nor the complex ethnic mix of peoples that often made up their villages and their homeland" (Rashid 2000, 32). According to political scientist William Maley (2002, 223), the Taliban were a "*pathogenic* force, whose view of the world conspicuously omitted the pragmatic moderation which historically had muted the application of tribal and religious codes in Afghan society." Many had grown up without mothers, sisters, or cous-ins in their lives, and the totality of their programs for the subjugation of women became a "fundamental marker that differentiated the Taliban from the former Mujaheddin" (Rashid 2000, 33). According to Pakistani journal-ist Ahmed Rashid (2000, 32), "these boys were what the war had thrown up like the sea's surrender on the beach of history. . . . They had no memories of the past, no plans for the future . . . [only a] simple belief in a messianic, puritan Islam which had been drummed into them by simple village mul-lahs" (Rashid 2000, 32). They were inadequately socialized for anything but a radical, passionate, brutal revolutionary movement that offered the security of "certainties and a clear way forward" (Marsden 1998, 71). Their religious passion was fueled by outrage against the corrupt practices of duel-ing *mujahideen* leaders and a burning desire to create a pure Islamic state and nation. Also affecting their agenda was adherence to "an unstated but prevalent Pashtun ethnic identity" (Roy 1998, 209) and to the Sunni sect. Thus, the Taliban were hostile to Afghanistan's non-Pashtuns and members of rival sects such as the Shiites (Maley 2002, 223).

This group of students came together in Kandahar in 1994 and soon devel-oped a military arm, declaring themselves the "Islamic Movement of Taliban." Pakistan, to extend its influence in the region and secure Afghanistan for the laying of oil pipelines, provided funding, diplomatic support, training for fighters, ammunition, and an estimated 80,000 to 100,000 troops (Maley 2002, 221–222). The Taliban were also backed by trucking mafias and drug barons who needed order restored for business reasons. The "undisputed leader of the Taliban, from its inception to its collapse," was Mullah Muhammad Omar, a pious, one-eyed former *mujahideen* (Maley 2002, 223). Omar later took the title of *Amir al-Momineen* ("Commander of the Faithful") and sought legitimacy by displaying himself in public with Afghanistan's most sacred treasure, the Cloak of the Prophet Muhammad. When the Taliban took over Kandahar (Afghanistan's second-largest city) in late 1994, their remarkable success in bringing order to a city of warlords and anarchy brought popular acclaim. The local population was influenced by "their distinctive white turbans and obvious religious fervor and purity, [which] lent [the Taliban] an almost supernatural aura" (Marsden 1998, 46). Omar emerged as a Robin Hood figure because he was perceived as "helping the poor against the rapacious commanders" (Rashid 2000, 25). To an exhausted and traumatized population, the Taliban posed as "the cleansers and purifiers of a guerilla war gone astray, a social system gone wrong and an Islamic way of life that had been compromised by corruption and excess" (Rashid 2000, 23). This reputation for restoring order was helpful to the Taliban in subsequent military campaigns, and they steadily acquired more and more territory, quickly controlling 12 of the nation's 31 provinces. When they encountered resistance (usually clan, ethnic, and sectarian), the Taliban responded ferociously, fighting not just for power as their enemies did, but out of religious conviction. Indeed, in 1996, Omar declared *jihad* ("religious war") against the regime in Kabul (Rashid 2000, 42).

The success of Taliban campaigns depended in part on the leadership's ability to gain the people's support, but also on their use of extreme violence. The Taliban laid siege to Kabul for 18 months, shelling the city mercilessly and killing many civilians. After the winter of 1996–1997, they controlled Kabul and most of the south. By May 1997, they controlled most of the north, but when they sought to establish the kind of Islamic rules they had forced on Kabul and other towns, the population of Mazar-e-Sharif rebelled, massacred Taliban troops, and forced them out of the city. The Taliban's retreat has been described as ethnic cleansing (Rashid 2000, 74–78). They devastated prime agricultural land in the Shomali Valley, poisoned water wells, and blew up irrigation channels to keep local Tajiks from returning. When they retook Mazar-e-Sharif, Mullah Omar gave the soldiers permission to kill for two hours, but they killed for two days—everything that moved. Approximately 2,000 people were executed, and the bodies were left in the street for six days. Campaigns against the Shiite Hazaras were particularly brutal, because the Taliban saw them as hypocritical, inauthentic Muslims. In a stark portrayal of the potential for brutality in ethnic and religious extremism, some lucky Hazaras were allowed to "convert" or leave the country—others had their throats slit, were lined up and shot, or left to expire in sealed truck containers (Rashid 2000, 74–78).

Mullah Omar's holy war was against fellow Muslims who resisted the imposition of Taliban religious dictates and their political dominance as well. *Jihad* also extended to the cultural artifacts of enemies. Thumbing their noses at the world community, the Taliban members destroyed materials that supported modernity and secularism. In an attempt to impose orthodoxy and expunge from Afghanistan identities that were not primarily related to their form of Islam, they sought out texts in non-Pashtun languages, especially Persian materials. Persian materials were deemed particularly offensive and deserving of destruction because Persian was the language of poetry and philosophy, and the Taliban believed that only religious texts should have status. Persian was also associated with Shi'a-ism (a creed of a rival sect and the national religion of their neighbor and competitor, Iran), and Persian texts bore witness to a glorious pre-Islamic history, a secular identification that looked to a multicultural, cosmopolitan past rather than confining itself to the era of the prophet that inspired the Taliban. The Taliban tried to extinguish the national tradition of reading the *Shahnamhon* (*Epic of Kings*), an epic poem that retold the Persian creation myth and, according to some, served as the cultural memory of Afghanistan (Loving 2002, 71). Books containing the poem had always been passed from hand to hand and even illiterates memorized hundreds of its lines (Loving 2002). The Taliban wanted to eliminate all texts that competed with Koran: the central belief system of Afghanistan was to be purged of complexity and multiculturalism. The Taliban conducted house-to-house searches for banned books, and families preemptively burned their personal collections. In the massive offensive of 1998, Persian materials, including street signs, were obliterated, and librarians and scholars of ancient Persian were attacked and executed (Loving 2002). Word spread about the Taliban's policy of destroying libraries and bookstores in each conquered region: "It was a campaign not only against libraries but also against the other ethnic languages spoken by Afghanistan's diverse population" (Loving 2002, 72).

One of the Taliban's primary targets was the Hakim Nasser Khosrow Cultural Center. The center had opened in Kabul in 1987 as a public library and was known as the "jewel" of Afghanistan's libraries because of the quality of its modern texts, the depth of its collection, and its rich Persian artifacts (Loving 2002, 70). The highlight of the collection was an illuminated manuscript of the *Shahnameth* dating from the eleventh century. It was one of only six original copies of the masterpiece. The collection also included several manuscripts from the tenth century, restored texts in ancient Persian, Koranic manuscripts, artwork, carved miniatures, Timurid calligraphy, handwritten letters, and ancient stamps. When civil war engulfed Kabul in 1992, the library was moved to Pol-e-Khomri. Particularly in 1996, with the influx of scholars fleeing Taliban-occupied Kabul, the city and the library became what its director described as an "oasis for scholars" and "the only light in Afghanistan" (Loving 2002, 71). The center preserved a secular atmosphere, admitted both men and women, and followed a charter that forbade proselytizing and bringing exterior conflicts into the building. Refugee intellectuals, scholars, poets, and artists clustered within the building, where "there was freedom, there was life" (Loving 2002, 71). The library and cultural center was the treasured possession of ethnic, religious, and scholarly groups who were resisting the Taliban. It contained materials in Persian—an affront to that Pashtu-speaking group. Its rich collections defied their narrow fundamentalism: it was a secular haven, a center for humanism, learning, and scholarly endeavors that linked Afghanis with the outside world. After the conquest of Pol-e-Khomri in 1998, the Taliban drove up in Toyota 4x4 trucks, fired rocket launchers through the doors, and machine-gunned the videorecording studio and printing presses. The soldiers' eagerness to damage the center quickly degenerated into a frenzy of destruction, in which rockets were launched into the stacks; statues and artifacts smashed; and books were torn apart, stomped on, and removed and thrown into an adjacent river (Loving 2002). Eventually, not a single book was left.

The world first awoke to the nature of the Taliban movement when, after seizing Kabul in 1996, they murdered the former president, Mohammad Najibullah, and his brother and put their mutilated bodies on public display (Maley 2002, 236). In the next two years, the international community increasingly distanced itself from the regime. Unlike most modern regimes, the Taliban made no pretense of caring about the physical well-being of its people, yet made it difficult for aid organizations to operate and for the people—especially women—to help themselves. In 1998, the U.N.'s Koffi Annan declared that 50,000 armed men were holding the whole population hostage (Boustany 1998). Journalists and human-rights activists reported on public executions and the gross abuse of women. Questions swirled as people tried to comprehend the motivation and impetus behind the violent programs that targeted sin and that appeared, on the surface, to be impossibly anachronistic and surreal. Taliban religious beliefs became key to understanding their conflation of both politics and religion and purification and destruction.

The practice of Islam ranges, as do most religions, from liberal to conservative. For some Muslims, Islam is a progressive and peace-seeking force. For others, it is the foundation for militant dogmatism and exclusionary violence. The Taliban falls at the extreme conservative end of this spectrum (Marsden 1998, 59). The foundational myth of the Taliban was a dream by Mullah Omar, in which he led "pure" young students on a campaign to cleanse Afghanistan of the corruption and debauchery of warring commanders (Maley 2002, 220). Their ultimate goal was to rescue the country from the chaos of civil war and, simultaneously, from the processes of modernization, secularization, and Westernization that threatened to overwhelm its traditions (Marsden 1998, 59). They were building on conservative rural and patriarchal traditions, but as fundamentalists, they were selectively using the Koran and Sharia (an Islam-derived law system) to legitimate a set of rules, issued as decrees, that were designed to regulate and control behavior and form the basis for a purified Islamic society. The Sharia actually extends beyond law: it is "the totality of religious, political, social domestic and private life" ("Sharia" 2005). Like other twentieth-century revolutionaries, the Taliban used ideas as a means of ensuring conformity, making behavioral expectations concrete, and simplifying behavior (Taylor 1991). The state was defined as the "collective embodiment of the Islamic values espoused by society," and the Taliban charged themselves with enforcing these values (Marsden 1998, 69).

The Taliban members were primarily rural, and they viewed urban areas as centers of corruption, liberalism, and decadence (Marsden 1998, 65). As a result, they concentrated their efforts on purifying the cities by enforcing their strict interpretations of Islamic laws. For the most part, they left rural areas alone. Once in power in Kandahar and later in Kabul, Taliban leaders put into effect draconian codes that were designed to erase any distinction between the public and private sphere. One document, issued by a deputy minister, banned 16 common practices, including drum playing, pigeon feeding, beard trimming, Western hairstyles, kite flying, music and dancing at weddings, gambling, interest charges, washing clothes by ladies along the streams, addictions, the taking of women's measurements by tailors, and sorcery (Grazda 2000, 100). The decree banning sorcery instructed: "To prevent sorcery. All the related books should be burnt and the magician should be imprisoned until his repentance" (Rashid 2000, 219). The rationales were simple. A religious text, for example, stated that the Prophet Muhammad did not trim his beard all his life: therefore, all Afghani males should let their beards grow. Many aspects of modern life were banned, including movies, television, cassettes, photography, and radio broadcasts (except those publicizing decrees and leading prayers). In charge of enforcing these rules was the religious police, the *Amar Bil Maroof Wa Nahi An al-Munkar* ("Department of the Promotion of Virtue and the Prevention of Vice"). "Armed with whips, long sticks, and kalashnikovs [submachine guns]," they combined religious zealotry with police powers (Rashid 2000, 105), administering the code without due process and using intimidation to control a populace that they believed was addicted to sin (Maley 2002, 234). Punishment was often public and summarily dispensed. Major punishments, including the amputation of limbs, lashings, stoning of women, and executions, were staged weekly in Kabul in 1998. Indeed, after aid agencies rebuilt the bombed-out soccer stadium, the inaugural event, attended by 10,000 men and children, was the execution, between the goalposts, of a murderer by the victim's family (Rashid 2000, 5).

The most publicized and restrictive edicts were directed at women. Immediately after taking over Kabul, the Taliban banned women from employment, which cost the educational system 70 percent of its schoolteachers—a loss somewhat ameliorated by another decree forbidding girls to attend school at all levels. According to the Taliban: "We have given women the rights that God and his Messenger have instructed, that is to stay in their homes and to gain religious instruction in *hejab* [seclusion]" (Marsden 1998, 98). Because women were the primary vehicle for passing on Islam to the next generation, they had to be protected from the corruption of all but Taliban-sanctioned teachings; they had to be protected from all influences that could weaken society from within. Women had to be protected from men, and men had to be protected from the women's innate corruption. Women were not allowed to go outside of their homes unless accompanied by a male relative. (At one point, in a move that expressed fanaticism or harassment, or both, they wanted foreign aid workers to adhere to this rule also.) Women had to be covered from head to toe by *burkhas* (voluminous robes) and even the sight of a stocking was grounds for beating a woman with electrical cables (Burns 2002). Within their homes, women lived in darkness, because their windows had to be blackened so that no man might catch a glimpse of them. Severity of punishment for women was almost unbounded: in one case, a woman was publicly stoned to death for trying to leave Afghanistan with a man who was not a relative (Marsden 1998). Observers had various insights concerning such extreme policies. Perhaps, given the foot soldiers' simplistic view of gender policy, incarceration in the home was easier to implement than more nuanced policies (Marsden 1998). Or, according to Nancy Dupree (1998), an expert on Afghanistan who lived in Pakistan, the restrictions, especially those on women, served a wider purpose: they asserted the right to interfere in even the most intimate aspect of people's lives. Maley (2002, 243) has posited that the abysmal treatment of Afghan women, even in the face of international protests, reflects deep tensions between "a vision of the world as governed by rules of an evolving international society, and a vision of the world as ruled by the word of God."

The same tension defined the Taliban's stance on learning and culture and led to policies of biblioclasm like those of Omar the Caliph in 640 A.D.: if a book agreed with God, it was redundant, and if it disagreed, it was pernicious. The Taliban followed the same code as other fundamentalists. In their intellectually closed world, reading anything but approved religious texts was perceived as unnecessary and potentially contaminating. All intellectual pursuits implied autonomy and independent cognitive functioning, both threatening to religious orthodoxy. The Taliban monitored bookstores and jailed employees for selling forbidden books. The owner of Kabul's two largest bookstores, Shah Muhammad, reported weekly visits from the Taliban, during which they searched for contraband, removed and destroyed books, and defaced jacket photos (Sullivan 2002). In 1999 alone, $40,000 worth of books from his shops were burned. After the fall of the Taliban, National Library Director Fazlollah Qodsi estimated that tens of thousands of books were lost under Taliban rule. Lost also were basic texts that supported a secular civil society, including every copy of the Afghanistan Legal Code (Greenstein 2002). Furthermore, 8 of Kabul's 18 libraries were shut down, and 7 more were converted into residential buildings (Kniffel 2002, 22).

Policies concerning higher education were further evidence of the regime's hostility to secular institutions. Kabul University, founded in 1932 as a medical school, was once one of Asia's finest universities. By 1979, when the Soviets invaded, it was serving 10,000 students, including some from Iraq, Indian, Russia, and Iran (Talab 2002, 1). About 60 percent of the student body were women. During the years of factional fighting over Kabul, the physical infrastructure of the university sustained heavy damage: the buildings were damaged by artillery attacks; the laboratory equipment, including microscopes, was smashed and sold for scrap; the campus gardens were mined; and dead bodies were stuffed down the wells (Talab 2002, 1). The university was closed for long periods, and when it was able to function again, few resources were available: there was no electricity, phone service, computer equipment, faculty pay, or even cadavers for the medical students. After taking Kabul in September 1996, the Taliban, citing the need to rid it of "corrupting Western influences," shut down the university for nine months, expelled the women students, and discharged female faculty (Lloyd 1999). When it reopened, poorly educated mullahs required students to spend 12 of their 36 classroom hours studying the Koran (Burns 2002, 12). Certain courses, particularly in the humanities, were prohibited. Dr. Aziz Ahmad Rahmand, a professor of contemporary Afghan history, described the Taliban as "monsters": "I myself was a victim of their totalitarian ways. I had to grow a ridiculous beard, they ransacked my library, they banned me from teaching any twentieth-century history" (as quoted in Burns 2002, 12).

The university's library suffered a similar decline. Built in 1963, the library had employed 50 librarians and 80 workers in 1992. The collection of 200,000 books included 5,000 manuscripts, 10,000 books on Afghanistan studies, 10,000 bound volumes of periodicals, 3,000 rare books, 10,000 electronic materials, 2,000 photo albums, 5,000 calligraphic specimens, and a sizable collection of national archival and documentary materials. It had modern heating, lighting, and telephone systems. It used modern classification systems, operated a conservation center, maintained a union catalog for the city of Kabul's public libraries, and served as a collection point for U.N. materials. But during the civil war and the Taliban's siege of the city, the building, once "brimming with readers," was shelled extensively (Kniffel 2002, 22). Upon returning to the city after the Taliban's takeover, Abdul Rasoul Rahin (1998), the library's director, was overwhelmed by its condition. He counted 25 holes in the walls and roof and described the library's great hall, once large and beautiful, as a "mere path through rubble." Little remained of the collection except scattered piles of 20-year-old books that had not been considered worthy of looting. The unique Afghanistan Studies collection was a "mass of ashes" (Rahin 1998, 71). The audiovisual collection, which had included graphics, maps, films, microfiche, and filmstrips, was totally gone. Rahin and a small remnant of library staff restored order, did some basic repairs, and collected items for a "Museum of Library War-time Fragments." An embittered Rahin videotaped a documentary of the past, present, and future of the library, but soon left Kabul because the environment under the Taliban was "not conducive to cultural restoration. The fundamental Islamic groups [had] a threatening way of ruling" (Rahin 1998). Under the Taliban, the library, such as it was, was poorly used. The women were banned and the young men avoided appearing in public places for fear of being drafted. A Reuters news-service article quoted a librarian as saying, "They [the Taliban] said we didn't need books," and another Afghani reported that staff had to hide the anatomy books (Kniffel 2002, 22).

By leaving, Rahin was spared the repressive attentions of the ruling Taliban regime. The library, however, was not. After the Taliban's 1996 takeover, the randomness of the destruction had abated and books were targeted because of their content, the languages they were written in (non-Pashtu), or their representations of Afghanistan's Persian heritage. Afghan librarians felt that the Taliban had embarked, from the beginning, on a planned campaign to extinguish Afghan nationalism that was associated with the use of Persian (Loving 2002). With the destruction of libraries came attacks on the country's museums and historical documentation. The National Museum's astonishingly complete record of thousands of years of Afghan history, from the prehistoric to the present (as represented in ethnographic materials), had given "substance" to the concept of Afghanistan as a secular and modern nation (Dupree 2001, 4). A case is made by Dupree (2001, 4) that the Taliban's attempts to destroy evidence of Afghanistan's glorious past and confine Afghan heritage solely to Islam were designed to rob Afghans of their uniqueness, place in history, and identification with anything beyond religious fundamentalism.

By creating libraries and museums and preserving cultural artifacts and sites, earlier regimes in Afghanistan had created an institutional base for a modern state. The preservation, use, and display of Afghan cultural items signaled national pride and also membership in an international community in which each nation's cultural resources made a unique contribution to the common heritage of the world. When libraries become battlefields for the clash of extremist and humanist values, librarians are forced to conceal their humanistic beliefs. With freedom, this orientation has reemerged. In 2002, after the Taliban were forced from Kabul, the chief librarian of the Kabul University Library quickly appealed to international visitors for books: "The Afghan people are in darkness, and we ask the Western countries to help us shine some light" (Burns 2002, 12). A sign posted over the door of the Kabul Museum now reads: "A nation stays alive when its culture stays alive" (Sullivan 2002, A1).

This identification with a global civilization, as evidenced by veneration of cultural objects, was antithetical to everything the Taliban believed in. "We are not against culture, but we don't believe in these things," said Taliban Foreign Minister Wakil Ahmed Muttawakil ("Fallen Idols" 2001, 2). Even more theocratic than nationalistic, they believed that nationhood was irrelevant to the cause of living in accordance with Islamic principles and ethnic codes. Religion (and to a lesser extent ethnicity), not culture, was the sole basis for identity. The institution of the museum has been characterized as signifying a post-Enlightenment shift from "cult to culture that has indexed the transition to modernity in the West" (Flood 2002, 652). By destroying and vandalizing cultural institutions, the Taliban were shifting "cult" or spirituality back to center place and reversing the progress of modernity. Eventually, images of all kinds were designated as "idols" and campaigns against photographs, films, paintings of human beings and animals, and statues were targeted for destruction. One of the greatest tragedies of these campaigns was the loss of the Graeco-Buddhist Buddhas and bodhisattvas for which Afghanistan was famous.

The Taliban's iconoclastic attacks increased as they settled into the task of governing Afghanistan—a frustrating task for which they were inadequately prepared and temperamentally unsuited. Building and administering a state were not priorities. The Taliban leadership remained focused on their original goals of eradicating corruption, maintaining law and order, and achieving complete military conquest. Cabinet ministers were field commanders who rotated in and out of combat and left their offices unmanned. There was no constitution and only a token assignment of governmental responsibilities; indeed, most government workers had been dismissed and replaced with clerics who knew little about administration, finance, or public works (Constable 2001). The Taliban rarely issued policy statements or held press conferences (Rashid 2000, 5). Few records were kept as orders were issued on walkie-talkies or scraps of paper (Constable 2001). Mullah Omar lived in Kandahar and became increasingly isolated and secretive. His decisions about running the state emerged slowly through consultation. By 2000, he sought advice mainly from a core group that included extremist religious leaders, elderly parochial judges of the Supreme Court of Kandahar, loyal staffers, and followers of Osama Bin Laden (Maley 2002).

A hard-line fundamentalist and dedicated puritan in his own right, Bin Laden encouraged Taliban insularity, extremism, and an ambivalence toward the international community, which eventually led to abuse of aid workers and their withdrawal from the country. The Taliban wanted international recognition of the legitimacy of their regime, but seemed unable and unwilling to understand how their actions violated Western mindsets and norms. Western reactions to their gender policies were inexplicable to them because they perceived their policies as "protecting" women. The modern burden of statehood—the construction of a social infrastructure that would alleviate wretched living conditions—concerned them little because, in their eyes, their imposition of moral and legal order had addressed these issues (Gouttierre et al. 2001). When the Western world reacted to them as criminally negligent administrators and zealots who brutalized women, they interpreted the United Nations and Western nations as conspiring against Islam and Sharia law (Rashid 2000, 64). The Taliban refused to compromise with international values, which they equated with Western values, and instead demanded that the West should respect and accommodate to their value system (Marsden 1998, 81–82). After the Taliban interfered with the U.N.'s delivery of vital aid supplies and harassed staff members, the agency left in

February 1998. By July 1998, the Taliban's obstructive and abusive behavior led to the shutdown of all nongovernmental organization offices, despite the fact that many Afghan women and children were left without food and health care (Rashid 2000, 72).

In the end, however, it was the harboring of terrorists that precipitated their downfall. When the Taliban refused to hand over Bin Laden even after he was implicated in the October 12, 2000 bomb attack on the USS Cole in the harbor of Aden, Yemen, which killed 17 sailors, the United Nations expanded previous sanctions, imposed arms and flight embargos, and seized the Taliban's overseas assets. The Taliban intensified their violent behaviors, including the practice of destroying cultural items. Their tactical and ideological vandalism seemed also to have a cognitive component. The Taliban were demonstrating that they were in control and could do what they wanted (Vogelsang 2002, 333). They were, as well, protesting their exclusion from the international community and that community's dedication to universal, as opposed to religious, values (Flood 2002). It was as if they were saying, "So the outside world tightens sanctions. . . . [Our] children are starving, but the West is concerned about statues and monuments. . . . We'll show them" (Gouttierre et al. 2001, B4). Their campaigns were designed to obliterate objects that offended Islamic beliefs, but this cloak of instrumental iconoclasm barely concealed their expressive motives (Flood 2002). Their "idol-bashing" seemed little more than a "primal scream prompted by international isolation" (Maley 2002, 241). Mullah Omar cited the religious judgments of the *ulema* and the rules of the Supreme Court as sanction for the destruction of the "shrines of unbelievers": "God Almighty is the only real shrine and all fake idols should destroyed" (Flood 2002, 655).

The Taliban stepped up its campaign against what Omar called the "gods of the infidels," idolatrous symbols that defiled Islam (Satchell 2001). In March 2001, in an act of "studious insolence," a measure designed to provoke the outside world, the Taliban destroyed the ancient Bamiyan Buddhas, 174-foot and 125-foot statues carved out of sandstone cliffs by Buddhist monks between the second and fifth centuries, when the Bamiyan Valley was a center of Buddhist learning. Once beautifully decorated with plaster, paint, gilding, and jewels, by the twentieth century, the battered Buddhas were rugged survivors. They had withstood erosion of snowmelt and natural disasters such as earthquakes; they had survived vandalism during the invasions of Genghis Khan and Tamerlane in the thirteenth and fourteenth centuries. More recently, they had acquired scars from the civil war that had pitched their local custodians, the Shiite Hazaras, against rival ethnic and religious groups. The base of the larger Buddha had been used as an ammunition dump in the 1990s, and its face had been blackened by burning tires (Romey 2001). The smaller Buddha's head had been blown off. But in 2001, the Buddhas did not have a chance as the Taliban's antiaircraft fire, rockets, and cannon, tank, and mortar shells blasted them from their nooks forever (Shukla 2001). Journalists who were trucked in to Bamiyan to report on the destruction were confronted with two gaping holes and a message scrawled on the cliff face: "We must confront the idols of non-Muslims and destroy them" ("Fallen Idols" 2001, 1). At the same time, the Taliban entered 25 caves within the valley and eradicated wall paintings that dated back to between the third and seventh centuries and the Persian Sassanid era. In retrospect, art historian Nigel Spivey (2002) wondered whether the Taliban may in fact have been reacting to a "potent lingering holiness" from a once-active community of Buddhist monks: Did the "genius" of the place linger and "worry at the minds of the Taliban chiefs?"

The loss of the Buddhas set off shock waves all over the world. Although some Muslims saw it as an understandable response to external repression, others distanced themselves from the desecration. Iran's foreign ministry pointed out that, "unfortunately, the Taliban's destruction of the statues has cast doubts on the views offered by Islamic ideology in the world" ("Fallen Idols" 2001, 2). Far more telling than the reaction of this hated rival was the concern expressed by leaders of Afghanistan's closest ally, Pakistan, that iconoclasm on this scale would discredit Islam in general ("Afghan Iconoclasts" 2001). An editorial in Pakistan's leading newspaper, the *Dawn*, stated: "Islam is a religion of harmony and peaceful coexistence. . . . Buddha was an apostle of peace and non-violence. Certainly he deserves better treatment than what he has hitherto received at the hands of blind zealots in Afghanistan" (Romey 2001, 16). *Time* magazine writer Robert Hughes (2001) assessed the Taliban's actions as extremist and unlike traditional Islamic responses to images: not an iconic religion, Islam forbids depictions of its prophet but makes "no injunction to destroy the images of other faiths." Art historian Finbarr Barry Flood (2002, 652), a scholar of Islam who has examined Islamic iconoclasm through the centuries, pronounced total obliteration to be atypical of Islamic responses to images, a broad spectrum that ranges from aesthetic appreciation, awe, fascination, even scholarship, to a revulsion that has sometimes been expressed by ritual defacement. He feared that the Bamiyan incident would come to define the Islamic stance toward other religions, reinforcing the problematic and widespread notion of Islamic culture as "implacably hostile to anthropomorphic art" and hopelessly out of step with modern Western civilization (Flood 2002, 641).

As often when confronted by violent cultural destruction, observers disagreed over the question of whether the perpetrators understood what they had done. Several commentators likened the Taliban to Mao's Red Guard and described them as "a group of mindless fanatics who have gone about destroying their own history, culture, and traditions" (Gouttierre et al. 2001, B4). Another argued that they had displaced the Maoists in setting a new standard for "ideological vandalism" (Hughes 2001). Others thought that perhaps the Taliban were simply parochial and oblivious, a position fostered by Taliban leaders themselves who professed to be mystified by the world's reaction. Mullah Omar's ingenuous statement, "All we are breaking is stones," was widely quoted (Romey 2001, 16), and in one sense, it contradicted his professed goal of ridding the country of false idols. It also clashed with his "artful mining of the Islamic past for authoritative precedent" (Flood 2002, 652). Mullah Omar had responded, on Radio Shari'a, to the Metropolitan Museum of Art's offer to purchase and remove the Buddhas by posing the question: "Do you prefer a breaker of idols or a seller of idols?" It was an allusion to the response of esteemed Sutan Mahmoud of Ghazna (971–1030 A.D.) to an offer concerning the ransom of an icon, and it seemed to levy an accusation of moral turpitude at the West (Flood 2002, 652).

Besides destroying the Bamiyan statues, the Taliban stepped up their attempts to purge cultural institutions. According to an eyewitness, in February 2001, a group of senior Taliban officials accompanied by armed guards entered the "nearly gutted bulk" of the National Museum and gained entry to the storeroom of remaining artifacts. "From [that] afternoon until evening they broke statues" and then came back many times (Lawler 2002c, 1202). In the National Gallery, artists and curators sped up their concealment of artistic images. At the museum, Mohammad Yousof Asefi, a physician and leading painter, had braved imprisonment, torture, and death to paint "watercolor masks" over the forbidden images of people and animals (donkeys, birds, and cows). He had matched the background colors perfectly and had saved many paintings, including 80 in the last year of the Taliban's regime. Asefi saved a few of his own paintings, although 26 of his were stolen or destroyed. "I have worked in the arts in our country for twenty years, and I could not be responsible for letting our history and culture be destroyed," he explained later to a journalist (Sullivan 2002, A1). Paintings that were not camouflaged were routinely destroyed.

Shortly after the destruction of the Buddhas, the Taliban began paying visits to the government-run national film studio and archives, which had made and preserved newsreels, documentaries, and feature films since 1968 (Sullivan 2002). Finally, they made a bonfire of 1,000 films and scattered others about. The eight remaining employees (out of 160 people who had once worked there) hid as many films as possible and even destroyed the electrical system so that the Taliban had no lights to search by. The films the employees saved, pieces of Afghanistan's visual history, included a documentary showing rival *mujahideen* bombarding Kabul in the early 1990s, and an old newsreel showing the former King Mohammed Zahir Shah arriving on the White House lawn and greeting President John F. Kennedy (Sullivan 2002). The films destroyed by the Taliban were an incalculable loss to the historical memory of Afghanistan.

The Taliban pursued cultural destruction until the terrorist attack on September 11, 2001, and the resultant invasion of Afghanistan by the United States. The regime fell quickly, an indicator of its problematic legitimacy (Maley 2002, 67). The leaders had not led a willing populace toward realization of a commonly held vision, but instead distorted the common bond of Islam into a rationale for tyranny. Promising an end to anarchy, they had made a wilderness and called it peace (Maley 2002, 228; Rashid 2000, 74). The Taliban, like the Khmer Rouge in Cambodia, inverted usual notions of progress and posed regression as the way forward. A pure society was a primitive one in which all modern and cosmopolitan influences had been expunged. The two regimes had tightened their grips on the population and used the nihilistic destruction of culture as a tactic to effect change and make way for a new society. In the name of transformation, they waged total war on their own societies. Their battlegrounds were every home and institution, and they fought to control the consciousness of each member of society. Each person was considered a potential enemy; if the person could not be "transformed" into a blank tablet for the regime's use, that person was eliminated. Because books and libraries sustained modernity and alternate beliefs and identities, they too had to be neutralized. All destruction was committed in the name of "truth," for the "good" of the people, and in pursuit of utopia. The Khmer Rouge called their sought-after paradise "Year Zero"; the Taliban called theirs "the rule of Sharia" (Bergen 2002). The cumulative history of twentieth-century extremism, to which the Taliban made a significant contribution, illustrates all too well the corrupting influence of unchecked power, especially when wielded by self-righteous fanatics. The Taliban demonstrated the potential for unbounded religious fundamentalism to lead to purification campaigns that rationalize murder and cultural devastation on a horrific scale.

REFERENCES

"Afghan Iconoclasts." 2001. *Economist* 358 (8212):19–21.

"Afghanistan." 1999. *Encyclopedia Americana International Edition*, Vol. 1. Danbury, Conn.: Grolier, 242–255.

Amirkhani, Gholamreza. 2001. "Afghanistan's Lost Splendor." *American Libraries* 32 (11):19.

Bergen, Peter L. 2002. *Holy War, Inc.: Inside the Secret World of Osama Bin Laden.* New York: Touchstone.

Boustany, Nora. 1998. "Busy Are the Peacemakers." *Washington Post*, 10 January, p. A27.

Burns, John F. 2002. "For Women in Kabul, This Test Is Welcome." *New York Times*, 10 February, sec. 1, p. 12.

Constable, Pamela. 2001. "Kabul Good Riddance, Taliban Told Mullah's Fiery Sermon Accuses Militia of Ignoring Suffering." *Washington Post*, 8 December, p. A16.

Dupree, Nancy. 1998. Afghan Women under the Taliban." In *Fundamentalism Reborn?: Afghanistan and the Taliban*, ed. William Maley. New York: New York University Press, 145–166.

Dupree, Nancy Hatch. 2001. "The Lost Treasures of the Afghans." *UNESCO Sources* 134:4.

"Fallen Idols: Afghanistan's Taliban Destroy Ancient Statues." 2001. *Current Events* 100 (23):1–2.

Flood, Finbarr Barry. 2002. "Between Cult and Culture: Bamiyan, Islamic Iconoclasm, and the Museum." *Art Bulletin* 84 (4):641–659.

Gouttierre, Thomas E., Larry P. Goodson, and Sarah E. Fraser. 2001. "He Doesn't Understand What He Did." *Chronicle of Higher Education* 47 (31):B4.

Grazda, Edward. 2000. *Afghanistan Diary 1992–2000.* New York: Powerhouse Books.

Greenstein, Michelle. 2002. "Michelle Greenstein Discusses Return of a Legal Code to Afghanistan." *National Public Radio*, June 7, 2002.

Hughes, Robert. 2001. "Buddha Bashing." *Time* 157 (11):52–53.

Kniffel, Leonard. 2002. "Afghanistan Reports Reveal Devastated Libraries." *American Libraries* 33 (3):22–24.

Lawler, Andrew. 2002a. "Afghanistan's Challenge." *Science* 298 (5596):1195.

Lawler, Andrew. 2002b. "Resuscitating Asia's Damaged Heart." *Science* 298 (5596): 1196–1200.

Lawler, Andrew. 2002c. "Then They Buried Their History." *Science* 298(5596):1202–1203.

Lloyd, Marion. 1999. ""Kabul U. Struggles Amid the Ruins." *Chronicle of Higher Education* 45 (19):A45–46.

Loving, Matthew. 2002. "Darkest Days: From Exile in Paris, Afghan Librarian Latif Relives the Nightmare." *American Libraries* 33 (5):68–72.

Maley, William. 2002. *The Afghanistan Wars.* New York: Palgrave Macmillan.

Marsden, Peter. 1998. *The Taliban: War, Religion and the New Order in Afghanistan.* New York: Zed Books.

Rahin, Abdul Rasoul. 1998. "The Situation of Kabul University Library: Its Past and Present." *World Libraries* 8 (2):69–73.

Rashid, Ahmed. 2000. *Taliban: Militant Islam, Oil and Fundamentalism in Central Asia.* New Haven, Conn.: Yale University Press.

Romey, Kristin M. 2001. "Cultural Terrorism." *Archaeology* 54 (3):16–17.

Roy, Olivier. 1998. "Has Islamism a Future in Afghanistan?" In *Fundamentalism Reborn?: Afghanistan and the Taliban*, ed. William Maley. New York: New York University Press, 199–211.

Satchell, Michael. 2001. "Blotting Out History." *U.S. News and World Report* 130 (10): 48.

"Sharia." 2005. *Encyclopedia of the Orient*, ed. Tore Kjeilen. http://I-cias.com/e.o/sharia.htm. October 16, 2005.

Shukla, I. K. 2001. "Theoterrorism as Statecraft." *Humanist* 61 (3):4–5.

Spivey, Nigel. 2002. "'Shrines of the Infidels': The Buddhas at Bamiyan." *International Magazine of the Arts* 155 (485):28–34.

Sullivan, Kevin. 2002. "Artists Trick Taliban Police, Save Art." *Washington Post*, 2 January, p. A1.

Talab, Rosemary. 2002. "Kabul University Library in Afghanistan: Postwar Emergence." *International Leads* 16 (3):1–2.

Taylor, Maxwell. 1991. *The Fanatics: A Behavioural Approach to Political Violence.* London: Brassey's.

Valéry, Paul. 1962. *History and Politics.* Vol. 10 of *The Collected Works of Paul Valéry.* Trans. Denise Folliot. Ed. Jackson Matthews. Princeton, N.J.: Princeton University Press.

Vogelsang, Willem. 2002. *The Afghans.* Oxford: Blackwell.

Part III

War, Power Vacuum, and Anarchy

After institutionalizing their values and power internally, ideologues may seek to colonize rival states. Again, libraries are pulled into the fray. They may be targeted deliberately, for the same reasons that enemy civilians are victimized. They may also become collateral casualties of the ensuing wars. The high stakes involved in global wars of the twentieth century—essentially, control over belief systems—spurred them to become totalistic struggles over the survival of a way of life. The aggression of rogue regimes brought, from the democracies under attack, a staunch defense that vested these states in extremism as well, leading to the distanced but nonetheless tragic cultural violence inherent in strategic bombing.

The violence of war involves both the tactical methods of combat and the breakdown of controls that inhibit random violence. Violent regime change in particular may cause a vacuum of authority that occurs as groups fight over control of the social center. With a population that has been brutalized, a power vacuum invites anarchy and the opportunity for iconoclasm. As mobs act out their rage against symbols of the establishment, libraries again enter the line of fire. In 2003, it was the American leadership's extremism that resulted in the invasion of Iraq and provided the conditions for pillage and arson.

CHAPTER 8

Dueling Ideologies and Total War, 1939–1945

> The industrialization of war has efficiently erased all those elements which once gave war a kind of qualified humaneness.
> —Eric Carlton, *Militarism*

Western nations of the twentieth century paid a high price for the rogue ambitions of fanatical regimes whose unchecked paranoia and perceived supremacy led them into violent and aggressive campaigns against groups that challenged their hegemony. Internal purges of those elements that could not or would not find a place within ideological templates were followed by attacks on neighboring nations, and regional skirmishes escalated into total war. Beginning in World War I and coming to full development in World War II, a new style of warfare invested both instigators and their enemies in all-out battle. It was high-stakes, unbridled warfare in which the opponent's defeat had to be unconditional, and humanistic concerns were decidedly secondary to practical matters of strategy. Distinctions between civilians and troops, cities and battlefield eroded, and technological capabilities and modern weaponry drove military tactics to the extremes of rationalized virulence.

In World War II, both sides perceived themselves as struggling for their very survival in a fight over mutually exclusive ideas. Their devotion to these ideas enabled the perception that theirs was a just war. Both sides clung tenaciously to a notion of war as the legitimized use of purposeful violence to attain political objectives. Both backed their campaigns with mass mobilization of troops *and* civilians, newly evolved technological capabilities, and industrialized economies. The ensuing totality of engagement fostered an excess of militarism, the crossing of traditional and moral lines, and the breaching of international prohibitions against the destruction of cultural institutions and artifacts. All resources of the enemy—even books and libraries—became pawns in campaigns to impose political dominance, shatter morale, and force surrender. Human life and material artifacts were victims of the ideas that gave life to parallel nationalisms: the commitment to racial supremacy and national expansion that drove the Axis Powers, and the Allies' commitment to democracy, borders, and—something a little more nebulous—the traditions of Western civilization.

For the aggressors of World War II, Germany and Japan, war was a means for achieving ideological visions. In Europe, where Germany's invasion of Poland initiated international conflict in 1939, the war masked genocide, ethnocide, and other programs that advanced National Socialist agendas of racial purification and expansion. In Asia, military aggression was similarly driven. The Japanese Imperialists invaded first China and then all of its neighbors, using indiscriminate violence to achieve dominance for the Yamato race. Both the Germans and Japanese of this era burned books and libraries, in apparent recognition that cultural artifacts and institutions contain some element of a people's will to freedom. Indeed, they seem to have recognized that books carry ideas that, explicitly or otherwise, oppose ideological mandates, and that libraries—collections of such ideas—stand as pillars of the opponents' identity. By the end of their occupation, the Nazis had destroyed approximately six million Poles (including three million Jews) and three-quarters of the written heritage of Poland. The Japanese Imperialists killed as many as five million Chinese and obliterated millions of their texts as well. They killed hundreds of thousands of Filipinos and burned most of the libraries and archives in the Philippine Islands. The purposeful pairing of human and cultural destruction employed in these campaigns was a signifier that modern war had become "total."

The totality of engagement was forced on all participants. A powerful factor influencing the evolution of total war was the concurrence of human and cultural destruction that occurred as the result of air campaigns. In one of the most unfathomable events in the history of democracy, hundreds of thousands of lives and millions of texts were destroyed by anti-extremist, democratic regimes that espoused humanism, intellectual freedom, and the preservation of knowledge. During Britain's bombing of German cities and the United States's bombing of Japanese urban centers, millions of books, manuscripts, and print records were burned (along with buildings and human beings) as the Allies directed sophisticated campaigns against whole peoples and their means of resistance. To varying degrees, and at times with the full knowledge of their people, the Allied powers embraced the logic of total war, particularly in the area of airpower policy and tactics, and their campaigns reached a scale of destruction comparable to that of their enemies. Because the Allies, unlike their adversaries, did not accrue long-term ideological advantage from such destruction, their campaigns raise the question of what it is about the logic of total war that involves *all* participants in wanton militarism. Nevertheless, we must ask what mindsets make the coupling of human and cultural casualties a matter of tactics, excuse the breach of international prohibitions against cultural destruction, and throw open the door to both the instrumental and collateral destruction of textual heritage?

The military tactics employed during World War II marked a turning point in a change of consciousness regarding the tactics and parameters of war that had been gradually taking place for centuries. The Peace of Westphalia, the agreement that ended the Thirty Years' War, laid the foundation for a system of independent, competing states in Europe and also for a new concept of war. Previously, wars were waged by monarchs seeking to promote their own dynastic interests, but after the agreement in 1648, governments conducted the wars and employed armed forces to act on behalf of their respective states (Van Creveld 2000). Frequent wars encouraged rival nations to develop their armies. Military officers attended academies and received advanced education in tactics and strategy. The armaments industry boomed. After the French initiated the first mass conscription of modern times, armies became huge; one million soldiers are said to have died in the Napoleonic Wars, a huge and unprecedented casualty rate. By the end of the nineteenth century, the size of armies and the cost of weapons and ordinance required to sustain "killing capacity" during war (Feldman 2000) demanded an unstinting flow of money and men, necessitating mass mobilization and broad public support for war (Forster 2000). Because a government's ability to achieve its military objectives depended on its citizens' identification with their government's objectives and willingness to make sacrifices, the ideas justifying war became very important for achieving consensus (Howard 1983). Regimes facing conflict fostered nationalism along with competitiveness that encouraged a collective sense of both victimization and entitlement.

It was from the more contained wars of the eighteenth and nineteenth centuries that a doctrinal platform for the conduct of total war was built. Theorists in Europe (usually military officers) tested their ideas on the battlefield during war; in times of peace, their theories were systematically taught to officers as part of the professionalization of the military and the development of specializations within the armed forces—for example, the twentieth-century development of air force units. German military theorist Carl von Clausewitz (1780–1831) forever changed the way militaries and governments thought about war. He described war as a "great socio-political activity, distinguished from all other activities by the reciprocal and legitimised use of purposeful violence to attain political objectives" (Howard 1983, 1). Clausewitz laid the foundation for the notion that war naturally invested participants in extremism. Through incrementalism, he argued, military operations escalate to the use of all conceivable means; he saw war as "an act of force which theoretically can have no limits" (Garrett 1993, 132). This principle was demonstrated in the notoriously brutal American Civil War campaigns of General William Tecumseh Sherman, who burnt a path behind the lines in an effort to break the spirit of the South. It was an act that foreshadowed twentieth-century total war. Sherman is known to have said that those responsible for the successful conclusion of a war could not be held accountable for the methods used to meet that end (Garrett 1993).

World War I can be considered the first total war. By all measures, it was catastrophic. Thirty-six countries mobilized 70 million men, and more than 10 million lives were lost. It was also momentous in terms of the evolution of war itself. By 1914, the key elements of total war were in place: nationalism, racism, mass armies, modern weapons, industrialized economies (Forster 2000). The scale of this war and its unbounded consumption of raw materials led to the unprecedented levels of mobilization of human and material resources. As populations succumbed to chauvinism and bought into the ideological stakes of the conflict, the war came to be characterized by erosion of the distinction between soldiers and civilians. Breaking will on the home front was as sure a route to victory as triumph on the battlefield, because civilians provided the moral and economic background to armies and navies (Forster 2000). By the end of World War I, aircraft technology had changed the natural order of things, adding "a third dimension to war" that allowed direct attack on enemy rear zones, cities, economies, and, perhaps most important, civilian populations (Buckley 1999, 2). The 1917 Gotha bombing raids on Britain, which killed 1,400 people, brought modern war past a basic threshold of discretion concerning the parameters of military conduct, establishing the ominous precedent that civilians and cities could be legitimate and even important targets of air strikes (Garrett 1993).

At the onset of World War I, nineteenth-century restraints with regard to destroying cultural sites (including libraries) were still in place but beginning to erode. A case may be made that the deliberate destruction of libraries and other cultural resources as a strategy of twentieth-century war began, in 1914, with the Germans' annihilation of the centuries-old library at the university in Louvain, Belgium, considered that country's Oxford. Enraged and made fearful by perceived civil resistance, German troops went on a six-day rampage. Along with looting, taking hostages, and executing civilians, they burned the medieval city and its library. Lost were 230,000 volumes, including a collection of 750 medieval manuscripts and more than 1,000 incunabula (books printed before 1501). Louvain may have reflected evolving policies of *Kriegsbrauch*, which stipulated that "[W]ar cannot be conducted merely against the combatants of an enemy state but must seek to destroy the total material and intellectual (*geistig*) resources of the enemy" (Tuchman 1962, 321).

By World War II, the vision of Erich von Ludendorff (who had commanded German troops in the previous war) was in place: war had become "the highest expression of the racial will to life" (Wallach 1986, 15). Violence to cultural materials and institutions was an organized part of the Nazis' overall plan of dominance (Borin 1993). For the Nazis, the destruction of books and libraries was both ideological and tactical: it weakened the spiritual foundations of the enemy's national pride and cultural identity, struck a blow to morale, and pushed the population toward hopelessness and surrender. The Clausewitzian principle of reciprocal action was seen in World War II as opponents rationalized ever more ruthless types of military actions based on the premise that their enemy would do the same. The archetype of reciprocal action is the use by the United States of the atomic bomb on Japan. Carpet bombing of cities in general illustrates Clausewitz's observation that if winning means destroying the enemy's capacity to resist, then the potential victor's "self-defense" makes imperative the destruction of anything supporting that capacity. In other words, "there is no stopping place short of the extreme" (Howard 1983, 49). In fact, during the twentieth century, wars became brutal contests and "supreme emergencies" in which survival justified the complete dismissal of even wartime ethics (Garrett 1993)—the very expression of Clausewitzian theory.

In both world wars, the German troops' destruction of libraries tended to be deliberate, purposeful, and fully rationalized. Although frequently overlaid with vindictiveness, it was primarily used as a terror tactic (an instrument of intimidation) and as a tool of subjugation, colonization, and other ideological imperatives. The burning of Louvain's library is an example of book destruction as terror, and it was a precursor to more aggressive campaigns in World War II in which libricide became policy. Certainly, Louvain's destruction shocked the world, and the implications of destroying such a library were not lost on the public. The British *Daily Chronicle* characterized it as war not only on noncombatants but on "posterity to the utmost generation" (Tuchman 1962, 321). Postwar reparations funded the rebuilding of the library, but it was destroyed again by the Germans in 1940, in part, as an act of revenge for the devastating effect of reparations on the German economy. Revenge for British raids on Germany, especially on historical Lubeck and the cathedral city of Cologne, had some part in driving Hitler's 1942 decision to order raids against Britain that targeted British cities of particular historical and cultural significance. Baron Gustav Braun von Stumm, Deputy Head of the Information and Press Divisions of the Foreign Office, gave the game away when he announced, "Now the Luftwaffe will go for every building which is marked with three stars in *Baedeker*," the widely used guidebook (Rothnie 1992, 131). According to historian Niall Rothnie (1992, 139), the tragedy of the Baedeker blitz was that it served no purpose: it was "the product of Hitler's anger, a knee-jerk response of no importance to global strategy." But this does not take into account the Nazi pattern of destroying culture as a means of asserting dominance and creating terror. What was unusual about the Baedeker raids was that the Nazis overtly targeted the culture, not just of people they deemed inferior and sought to enslave or eradicate, but also of the British, their racial equals. The Baedeker raids signaled to the world, once again, the Nazi regime's willingness to pursue antihumanistic campaigns of devastating dimensions for malicious and tactical as well as ideological reasons. The air raids on Canterbury, Exeter, Bath, York, and other cities resulted in the loss of thousands of books. It did not, however, demoralize the British people. In fact, it stiffened their resistance.

The Nazis' practices of mass murder and deliberate cultural destruction were driven by a runaway German nationalism that achieved its logical extreme in total war. The Nazis' annihilation of six million Jews brought reality to the term *genocide* and in turn, libricide became a component of the "final solution" for the "Jewish problem." In this campaign, the Germans destroyed all Jewish texts except those confiscated for use in studying the Judaic culture in the interest of eradicating it worldwide. In Eastern Europe and Russia, Nazi racism extended to the Slavs, an "inferior" race, and methodical and violent ethnocidal policies were put in place to facilitate colonization and achieve *lebensraum*, room for German settlers. In Poland, the Germans initiated a reign of terror aimed at dismantling the Polish nation as a cultural entity by murdering the educated classes and those who might provide leadership for a resistance effort or cultural regeneration. Hitler told his occupying forces to liquidate Poland's elite classes and "watch out for the seeds that begin to sprout again, so as to stamp them out again in good time'" (Lukas 1986, 8). Political statistician R. J. Rummel (1992) has calculated that the Nazis eventually killed one out of every six Poles and Soviet citizens under their rule, these often being members of the intellectual community.

The eventual genocide of the Polish people became a matter of official policy intended to be long term. A preliminary step was cultural nullification (necessary to short-term colonization), initiated with the postinvasion confiscation of the entire property of the Polish state, including its libraries. Public library stocks were collected and stored in central locations. Then, by decree, all Polish book collections, including those owned by private persons, had to be surrendered to the authorities. Some collections, including the library of the Polish Parliament, were sent to Germany for use in museums, research institutes, and educational facilities; others were preserved for use by German administrators (Dunin 1996). But in general, the nation's books were looted, destroyed, pulped, or left to molder in undesirable conditions. School libraries—expendable under Nazi education policies—were used for barracks and their collections destroyed. Polish children were allowed but a few years of education; the ability to read would be irrelevant to their lives as peasants (Kamenetsky 1961).

When the Germans began to lose the war, their frustration added fuel to their campaigns. In 1944, as part of efforts to make good on Hitler's pledge to make Warsaw a "second Carthage"—a reference to the Romans' annihilation of that city-state and its culture (Borowiec 2001, 99)—German squads deliberately torched Poland's most prestigious libraries. As outlined in contingency plans for defeat, the Nazis burned many of the illustrious collections they had gathered earlier for "safekeeping" and use by the Germans. They burned prints, manuscripts, and maps from the university library, the Zamoyski Library, the National Library, and Rapperswil Library. The National Library lost nearly all of its 700,000 volumes; the Central Military Library, which contained 350,000 books concerning the history of Poland, was utterly wrecked. One million books were lost from the university library in Warsaw, and many research and special libraries were destroyed (Bilinska 1946). On the eve of evacuation, the main stacks of the Warsaw Public Library were burned; it had housed 300,000 books and had functioned as the center of a national network of branch and children's libraries. Some scholars estimate that, altogether, Poland lost about 90 percent of its school and public-library collections during German occupation, 70 to 80 percent of its specialized and private collections, and about 55 percent of its scientific collections (Dunin 1996). According to another estimate, 15 million out of 22.5 million volumes in Polish libraries were harmed (Sroka 1999). These estimates are based on Nazi records from annexed areas. Figures for the rest of Eastern Europe are much less exact, though also devastating. Estimates, though most likely inflated, of Russia's loss of books during Germany's invasion total 100 million volumes (UNESCO 1996).

These details are included because they quantify the violations committed by German nationalists and give some sense of the scale of a destruction that was rationalized by recourse to the imperatives of National Socialism and the triumph of the German race. The depth of Nazi extremism is graphically represented by this cultural vandalism that comprehensively expressed the full range of motives: it had playful, malicious, vindictive, tactical, and ideological components. Their actions and their self-professed moral exemption put the world on notice and guaranteed that the wars they set in motion would be total and devastating.

At the same time that the Germans were seizing *lebensraum* in Eastern Europe, Japan's imperialistic regime was pursuing a course of territorial expansion similar to Germany's. Oppressed by a centralized and authoritarian government, the Japanese people had been schooled for war throughout the 1930s. Citing racial superiority (as the Germans also did), a divine mandate to dominate Asia, and the need to redress ongoing economic victimization, Japan's militarists formulated an ambitious plan. It was a vision of Japanese rule throughout a Greater East Asia Co-Prosperity Sphere, stretching from Manchuria through the Philippines, Netherlands Indies, Malaya, Siam, Burma, and possibly Australia, New Zealand, and India (Tuchman 1984). But first, China had to be subjugated. In 1937, the Sino-Japanese War began, setting the stage for eight years of aggression and immense violence. Against the Chinese, who were despised as the most inferior of all Asian races, total war was justified by expansionist goals (Markusen and Kopf 1995). Japan's tactics included germ warfare, and in parts of China, an avowed policy of "Loot all, Kill all, Burn all" was in force. Resistance was mercilessly suppressed. In the 1937 "rape" of Nanking, one of China's greatest literary, artistic, and political centers, one-third of the city was burned and some 200,000 people killed (Chang 1997). The Japanese occupation of China from 1937 to 1945 resulted in the deaths of between 10 and 15 million people (Frank 1999). Throughout Asia, Japanese troops killed, raped, and burned in a similar manner.

Japan's policies of achieving dominance through violence and terror resulted in a loss of books (through looting and burning) that paralleled, in quantities, the loss of lives. Although the transfer of valuable Chinese books back to Japan for sale to collectors abounded (Fung 1984), many more books were simply casualties of the devastation caused by troops. Between 1937 and 1945, vandalism, looting, burning, and bombing resulted in the loss or dispersion of 10 million books and between 2,000 and 2,500 libraries (Lin 1998). College and university libraries were prime targets; for example, one-quarter of a million valuable books and manuscripts (some irreplaceable) were lost in the Japanese bombing of the Nankai University in Tianjin in 1937. In the Philippine Islands, the Japanese carried off valuable scientific and other works and then burned nearly every collection within the nation (Shaffer 1946). Almost all the rich depositories of Filipiana materials (books, manuscripts, maps) were burned (Zaide 1990). In 1945, Manila endured an orgy of murder and rape that killed about 100,000 civilians (Frank 1999). By the war's end, Manila had also lost its National Library, the University of the Philippines Library, religious archives, and many private holdings (Zaide 1990).

In Europe, Germany's programs of libricide were designed to advance National Socialism and German world domination. In Asia, libricide advanced a similar ideology of national superiority and imperialistic aspirations. Both campaigns drew strength from racism, deeply embedded in an authoritarian culture, as well as from a "bitter grievance against the democratic Western world" that contributed to "a chemistry of revenge and frustrated self-idealization" (Taylor 1993, 34). In both arenas, violence to culture was goal-driven and expedient, designed to colonize nations perceived as inferior and to aggrandize the home country, which was idealized as the font of all cultural greatness. In her book on Nanking, Iris Chang observes, about the behavior of the Japanese during World War II, that it was less a product of a dangerous people than of a dangerous government in a vulnerable culture that, during dangerous times, was able to sell dangerous rationalizations to those whose human instincts told them otherwise (Chang 1997, 220). The same could be said for Germany during this period. Although destined for success according to Clausewitzian theory, both countries' aggressive campaigns incited a backlash that would eventually bring ruin to their homelands. Believing the fate of Western civilization to be at stake, the Allies resorted to carpet bombing and then use of the atomic bomb as the logic of total war took hold: these tactics were—or seemed—the only way to bring defeat to these murderous rogue nations, the nature of whose threat went far beyond political subjugation to obliteration on all levels, including historical.

In World War I, both the Germans and Allied commands experimented with aerial support for ground troops, and the idea of bombing urban centers was introduced. In the postwar years, air-strike advocates in Britain, the United States, and Germany developed military air capability and promoted doctrines of airpower that they believed—in the event of another war—would prevent a return to the carnage of trench warfare. The British Royal Air Force (RAF) was developed by a group that believed that the objective of air attacks was to dislocate the enemy's economy *and* produce utter terror and panic in the civilian population (McKee 1982). Its organizer and chief of staff from 1918–1929 was

Lord Hugh Trenchard, who posited that the effect on morale of laying waste to an enemy's cities (particularly its capital) would be 20 times more effective than physical damages. At the same time that Hague Conference participants in the 1920s were drafting and passing aerial warfare rules to prohibit aerial bombardment for the purpose of terrorizing civilian populations, proponents of bombing were advocating its use for the very same purpose. The "airpower ethic" was an argument that future wars would be more humane because, in the long run, they would be over faster and cause less bloodshed (Crane 1993).

In the early months of World War II, ethical considerations prevailed. The first British payloads were five million leaflets inviting the overthrow of Hitler. For the first six months of the air campaign, British Bomber Command was expressly forbidden to bomb targets where civilians could get hurt (Morrison 1982). Eventually, precision attacks on industrial and military targets were approved, but British bombers were unable to hit designated targets (and for much of the war, they lacked the technological capacity for the approved precision). In addition, their planes were neither sturdy enough nor sufficiently armed for daylight operations. So, in the context of these constraints and devastating losses in the first two years of the war, Bomber Command quietly shifted to area bombing with blind nighttime raids that targeted the centers of German cities. Ethical concerns had been displaced by a desire for retaliation against Germany for attacks on Warsaw and Rotterdam and for the Blitz, a series of attacks on Britain in 1940 and 1941 that killed 40,000 civilians. In December 1940, the first deliberate British area bombing was a raid on Mannheim, requested by Winston Churchill as a reprisal for the German assault on Coventry (Levine 1992). The devastation of Germany's cities by the British became routine after 1942. Over the next three years, three-quarters of the British bombs dropped over Germany targeted city centers, and 30 percent of Britain's war expenditures were devoted to bombing offensives. Bomber Command delivered severe blows to 80 percent of German urban areas occupied by more than 100,000 people. An estimated 300,000 to 600,000 German civilians were killed. One million people sustained serious injury, and more than three million homes were destroyed. For every ton of bombs Germany dropped on Britain, the rogue nation received 315 tons in return (Garrett 1993). Wartime censorship made it possible to conceal the full impact of such strategies from the British public and avoid public backlash.

Bomber Command's area bombing of German cities was based, according to total war premises, on the necessity of shattering the Germans' morale as well as the fabric of their civil and economic life (Garrett 1993). The violence escalated as Britain's civil and military leadership, convinced that they were waging a war against evil itself, rationalized total-war tactics as necessary and even humane: Germany was to be brought to its knees by the devastation of its cities and production capabilities. In theory, "the speed of such a success and the saving of Allied—and in the end German—lives would justify civilian casualties" (Clayton 1999, 37). Prime Minister Churchill declared in 1943 that to achieve the defeat of the Nazis, there were "no lengths of violence to which we will not go" (Garrett 1993, 31). Because the heart of Germany's social, political, and industrial infrastructure lay in its cities, so much the worse for Germany's cities (Garrett 1993).

In June 1943, a series of raids culminated in attacks on Hamburg that killed more than 31,000 people and destroyed 74 percent of the city's densely populated areas. British bombs blanketed the city and set off huge fires in areas with a high concentration of tall buildings. As a result, the air above the city became superheated and the flames were drawn out explosively. The resulting firestorm had the characteristics and power of a tornado, picking people up and sucking them into the flames. Many victims were reduced to ashes by heat that rose to more than 1,000 degrees; others who escaped the flames died of asphyxiation (Sebald 2003, 28). The physical devastation of buildings was extraordinary: block upon block was reduced to rubble. The bombing of Hamburg demonstrated the effectiveness of firestorms, and after this, the phenomenon was deliberately replicated (McKee 1982).

The word *firestorm* has actually become synonymous with Dresden and the events of 1945. By February of that year, the majority of Germany's cities had sustained significant damage, but few bombs had fallen on the city of Dresden and its citizens felt relatively secure. Dresden, known as Germany's Florence, was a famous cultural site, with an old town center densely packed with tall wooden buildings, an undefended city devoid of first-order industrial, strategic, or military targets. According to a British Home Office intelligence memo in 1947, "The Dresden population appears to have believed that an understanding existed between ourselves and the Germans that we would spare Dresden if Oxford was not attacked" (Irving 1963, 73). Certainly, among the city's citizens, there was a "widespread, positive, but fatal legend of Dresden, the city that would never be bombed" (Irving 1963, 73). But the head of Bomber Command, Arthur Harris, was unsentimental about preserving culture, devoted to area bombing, and in search of new targets to maintain the momentum of previous attacks. In addition, there was strategic advantage to an attack on Dresden because this action would support Russian offensives from the east by disrupting German transport systems. There was also a political payoff, in that a demonstration of Allied firepower might impress the Russians and affect diplomatic negotiations as to the fate of contested lands. And, even this late in the war, Britain's leaders were by no means sure of ultimate victory. They had lost many bombers to German defenses, and the convulsive counteroffensive launched by the Germans, the Battle of the Bulge, was sobering. German V1 flying-bomb and V2 rocket attacks on Britain in summer 1944 bred fears that Germany might yet develop new and more powerful weapons. "Inevitably, war-weary minds turned to a strategic air knockout blow that might end the war in Europe" (Clayton 1999, 38). It was, of course, prewar airpower dogma that a nation could be terrorized into surrender. Dresden's reputation and characteristics made it the perfect site for a spectacular firebomb raid, "the *coup de grace* to German morale" (McKee 1982, 99). In the throes of total war, British strategists gave in to the temptation that extremists find so irresistible: the notion of taking an idea to its logical conclusion, regardless of ethical considerations, and cold-bloodedly rationalizing the desirability, even necessity, of excessive and violent tactics.

According to historian David Irving (1963), the full "Hamburg" treatment was employed against Dresden on the night of February 13–14, 1945: first the windows and roofs were broken by high-explosive bombs; then incendiaries rained down, setting fire to the houses. Storms of sparks, in turn, set fire to curtains, carpets, and furniture. A second attack released high-explosive bombs to spread the fires. The resulting firestorm burned eight square miles; estimates of the dead range from 30,000 to 135,000. A great cultural center, "hundreds of beautiful buildings of all periods, set within a cultured, cosmopolitan and balanced whole," and tens of thousands of artifacts and books were lost overnight (Russell 1999, 125).

By the end of the war, bombing had resulted in the devastation of 131 German cities, in which 600,000 civilians fell victim and three and a half million homes were destroyed (Sebald 2003). The Germans suffered irreparable losses to their print heritage. The Magdeburg *Stadtbibliothek*'s 140,000 volumes were a total loss; the *Stadtsbibliothek* in Bremen lost about 150,000 volumes, including many rare and precious works (UNESCO 1996). In Frankfurt, the Municipal and University Library lost 550,000 volumes, 440,000 doctoral dissertations, and 750,000 patent documents. The library of the University of Munich lost 350,000 academic books in three air raids in 1943 and 1944, and Darmstadt lost more than half a million books in a single night in September 1944 (Flood 2002, 374). Altogether, Germany lost between one-third and one-half of its books, many as a direct result of Allied attacks.

Although a successful technical achievement, the attack on the undefended city of Dresden was also the "greatest Anglo-American moral disaster of the war against Germany" (Johnson 1991, 404). A certain level of revulsion at the intense violence, egregious loss of lives, and the targeting of a world-famous cultural site set in at both civil and military levels, and has lingered over the years. The attack seemed uncivilized, especially because the Allies viewed the war as a struggle against barbarians for the survival of Western civilization. As one aviator later expressed it thus: "We had turned the evil of our enemies upon them a hundredfold, and, in so doing, something of our own integrity had been shattered, had been irrevocably lost. We who had fought this war could feel no pride. Victors and vanquished all were one" (Critchell 1963, 384). In response to widespread criticism, Churchill gave orders to pull back from area bombing and concentrate on military objectives, but a defiant Harris continued area bombing until the end of the war.

In some respects, the United States Army Air Forces fought a different kind of war in Europe, for the most part holding true to American prewar airpower policies that emphasized precision bombing. The Americans resisted British pressure to join in the wholesale bombing of German cities and enunciated a policy of pinpoint assaults on key industrial and military targets, although there was some slippage. This approach was feasible because the Americans had more accurate bombsights and thus, the technical capability of staging precision attacks. Their planes were better equipped to survive enemy defensive measures during the daylight raids required for effective targeting. In addition, key government officials felt that the American public would react negatively to indiscriminate attacks on cities, and outspoken American military-command leaders in Europe resisted British pressure to participate in area bombing, even expressing a certain level of disdain for it. As General Ira Eaker, commander of the Eighth Air Force, stated, "We should never allow the history of this war to convict us of throwing the strategic bomber at the man in the street" (Garrett 1993, xiii). In some cases, the Americans developed policies to avoid hitting religious, cultural, or historical sites. Bomber crews in Italy, for example, were given maps that identified cultural sites that were to be exempted from targeting. Also in Italy, specific units, including art historians, shadowed ground troops in order to begin the immediate conservation of damaged buildings and artifacts. In Germany, American forces specifically asked the British to spare the historic university city of Heidelberg. The targeting of military and production sites nevertheless caused a significant amount of damage to cultural sites.

But compunctions and moderation were quickly abandoned when, as the war wound down in Europe, attention turned toward winning the war in the Pacific. For the Americans, defeating the Japanese was an urgent matter of self-defense, preservation of national values, and *raison d'état*—the same mission the British felt in Europe. American political scientist Carl Friedrich (1957, 4–5) later wrote, "Reason of state is nothing but the doctrine that whatever is required to insure the survival of the state must be done by the individuals responsible for it, no matter how repugnant such an act may be to them in their private capacity as decent and moral men." Normally priding themselves on the ethics and humanism of their society, American leaders, after years of war, felt that national survival and the necessity of ending ongoing carnage dictated the short-term abandonment of scruples.

Racism too was a significant factor in this switch in strategy in Japan. Leaders did not need to worry about the American public's condemnation of the use of extreme tactics in Japan because, while "public hatred was directed at Hitler and Mussolini rather than at their subjects . . . [it was] aimed against the Japanese people as well as the emperor" (Crane 1993, 59). "Dehumanizing, demonizing stereotypes of the enemy are a common feature of modern, total war" (Markusen and Kopf 1995, 191), and through propaganda, the American people had been encouraged to hate the Japanese. According to John Dower (1986, 9), author of *War without Mercy: Race and Power in the Pacific War*, an endless stream of evidence was cited "to substantiate the belief that the Japanese were a uniquely contemptible and formidable foe who deserved no mercy and virtually demanded extermination." American civilians and leaders were appalled by reports of Japanese violations against prisoners of war and populations in occupied territories where, indeed, the Japanese had made Asia a "charnel house of atrocities" (Daws 1994, 363). Intelligence reports indicated that Asian noncombatants were dying at a tremendous rate as the Japanese dug in and conditions deteriorated in occupied territories; the minimum plausible range for deaths for Asian noncombatants each month in 1945 was later estimated to be more than 100,000 and possibly higher than 250,000 (Frank 1999). American commanders were horrified by the suicidal resistance that led to the loss of 97 percent of the Japanese troops defending Saipan and, in the same battle, the "carnival of death," in which 10,000 Japanese civilians committed mass suicide (Frank 1999, 72). On Okinawa, at least 62,000, and maybe as many as 150,000 civilians, chose death over surrender. These incidents strengthened the American perception of the Japanese as fanatics. The projected losses of both American invasion forces and Japanese troops and citizens defending their homeland were staggering, so when precision bombing failed, the Americans chose firebombing. It was thought that such an extreme measure would break the morale of the Japanese people, who would then pressure the government to surrender. This was, of course, the same airpower doctrine that had driven the reasoning of the British military leaders earlier.

The Americans' abandonment of the restraints practiced in Europe was incremental, aligning once again with Clausewitz's theory of reciprocal action, that opponents rationalize ever more ruthless types of military actions based on the premise that their enemy would do the same. The initial decision to firebomb Japan's cities was taken after high-explosive precision attacks on military and industrial targets proved ineffective because of weather conditions and the fact that Japanese industry was dispersed into small workshops adjacent to residences. The U.S.-government-sponsored Incendiary Committee recommended firebombing, predicting that the destruction would be immense. (Ninety percent of Tokyo was constructed of highly flammable wooden buildings, a fact of which the committee made note.) The committee projected that there could be 560,000 Japanese casualties if the city was firebombed. According to airpower historian Michael Sherry (1987, 363), the bombing campaigns were the inadvertent but inevitable product of an American "technological fanaticism" combined with racism and "a slow accretion of large fears, thoughtless assumptions, and incremental decisions." It was, in any case, a sure slide to the extremes of total war.

Just prior to invasion of Japan, Haywood Hansell, a commander resistant to firebombing, was replaced by Curtis LeMay, who embraced firebombing as an efficient solution to the operational problems that were prolonging the war. Later, when asked about the morality of this tactic, LeMay replied: "Killing Japanese didn't bother me very much at that time. It was getting the war over that bothered me. So I wasn't particularly worried about how many people we killed in getting the job done" (Hurley and Ehrhart 1979, 200). Total war is a product of such dispassion and also evokes it. George Orwell (1961, 281) defined nationalism as a habit of identifying oneself with a single nation, placing it beyond good and evil, and recognizing no other duty than that of advancing its interests. "There is," he observed, "no crime, absolutely none, that cannot be condoned when 'our' side commits it. Even if one does not deny that the crime has happened, even if one knows that it is exactly the same crime as one has condemned in some other case, even if one admits in an intellectual sense that it is unjustified—still one cannot feel that it is wrong. Loyalty is involved, and so pity ceases to function" (Orwell 1961, 301–302). A defensive loyalty based on exclusion is key to the ethical shift that allows extremists to do what they will. Revenge, tactics, and ideology came together for American militarists who wanted the consequences of imperialistic aggression to be seared into the minds of the Japanese people. The ultimate goal was to elicit the unconditional surrender necessary to create the conditions for occupation and postwar reform, which would involve uprooting the philosophies of fascism and militarism and democratizing Japan (Frank 1999).

The firebombing of Japan's cities began with the March 1945, attack on Tokyo, which eclipsed in scale the Hamburg and Dresden firestorms. It was a "sweep conflagration"—instead of sucking everything to the center, the fire spread outward, engulfing everything in its path and exploding as it went. People burst into flames; some airmen were nauseated by the overpowering stench of burning flesh that permeated the skies two miles over the city (Caidin 1981). An estimated 87,000 to 100,000 Japanese died. Between May and August 1945, LeMay's men experimented with techniques to maximize the effects of their attacks, and their B-29s laid waste to 180 square miles and 67 cities, killing more than 300,000 people and wounding another 400,000. Only the ancient city of Kyoto was exempted by Secretary of War Henry Stimsen, despite protests by the military, on grounds of religious and cultural significance (Schaffer 1985). Hiroshima and Nagasaki were left as potential targets for the new atom bombs.

Yet even the terror of firebombing failed to evoke surrender. The Japanese people were stoic, their leaders unmovable. Intercepted messages indicated that the Japanese army was preparing for a decisive, defensive battle that would feature the amassed might of its most seasoned troops and thousands of naval and aerial kamikaze vehicles, as well as mobilization for combat of all women aged 17 to 40 and men aged 15 to 60. Key figures in the Imperial High Command were prepared to sacrifice the entire population in a glorious defense of the homeland if this battle failed to convince the Allies to accept a negotiated settlement rather than unconditional surrender (Frank 1999). It was under these conditions that the concept of an aerial deathblow proved a "potent lure" for American leaders, helping to sanction the use of the atomic bomb (Crane 1993, 26). The bombing of Hiroshima and Nagasaki on August 6 and 9, 1945, marked the end of the war and a milepost in the evolution of total war. The use of nuclear weaponry testified conclusively to the "tendency for war to become as destructive as the existing technology and resources will permit" (Carlton 2001, 21). Violence had become industrialized. Whereas, in World War I, large armies acted as the "medium through which the imposition of heavy casualties would inflict pain on the civilian populations that supported the war," pain in World War II was administered directly (Keegan 2001, 57).

In Japan, as in Germany, human and cultural destruction (including the loss of texts) were, of course, paired. Figures are hard to come by, but by the end of the war, bombing had accounted either directly or indirectly for the destruction of 50 percent of the total book resources in Japanese libraries. When the occupation troops arrived in 1945, there were probably fewer than five million books in the country (Welch 1997). Three-quarters of all public libraries suffered heavy damage, with 400,000 volumes in public library collections lost in bombing raids on Tokyo alone (Boyer 1985; Welch 1997). Heavy damage was sustained by government libraries: more than 655,000 volumes in the Tokyo area were burned, including libraries of the Cabinet, Ministry of Foreign Affairs, Transportation Ministry, Bureau of Patents and Standards, and Finance Ministry.

The loss of books and libraries in World War II becomes more comprehensible if we recognize that the major players (Allied and Axis) paired human and cultural destruction as a tactic of total war. In terms of the wanton destruction of culture, distinctions can be made between the aggressors, Japan and Germany, and those for whom the war was primarily defensive. These distinctions can be made on the grounds of intent, that is, whether there was an *intent* to destroy books or a library *per se*, and the long-term instrumentality of the destruction. In the Axis powers' pursuit of empire, libricide was instrumental—they destroyed their victims' cultures as a tactic that would facilitate their eventual military and political dominance. The Germans methodically articulated and pursued policies of ethnocide, whereas the Japanese destroyed books and libraries in generalized reactions to resistance. For both groups, colonization was the goal and troops often engaged in shelling and burning libraries. Their leaders chose libraries as targets because they recognized, and feared, the support these institutions gave to the cultural vitality of a people and the countereffect their very existence asserted against colonization efforts.

The Allies, on the other hand, were clothed in a value system that abhorred cultural destruction, and did not intend to destroy libraries. Though massive in scale, their destruction of books and libraries was not calculated so as to gain long-term advantage. Indeed, it violated the very belief system of the Allied nations, to whom libraries were pillars of intellectual freedom and democratic humanism. At first glance, Germany's systematic destruction of Jewish libraries and Germany and Japan's destruction in occupied countries seems clearly distinct from the havoc wreaked on cities during Allied air raids. But, with further consideration, the Allies' violation of their own principles and the sheer scale of their destruction and disregard for cultural heritage are troubling. Although Allied air raids on Germany and Japan did not intentionally target the enemy's culture, there was a definite subtext about destroying the enemy's cities and infrastructure as a means of breaking the population's will. And the Allies as well as Axis powers broke codified international prohibitions against the destruction of cultural artifacts and institutions. To twentieth-century rogue leaders driven to extremes by ambition and ideological imperatives, the obligatory mandate of preserving cultural artifacts and institutions, bequeathed by the nineteenth-century humanists, must have seemed naive and weak-minded; for them, cultural destruction was merely a tool. For the Allies, who espoused humanism and even posed the war as being fought over the preservation of democracy and humanism, cultural destruction remained an ethical issue, even while their mission and tactics defied preservation. We can see this paradox in America's postwar efforts to promote libraries and reading in occupied Japan; the creation of libraries in the rubble of the cities they had so recently destroyed was rationalized as necessary to a viable civil society and democracy. It says much about the nature of total war, that to win, Americans (and the British in Germany) had to dismiss the principles of the very philosophy they were defending. They donned the blinkers of extremism and committed to militaristic and nationalistic mindsets that allowed them to rationalize any tactic, any cruelty. One might argue that the phenomenon of pairing human and cultural destruction to extreme ends was proof that war had spread to the heart of humanity itself.

REFERENCES

Bilinska, Helena. 1946. "Poland Faces Intellectual Famine." *Library Journal* 71 (4):1022–1023, 1034.

Borin, Jacqueline. 1993. "Embers of the Soul: The Destruction of Jewish Books and Libraries in Poland during World War II." *Libraries and Culture* 28 (4):445–460.

Borowiec, Andrew. 2001. *Destroy Warsaw!: Hitler's Punishment, Stalin's Revenge.* Westport, Conn.: Praeger.

Boyer, Paul. 1985. "The Cloud over the Culture: How Americans Imagined the Bomb They Dropped." *New Republic* 193 (7, 8):26–31.

Buckley, John. 1999. *Air Power in the Age of Total War.* Bloomington: Indiana University Press.

Caidin, Martin. 1981. *Black Thursday.* New York: Bantam.

Carlton, Eric. 2001. *Militarism: Rule without Law.* Burlington, Vt.: Ashgate.

Chang, Iris. 1997. *The Rape of Nanking: The Forgotten Holocaust of World War II.* New York: Basic Books.

Clayton, Anthony. 1999. "Dresden, 1919–1945." In *Dresden: A City Reborn,* eds. Anthony Clayton and Alan Russell. New York: Berg, 27–46.

Crane, Conrad C. 1993. *Bombs, Cities, and Civilians: American Airpower Strategy in World War II.* Lawrence: University Press of Kansas.

Critchell, Laurence. 1963. "The Distant Drum Was Still." In *Combat: The War with Germany,* ed. Don Congdon. New York: Dell, 380–384.

Daws, Gavan. 1994. *Prisoners of the Japanese: POWs of World War II in the Pacific.* New York: William Morrow.

Dower, John W. 1986. *War without Mercy: Race and Power in the Pacific War.* New York: Pantheon Books.

Dunin, Janusz. 1996. "The Tragic Fate of Polish Libraries after 1939." *Solanus* 10:5–12.

Feldman, Burton. 2000. *The Nobel Prize: A History of Genius, Controversy, and Prestige.* New York: Arcade.

Flood, John L. 2002. "Varieties of Vandalism." *Common Knowledge* 8(2):366–386.

Forster, Stig. 2000. "Introduction." In *Great War, Total War: Combat and Mobilization on the Western Front, 1914–1918*, eds. Roger Chickering and Stig Forster. Cambridge: Cambridge University Press, 1–15.

Frank, Richard B. 1999. *Downfall: The End of the Imperial Japanese Empire*. New York: Penguin Books.

Friedrich, Carl. 1957. *Constitutional Reason of State: The Survival of the Constitutional Order*. Providence, R.I.: Brown University Press.

Fung, Margaret C. 1984. "Safekeeping of the National Peiping Library's Rare Chinese Books at the Library of Congress 1941–1965." *Journal of Library History, Philosophy and Comparative Librarianship* 19 (3):359–371.

Garrett, Stephen A. 1993. *Ethics and Airpower in World War II: The British Bombing of German Cities*. New York: St. Martin's Press.

Howard, Michael. 1983. *Clausewitz*. Oxford: Oxford University Press.

Hurley, Albert, and Robert Ehrhart (eds.). 1979. *Air Power and Warfare*. The Proceedings of the Eighth Military History Symposium, United States Air Force Academy, October 18–20, 1978. Washington, D.C.: Office of Air Force History.

Irving, David. 1963. *The Destruction of Dresden*. New York: Holt, Rinehart, and Winston.

Johnson, Paul. 1991. *Modern Times: The World from the Twenties to the Nineties*. Revised Edition. New York: HarperPerennial.

Kamenetsky, Ihor. 1961. *Secret Nazi Plans for Eastern Europe: A Study of Lebensraum Policies*. New Haven, Conn.: College and University Press.

Keegan, John. 2001. *War and Our World*. New York: Vintage.

Levine, Alan J. 1992. *The Strategic Bombing of Germany, 1940–1945*. Westport, Conn.: Praeger.

Lin, Sharon Chien. 1998. *Libraries and Librarianship in China*. Westport, Conn.: Greenwood Press.

Lukas, Richard C. 1986. *The Forgotten Holocaust: The Poles under German Occupation 1939–1944*. Lexington: University Press of Kentucky.

Markusen, Eric, and David Kopf. 1995. *The Holocaust and Strategic Bombing: Genocide and Total War in the Twentieth Century*. Boulder, Colo.: Westview Press.

McKee, Alexander. 1982. *Dresden 1945: The Devil's Tinderbox*. New York: E. P. Dutton.

Morrison, Wilbur H. 1982. *Fortress without a Roof: The Allied Bombing of the Third Reich*. New York: St. Martin's Press.

Orwell, George. 1961. *Collected Essays*. London: Secker and Warburg.

Rothnie, Niall. 1992. *The Baedeker Blitz: Hitler's Attack on Britain's Historic Cities*. Shepperton, England: Ian Allen Publishing.

Rummel, R. J. 1992. *Democide: Nazi Genocide and Mass Murder*. New Brunswick, N.J.: Transaction.

Russell, Alan. 1999. "Dresden's Architectural Traditions and Its Surviving Heritage." In *Dresden: A City Reborn*, eds. Anthony Clayton and Alan Russell. New York: Berg, 117–143.

Schaffer, Ronald. 1985. *Wings of Judgment: American Bombing in World War II*. New York: Oxford University Press.

Sebald, W. G. 2003. *On the Natural History of Destruction*. Trans. Anthea Bell. New York: Random House.

Shaffer, Kenneth R. 1946. "The Conquest of Books." *Library Journal* 7 (2):82–85.

Sherry, Michael S. 1987. *The Rise of American Air Power: The Creation of Armageddon.* New Haven, Conn.: Yale University Press.

Sroka, Marek. 1999. "The University of Cracow Library under Nazi Occupation: 1939–1945." *Libraries and Culture* 34 (1):1–16.

Taylor, Jay. 1993. *The Rise and Fall of Totalitarianism in the Twentieth Century.* New York: Paragon House.

Tuchman, Barbara. 1962. *The Guns of August.* New York: Macmillan.

Tuchman, Barbara. 1984. *The March of Folly: From Troy to Vietnam.* New York: Alfred A. Knopf.

UNESCO Memory of the World Program. 1996. *Lost Memory: Libraries and Archives Destroyed in the Twentieth Century.* Paris: UNESCO.

Van Creveld, Martin. 2000. "World War I and the Revolution in Logistics." In *Great War, Total War: Combat and Mobilization on the Western Front, 1914–1918*, eds. Roger Chickering and Stig Forster. Cambridge: Cambridge University Press, 57–72.

Wallach, Jehuda. 1986. *The Dogma of the Battle of Annihilation: The Theories of Clausewitz and Schlieffen and Their Impact on the German Conduct of Two World Wars.* Westport, Conn.: Greenwood Press.

Welch, Theodore F. 1997. *Libraries and Librarianship in Japan.* Westport, Conn.: Greenwood Press.

Zaide, Gregorio F., ed. 1990. *Documentary Sources of Philippine History*, Vol. 1. Manila: Navotas Press.

CHAPTER 9

Anarchy and Acquisitive Vandalism, 1967–2003

Tyranny and anarchy are never far asunder.
—Jeremy Bentham, 1748–1832

When wartime leaders subordinate their people to militarism and ideological mandates and adopt ever more deadly technology, books and libraries are threatened with tactical, ideological, and collateral annihilation. That is to say, they are threatened with deliberate destruction planned or executed by leaders for the purpose of war, or they are written off as unavoidable casualties of combat. At the same time, at local and regional levels, the mere state of being at war and engaged in armed conflict carries another set of lethal consequences for libraries. Wartime leaders may permit the looting of books, manuscripts, and archives by civilians and troops because the destruction of the enemies' cultural infrastructure can serve to erase identity and break the will to resist. Sometimes, however, military leaders may simply lack the will and means to stop people from taking advantage of the chaotic social conditions that accompany armed conflict. When the mechanisms that normally prevent random violence break down, the resulting conditions are an invitation to undisciplined troops and opportunistic civilians to engage in playful, malicious (nonspecific), vindictive, and acquisitive vandalism. It is in such circumstances that libraries are stripped of infrastructure and books are sold on the open market or used as waste paper. The line between expedience and criminal ignorance becomes very thin at times. In World War II, Allied troops in Germany used rare chapbooks issued by publishers *Ensslin und Laiblin* as fuel for barbecues (Flood 2002, 375).

A state of war brings Darwinian struggles over resources to the surface and allows a survivalist approach to human interests, values, and dignity to overtake civility. In situations of civil conflict, revolution, and regime change, anarchical and iconoclastic mindsets can easily take hold of repressed individuals and groups who have existed on the periphery. Long denied a respected place in society, they seize the opportunity to act out their hatred of rival groups, a regime, the establishment in general, or civilization as a whole. The breakdown of controls that occurs when there is a power vacuum (whether in war or violent regime change) may result in the pillage and devastation of cultural institutions. Then all manner of obligations are cast aside. The notion of a cultural commons erodes, and artifacts and institutions become targets of opportunity.

Local wars and civil conflicts can exhibit the totality of engagement of larger wars (the conflation of home front and battlefield, racial and ideological tensions). But whereas tactical and ideological vandalism clearly drive cultural destruction in global and total war, a more confused picture emerges at the local level. The Nigerian Civil War, which lasted from July 1967 to January 1970, illustrates the chaotic cultural destruction that can result from an armed conflict characterized by tribal and anarchical elements. The war began with a government coup that diminished the power of an economically dominant ethnic group, the Ibos, at the national level. The coup also triggered the subsequent massacre of between 6,000 and 8,000 Ibos in northern Nigeria, where the group was a minority. As rival groups sought revenge against them for humiliations (some real, some imagined) and perceived economic and political discrimination, one million Ibos fled to the east, where they were a majority, and this became the center of conflict for the next three years (De St. Jorre 1972, 86). The Ibos claimed that as many as 50,000 of their people had been killed in the pogrom, a fact that they considered to be proof of the state's genocidal intentions. They declared the area in which they were the majority, Biafra, an independent nation. When the Nigerian government sent in troops, disrupted agriculture, and initiated a blockade that eventually resulted in the death by starvation of one million people, the Biafrans constituted themselves as a distinctive group fighting for survival. By the time the war was over, their cultural losses would be immense because combat centered on areas where significant library development had occurred in the decades preceding the conflict. In fact, the Eastern Nigeria Library Board was a pioneer in African public-library development and a model for the whole Nigerian federation (Okpa-Iroha 1971; Enu 1970).

There is a range of interpretations for the destructiveness and violence of the war. Political scientist Robert Melson (1996, 93) puts forth the case that it was a classic ethnic scenario in which a culturally plural, postcolonial nation, "a shaky and hardly legitimate postcolonial state," falls into the hands of an ethnic group seeking dominance over all others. The heavy loss of life and the destruction of most of the cultural institutions in the area certainly reinforced the Ibos' perception of the Nigerian regime as genocidal, ultimately interested in the extinction of the Ibo race and culture. John De St. Jorre (1972, 283), a journalist who covered the war on the ground in Biafra, saw the conflict in a different light. He described the war as primarily civil—a dirty, internecine "brothers' war" to keep the nation together. He interpreted the destruction as random, incidental, collateral, and expedient rather than deliberately ethnocidal. The looting, for example, was not a deliberate tactic of war, but the opportunistic seizure of raw materials or marketable goods by both troops and civilians in miserable straits. He points out that the Nigerian army was given a code of conduct that laid out rules for humane treatment and the protection of noncombatants, institutions, and property, but there was a gap between intention and execution. The army fought on a diet of marijuana and beer and was guilty of many excesses (De St. Jorre 1972, 283).

Certainly the extensive devastation of Biafran public institutions was aggravated by the "willfulness or ignorance" of the fighting men and civilians (Nwafor 1971, 42). Often all that was left of a library was a skeleton: the collections were looted, furniture and bookshelves stolen, and louvres, floor tiles, and electrical fittings ripped out (Enu 1970). The university library at Nsukka was almost entirely destroyed after the city fell to the Nigerian army. Shelves holding the Herbert Macauley Library collection of 40,000 books, pamphlets, periodicals, newspapers, personal papers, and photographs were stripped bare (Okpa-Iroha 1971). This same library's Africana, Afro-Americana, and Nigeriania collections were also lost, at great cost to the country's historical record. Losses included microfilms and photocopies of every newspaper in Nigeria since 1863 and copies of every published book and doctoral and master's dissertations on Nigeria since 1900. Books, documents, and microfilms were strewn about the campus and scattered in nearby streets and fields. Some books disappeared into private homes and some were sold. One-of-a-kind documents were tossed onto refuse heaps and used as wrappers in the market; the center leaves of books were ripped off and used as toilet paper (Nwafor 1971). Many private collections, especially those of lawyers, were lost as well (Oluwakuyide 1972).

The bitter fighting on the ground was but one aspect of the Nigerian civil war. Internationally, the Biafran rebel government waged a "war of words" with an ambitious propaganda campaign (Anafulu 1971, 32). The loss of the Directorate for Propaganda's library, which served the rebel Ministry of Information, is particularly noteworthy because it would have been a unique source of information about the conflict for future researchers (Enu 1970, 210). Lost were copies of news releases that propounded the rebels' cause; books, reports, and newspaper and magazine clippings on the conflict from all over the world; abstracts, cataloged and indexed materials, radio transcripts, and files on the government's positions. The library was abandoned in the last days of the war, when the Nigerian government troops gained control, and no attempt was made to save its materials because, according to librarian Joseph Anafulu (1971, 37) "no one felt safe being caught with a 'Biafran' paper or file on him." The fate of the university and ministry libraries represents the fate of other Biafran libraries and illustrates both the losses war can inflict on the historical record and the somewhat random nature of biblioclasm during civil war. The fact that the killing of Biafrans and the destruction of libraries stopped with the end of hostilities tends to corroborate the view that the Nigerian war was fraternal and the cultural destruction the result of combat and opportunistic vandalism rather than primarily genocide or ethnocide. The government was directing undisciplined troops from a distance.

With the coup that began the conflict, the Nigerian government had fallen into the hands of the military and, in response to rebellion, leaders naturally turned to military solutions to fight secession. It is safe to say that an excess of militarism often leads to war, and one can also make the case that waging war sets in motion an increased militarism. In the case of Nigeria, both accelerants came into play. Sociologists know that "the term 'military' implies an acceptance of organized violence as a legitimate means for realizing social objectives" (Lang 1968, 305). For leaders who engage in war, militarism "implies both a *policy* orientation and a *power* relationship" (Radway 1968, 300). They use various "constellations of values—often intellectualized as ideologies—not only [to] constitute the rationalizations and justifications for war, but . . . to provide the actual imperatives for warfare itself" (Carlton 1990, vii). Modern militarists are extremists who capitalize on traditional fears of "the other"; wars are often posed as the defense of one kind of nation or civilization against another, which only increases intergroup hostility (Burns 1933, 447). As militarists train their people in learned aggression and loyalty to the state, there is an implicit credence to the hypothesis of natural selection through war (Burns 1933, 447). Militarism naturally opens the door to violence and vandalism because it socializes participants in a war to consciously or unconsciously claim survivalist entitlements.

A sense of entitlement can make theft, within the ranks or leadership, rational and acceptable. If one is winning, one's (or one's country's) sense of superiority is reinforced, and one is entitled to either well-earned spoils or reparations for previous losses. If one is losing, there is the satisfaction of revenge. Jeanette Greenfield (1995, 309), an expert in cultural repatriation, has characterized the history of the world as "an intricate web of universal plunder, of fetishism, and of the cannibalization of cultures." Throughout history, victorious armies have looted their enemy's patrimony and resources as a matter of course; indeed, loot was a major incentive for underpaid soldiers and for generals in search of personal wealth and status (Chamberlain 1983). Greenfield cites the treasures, including books, gathered in by Napoleon's bureaucrats who followed in the wake of his victorious armies. By the twentieth century, Western opinion of the practice had changed and international codes against cultural destruction existed. Nevertheless, the century was rife with incidents of wartime looting: governments encouraged looting and vandalism as tools of domination and individuals and armies persisted in taking souvenirs or opportunistically plundering cultural commons with which they lacked sympathy.

Of course, some individuals looted simply because chaotic wartime conditions make it possible to do so. Indeed, war and its aftermath created conditions of excruciating temptation. At the end of the nineteenth century, Peking's Hanlin Academy Library was China's largest repository library, the home of irreplaceable, unique collections that spanned centuries. Its greatest treasure was the last surviving copy of *Yong Lo Da Dian*, a 22,000-volume encyclopedia that had been compiled in the 1400s, when thousands of scholars fanned out over the country and collected and copied China's literary heritage (Davis and Huanwen 1997, 62). All the facts of its loss cannot be firmly established, but it was burned in 1900 as 2,000 Allied forces came to the defense of their embassies, under attack by Chinese insurgents. According to one account, the Chinese set fire to the academy to get through to the adjacent British embassy, whereupon the British systematically destroyed the library buildings as a defensive measure (Davis and Huanwen 1997, 62). Most of the volumes of the famous encyclopedia were consumed in the flames, but some were taken by Westerners as souvenirs, as antique "specimens" of an exotic culture.

World War II created conditions that made illustrious collections vulnerable and easy prey. During and after World War II, rare manuscripts were unprotected in ruined monasteries in Italy, and some were, inevitably, lost (Chamberlain 1983, 179). Some individuals, whether out of cupidity or a passion to possess them, quietly abused their roles as protectors of cultural items cast adrift by war. In 1945, American Lieutenant Joe Tom Meador was part of an artillery battalion stationed in eastern Germany and assigned to guard the cave in which the renowned medieval Quedlinburg treasury had been placed for safekeeping. Meador obtained possession of two jewel-encrusted manuscripts and various reliquaries and religious objects. He sent them back to the United States by military post and eventually set up a little shrine in his Dallas apartment in the late 1960s. Until his death in 1980, Meador displayed the objects only to friends (Korte 1997, 150). Attempts by his heirs to have the objects appraised and sold triggered a decade-long international confrontation over ownership of the items, which the heirs claimed that Meador had found in a German gutter at the end of World War II (Honan 1997, 154). In 1990, the Germans offered to pay $3 million to Meador's heirs for the safe return of just the Samuhel Gospels, a jewel-encrusted ninth-century Carolingian manuscript. However, subsequent litigation resulted in the return of all items for less than this sum (Kline 1997, 157). In this case, original ownership was indisputable. Many looted items never find their way back to the rightful owner.

Accounts of pillage often illustrate the brutalizing effects of militarism and war on individual values. In 1991, a global audience was horrified by journalist Robert Fisk's accounts of the sacking of Kuwait City by Saddam's troops. Fisk (2002, 290), a British journalist with a special interest in the horrors of cultural destruction, expressed incredulity at finding *The Collected Works of*

Mahatma Gandhi lying on a chair in the Self Receptor Palace's still smoldering library. Trying to make sense of why people burn libraries and museums, Fisk (2002, 291) concluded that the Iraqi troops had overrun Kuwait like a medieval army laying waste to a vanquished city, but he had trouble equating this behavior with faces of Iraqi soldiers captured by U.S. forces, "defeated teenagers with their sad smiles." The troops, coveting books as luxury items, had looted them from private collections while Iraqi bureaucrats looted Kuwait's public collections and made off with the critical documents from the National Archives. Another opportunity for government and personal looting arose when, immediately following Iraq's withdrawal from Kuwait, Iraqi Shiites rebelled against Saddam's regime (see Chapter 4). Shiite written materials were decimated as government troops enacted a program of ethnic cleansing against the group. Iraqi authorities were reputed to have long encouraged soldiers to keep goods they seize during their operations: "The heads of the people are for me," officers tell their subordinates, "their property, for you" (Middle East Watch 1992, 37). War creates extreme situations in which abnormal behavior is perpetrated with Darwinian sangfroid, and leaders may accord troops the same moral exemptions they claim for themselves.

The *systematic* looting of public collections in Kuwait by Saddam's bureaucrats had imperialistic overtones similar to the Nazis' looting in Eastern Europe during World War II. In both instances, special teams methodically inventoried and confiscated valuable historic, archival, scientific, and reference collections in order to reduce the cultural patrimony of a conquered people and increase their own. Both cases are reminiscent of Napoleon, who sent the avid bibliophile and writer Stendhal to supervise the confiscation and loading of baggage wagons with the libraries of six conquered nations. In his 1983 book *Loot: The Heritage of Plunder*, Russell Chamberlain described the exuberant Napoleon as taking "symbolic possession" of his enemies' treasures like a "savage eating the heart of a noble enemy in order to ingest its powers" (Chamberlain 1983, 134). By asserting that a strong nation has a natural right to the cultural goods of a weaker one, and, further, that "all men of genius are French no matter in what country they may have been born," Napoleon justified the cultural sacking of European countries as "simply gathering in France's heritage" (Chamberlain 1983, 135). Napoleon's looting resulted, after his defeat, in the 1815 Convention of Paris, which ordered the return of pilfered items to the countries of origin and established looting of cultural property as unacceptable (Kaye 1997, 101). International prohibitions against cultural destruction proliferated in the nineteenth and twentieth centuries, making it even more shocking when Adolf Hitler willfully flouted these conventions and replicated Napoleon's flagrant collection of cultural trophies. But unlike Napoleon's pillaging, Nazi looting was also accompanied by the widespread destruction of books for purposes of colonization and genocide.

Less familiar than the biblioclastic exploits of Napoleon and Hitler, the "alpha and omega" of cultural looters, is Joseph Stalin's identification with these two figures (Chamberlain 1983, 9). In 1943, he had lists prepared of desired holdings in the countries he planned to occupy and made plans to strip museum and cultural institutions there (Akinsha and Kozlov 1995). Like Napoleon and Hitler, Stalin was going to build a huge museum that would honor his political ideology. The Soviets did pillage the countries they occupied in 1945 and 1946, claiming millions of objects (paintings, archives, and books) as reparations for the Nazis' destruction of 100 million volumes in a 1941 invasion (UNESCO 1996, 14). But complications in Stalin's plan arose from the focus of Soviet propaganda on demonizing fascists by posing the Soviets as innocent victims. Revealing the full extent of their own loot-ing and book destruction did not serve their purposes, and in a move that demonstrated their awareness of international disapproval of the looting of cultural property, the Communist Party leadership hid many of the cultural trophies that they had so resolutely gathered. It is precisely because looting and other forms of biblioclasm offend modern norms that it must be covered up. Unless, of course, a regime wishes to ignore such values, in which case, the regime will stage high-profile book-burning ceremonies, as the Chinese did during the Cultural Revolution.

With the onset of *Glasnost* and a freer press, information about Soviet loot-ing began to emerge. In October 1990, the *Literaturnaia Gazeta* described two and a half million World War II trophy books that had been received by Russia's Academy of Sciences, hidden in a church, and left to moulder (Grimsted 2001, 257). Other collections had been exposed to extensive cleans-ing operations: those with "degenerate bourgeois ideology" were destroyed and others relegated to special restricted collections (Grimsted 2001, 257). With the decline of Communist Party control came access to archives that established the complicity of the Soviets in the destruction of their own books and libraries while blaming it on the Nazis. Indeed, in Ukraine, where an estimated 46 million unique historical documents and more than 51 million books were lost (Fedoruk 1997), the Soviets may have destroyed more books and documents than the Nazis (Grimsted 2001, 198). As they evacuated parts of Ukraine in 1941, they put into effect Stalin's "scorched earth" policy, burn-ing materials that could not be removed (Grimsted 2001, 193).

Stalin is remembered as a "nation killer" because his socialist visions required suppression of the national identity of constituent republics within the USSR, and the suppression often took the form of ethnocide (Conquest 1970) or the transport of cultural artifacts to Russia and their re-description as Soviet rather than national treasures. Throughout the history of the USSR, Russia domi-nated Soviet culture. The centralization of cultural resources in Russia was posed as value neutral, the gathering in of the common cultural objects of the Soviet people. The party labeled attempts to retain local cultural heritage as the unenlightened manifestation of nationalism by those who were blind to the rightness of making everything in the USSR, including cultural resources, belong to everyone. That, as Belarusan Adam Maldis (1997, 79) wrote, meant that cultural items (including cultural property that had been removed from nations such as Belarus) really belonged to no one under the Soviet system. In the 1990s, after the Soviet Union broke apart, the newly independent states had a difficult time reclaiming their cultural heritage from Russia, where Russian nationalists were reluctant to give up their preeminence in the region. In retrospect, centralization was a euphemism for looting that ultimately benefited the power center. This distorted form of long-term, quasi-imperialistic looting was replicated by the Chinese Communist Party, which looted the texts and religious treasures of Tibet in the name of Communism but used them for the enrichment of the Chinese people (Knuth 2003).

The absolute power vested in governments during war (and other situations when totalitarianism holds sway) vastly expedites top-down policies concerning book destruction or official looting as conducive to colonization, ideological transformation, and surrender. The brutish and anarchic conditions of war prevalent on the ground allow for opportunistic looting, violent or retaliatory acts, or thoughtless vandalism. War masks motivation, clouds events, turns cultural items into flotsam, and provides the perfect host for biblioclasm.

In previous chapters, we have seen that violence against books and libraries may be a byproduct of internal ethnic conflict. When this is the case, the destruction is not likely to be coincidental. Local governments may turn a blind eye to attacks on others by their own ethnic group, or they may even take a direct role in commissioning attacks. The 2004 attack on the BORI Institute in India was a calculated attempt to advance Hindu nationalist worldviews by extinguishing secular and Muslim perspectives; no one was held accountable for this deed. In Kashmir, Muslim militants transformed enmity into public campaigns to purge the area of Hindu rivals; little effort was spent in curbing them until the 1990s, when their alliance with Pakistan sufficiently threatened India's possession of the area. In Sri Lanka, where Buddhist extremists were in charge of the government, the Jaffna Public Library was victimized in an escalation of ethnic political repression in 1981. In Iraq, an insurrection triggered Saddam's ethnocidal extinction of the Shiites and their renowned culture of learning.

Internal wars and armed conflicts produce the same opportunities for violence and vandalism as any war. However, in the unique instance of the transfer of power from one regime to another, the aggression that seeks outlet comes not from those in power but from the people. The moral worldview that inevitably comes under attack is the one associated with the deposed government. The hatred that drives destruction stems not from ethnic rivalry but from political disillusionment. As defined in Chapter 1, modern biblioclasm is an attack by extremists on books and libraries on the grounds that they undermine ideological goals, threaten orthodoxy or dominance, or represent a despised establishment or political, ethnic, or religious enemy. In regime change and insurrection, the extremists are frequently those who lash out against the status quo, an entrenched elite, and political enemies. As in all biblioclasm, there is a heavily symbolic element. The previously powerless are asserting themselves against a system that has oppressed them.

In the late 1980s and 1990s, as Communism lost its grip on Eastern Europe, ordinary people became indifferent and even hostile toward socialism for its failure to deliver a better way of life. They perhaps sensed that even their leaders had "lost faith in what they were pretending to do" (Hobsbawm 1993, 62). Occasionally, the precipitous fall of a regime provided opportunity for groups to vent their rage directly at the symbols of the autocrats who had enforced the regime. Throughout the region, books and records associated with despised individuals and the Communist Party were attacked and purged. According to archivist James O'Toole (1993, 254), records in Communist countries had great symbolic significance to the people because of their use by the government in the systematic violation of human rights. In January 1990, the *New York Times* reported that an angry mob in East Germany had stormed the former headquarters of the Stasi, the secret police. In what the newspaper called "a show of popular frustration," the mob broke up furniture and scattered surveillance files on the floor and stomped on them. Those records, at least temporarily, became the symbols of all that was wrong with the old regime. They did not destroy the files, however, perhaps because the new democratic leaders had publicized the importance of preserving evidence of former abuse and the identities of informers (O'Toole 1993, 254).

For Romania, a country with rich literary traditions, regime change brought violent confrontation, book destruction, and the loss of a treasured library. Whether the events that brought down Romania's dictator Nicolae Ceauşescu in eight days in December 1989 were orchestrated or spontaneous and revolutionary is a matter of debate. But there is no uncertainty about the passion of the people, who finally rebelled after years spent living under his tyranny. In Romania, "grotesque, even ridiculous, crimes committed in the name of communism" had become commonplace: beautiful villages and historic buildings were destroyed in ill-conceived communalization schemes as leaders sought to purge Romania of its past. Denied adequate food and electricity, a formerly prosperous people lived cold, hungry lives in ill-lit rooms (Galloway and Wylie 1991, 26). Furthermore, government policies that banned birth control and denied basic medical services had transformed Romania into "the septic abortion and child AIDs capital of Europe" (Galloway and Wylie 1991, 26). In stark contrast to the austerity imposed on the population, the Ceauşescus presided over the misery, living in luxury in 40 extravagant houses (Galloway and Wylie 1991, 4).

During Ceauşescu's rule from 1967 to 1989, the number of public libraries in Romania declined by two-thirds ("Romanian Libraries" 1990, 18). No books were permitted from the outside world, and there was little access to information; in fact, no telephone books were published. An exiled writer, Andrei Codrescu (1991, 129), remembered Romania as a place where typewriters had to be registered, photocopies were forbidden, and "writing was deemed more dangerous than bombs." One publication that existed in abundance was

42-volume sets of Ceauşescu's collected speeches and writings—and these were one of the first things targeted by the rebelling Romanians. After storming the Communist Party offices in Timisoara, protesters ripped Ceauşescu posters off the wall and swept his books from the bookcases, throwing them out the window. One observer watched in utter astonishment as these icons crashed into the street, deducing instantly that Ceauşescu must have fallen from power (Galloway and Wylie 1991, 114). This scene was repeated in Bucharest when crowds stormed the Central Committee building and threw thousands of Ceauşescu's books off the dictator's balcony. The people built bonfires with the books and danced for joy, tears streaming down their faces (Codrescu 1991, 36).

As anarchy engulfed Bucharest in late 1989, frenzied mobs attacked Ceauşescu's brutal security forces, the *Securitat*, who had barricaded themselves in public buildings, including the library of the University of Bucharest. For three days, loyalists fought against the crowds and against the army, which used tanks and cannons to dislodge the recalcitrant paramilitaries. In the chaos, this nineteenth-century library, a prominent and beloved building in the center of the city, caught fire and burned. Lost in the building were 500,000 books, 25 percent of its collection, including hundreds of rare and ancient volumes, manuscripts, photographs, microfilms, and documents ("Librarians Rally" 1990, 180). The people prevailed and in the aftermath of fighting, grief over the loss of the library was widespread and expressed by both the Romanian people and outsiders. Andrei Codrescu (1991, 117–118), an expatriate who returned from exile when the fighting died down, walked through the destroyed building 10 days after its destruction:

[Despite] heavy snowfalls, and frigid temperatures, the books were still smoldering. I walked over the smoking remains of the books and manuscripts of Romania's greatest writers. I picked up a few charred pages. These were the sacred pieces of the Romanian revolution, more holy in their way than the pieces of the Berlin wall, which had come happily down in peace. The books murdered here carried a greater weight and a headier promise. On the half page I was holding was a folk story poem I recognized from my childhood. It was about Ion Handsome-Lad who sacrifices himself for his father, the aging king. About the sad king, it is said: "One eye laughed/While the other cried": That was—precisely—how I felt. Elated by the victory, wrenched by its losses.

Many Romanians were convinced that loyalist forces had deliberately set fire to the university library. It was the sort of vindictive vandalism to be expected of those who had lorded it over the population during a dictator's rule. Inasmuch as the crowd's fury affected books and libraries, it found outlet in the destruction of Ceauşescu's works and then dissipated. The post-Communist government in Romania quickly asserted the civic and intellectual importance of books by opening discussions about rebuilding the university library, a key sign of stability and commitment to democracy.

In other countries, books have not been dissociated from the regime's tyranny so soon after an overthrow. When the new government is unable to engage the people's trust, violence against symbolic representations of the old power structure can become a recurring event and expand in scope. This was the case in Albania. By the end of the 1980s, Albania, as with other countries where the Communists were losing their grip, was a nation in turmoil. For 40 years, Enver Hoxha's hard-line Communist regime had imposed a strict form of Stalinist Marxist-Leninism that was "harder and more terrible than anywhere else" (AIM 1997). This country had become the most poverty-stricken in Europe, with incomes in line with those of the poorest Third World countries (Vickers and Pettifer 1997, 2). Like the Romanians, Albanians were cut off from the rest of the world as few entered or left the isolated fortress state. Hoxha's secret police, the *Sigurimi*, ensured ideological conformity to Marxist-Leninist ideals and Hoxha's mandates. Literary deprivation was policy, with a single government-run publishing company in existence (Vickers and Pettifer 1997). Only Hoxha's regularly published works, which eventually totaled 71 volumes, were widely disseminated.

Hoxha's death in 1985 provided an opening for reforms, but Communist mindsets were deeply entrenched and hard-line Communist rule persisted until 1989, when a mildly reformist government took over. The demise of Communism in other Eastern Bloc countries, including Romania and East Germany, brought high hopes for sweeping reforms, but the new government's nominal gestures toward reform soon disillusioned the demoralized, poverty-stricken Albanians. Unlike the Romanians, they had never revolted and acted out their hatred for the old Communist regime, and, through that, achieved a sense of true participation in a new order. In 1990 and 1991, living conditions deteriorated as the economy and infrastructure collapsed and food became scarce. The dreaded secret police, still in place, began to lose its grip, and as people lost their fear of the authority, crime and random acts of rape became commonplace. Some people tried to flee the country; some staged street protests; others looted and vandalized public buildings. Journalists Miranda Vickers and James Pettifer (1997, 28) described Albanian towns and cities during the "Winter of Anarchy" of 1991–1992 as increasingly dominated by a "radical, violent and confrontational street culture."

In February 1991, crowds looted and set fires in Tirana, the capital. In some ways, this event was a delayed insurgency, a revolutionary attempt to exorcise Hoxha and his brand of Communism, though many years after his death. The bookstore where Hoxha had once worked was burned, and Hoxha's works were used to stoke a huge bonfire in Skenderbeg Square. Government and public property alike became targets for the people's "revenge against communism": schools, hospitals, Communist statues and monuments, and government offices were vandalized (Vickers and Pettifer 1997, 31). Crime spread, and in many parts of the country, the people took the government's failed rhetoric of democracy as license to violently appropriate or destroy all common property. In 1992, the country's entire rail system was closed down after mobs stripped the trains at the Tirana railway stations of their seats and smashed all their fittings. The buses in Tirana had empty sockets where their headlights once were. School classrooms soon lacked seats, windowpanes, and everything else that could be carried away. One student explained to a journalist: "The state has been stealing from us for 45 years. Now it's our turn to steal it all back from the state" (Malcolm 1992, 12).

The extent of destruction indicated that, in Albania, alienation from the state was more severe than in any other ex-Communist country (Malcolm 1992, 11). The looting of public property, a function of opportunism and desperate need, reflected the erosion of identification with civil society and a public commons that had occurred during years of repressive Communist rule. Perhaps the lack of a strong literary tradition, such as that which existed in Romania and East Germany, was a factor. The most dramatic form the alienation took was the wholesale destruction of public property, including libraries and museums. Unable to inspire confidence and improve socio-economic conditions, government officials who had promised to rectify the mistakes of Communism and failed abysmally were voted out of office in multiparty elections in 1992.

The subsequent government, headed by Sali Berisha and the Democratic Party (DP), continued to struggle under the post-Hoxha legacies of Communism: a disintegrating economy, strikes, and shortages of food and electricity. The social welfare net that had been in place was removed, making for a rocky road to capitalism and democracy. People stole telephone wires to enclose their newly acquired land and even the taps from public water fountains. It seemed to some observers that there was a complete breakdown of morality and collective conscience (Vickers and Pettifer 1997, 269). A chronic state of crisis and social conflict had created the survival mode, sometimes seen in war, of everyone for himself or herself. The DP government became increasingly autocratic and enforced a return to a one-party system by using the police to suppress dissent. Initial optimism about the new regime quickly faded, as did residual illusions about the DP's commitment to democracy. In 1996, Berisha and his party were reelected in an election that many Albanians later believed was financed by certain government-condoned pyramid investment schemes that had cost many Albanians their life savings. The collapse of these schemes after the election led to street protests in the major cities and towns. The response of security forces was brutal: protestors, journalists, and political opponents were arrested and tortured. But they could not maintain control. Prisoners broke free from the jails and formed armed gangs that terrorized the population. Many parts of the country descended into anarchy as Albanians fought the police and each other. An estimated 60,000 Albanians were involved in blood feuds (Vickers and Pettifer 1997, 274). Angry Albanians looted police and military arsenals and were soon heavily armed; according to one estimate, half a million *kalashnikov* machine guns fell into civilian hands (AIM 1997). The soldiers refused to fight their own people and went home. Two thousand people would eventually lose their lives in street violence.

By March 1997, the year after the ill-fated election, groups of Albanians were driving through town centers and shooting off their rifles, looting businesses and warehouses, and setting fire to police vehicles, government buildings, schools, theaters, museums, and libraries (Human Rights Watch 1998). In Sarande, a small coastal town, terror reigned when port facilities, boats, the bank, the National Information Center, and the police station were ransacked by mobs and the library and social insurance offices set ablaze ("Armed Bands" 1997). One librarian died trying, in vain, to protect the books in the Berat public library (Sopova 1997, 79). In Vlore, the $7-million Professional Information Center, which had been set up with help from the Danish government, was stormed and set on fire. President Berisha's official villa was ransacked: the looters carried off doors, windows, even flowers from the garden ("Unrest Spreads" 1997). No cultural site escaped the public's rage. The Durres Archaeological Museum was seriously damaged and looted. The ancient site of Butrinti, placed on UNESCO's World Heritage List in 1992, was ransacked; its museum was looted and its records burned (Sopova 1997, 79). The Agricultural University of Kamza, the alma mater of 25,000 agricultural specialists since its opening in 1951, was plundered and destroyed. Losses included the university's 400,000-volume library, which was valued at $4 million ("Albanian President" 1997). The library had been funded by private contributions and was the largest scientific library in Albania.

"What kind of a war is this for heaven's sake?" observers asked (AIM 1997). It had elements of a civil war and an armed rebellion. DP President Berisha claimed it was a revolt by those who wished to return to Communism; someone else posed it as "a war of all against all" (AIM 1997). One journalist concluded that it was none of those and rather "a desperate revolt of a 'protesting party' against economic deception and political autocracy"—in other words, a national revolt that had slipped out of control into anarchy (AIM 1997). Finally, in April 1997, 6,000 United Nations troops came in to stabilize the country, supervise humanitarian relief efforts, and monitor a new election. The Socialist Party won, calm returned, and the UN force left in August.

It could be argued that with a population so alienated from its government and society and frustrated by dismal social and economic conditions, the generalized destruction of libraries was a protest only in form. Lacking the specificity that usually defines true protests, much of Albania's cultural losses seemed to stem from an unfocused insurrection. According to Stanley Cohen's (1973) typology of vandalism, the Albanians may have been indulging in a primitive form of play. It was malicious in that it was a nonspecific attack motivated by hatred or pleasure in destroying, vindictive in that it was carried out as a form of revenge (against a crooked, uncaring regime), and acquisitive in that its destructive actions were aimed (at least in part) at acquiring money or property. It was not primarily ideological, that is, oriented toward a specific social or political cause: the attacks did not target the contents of the collections per se. It was not tactical in the strict sense that it was a considered, planned initiative to reach a goal beyond money, although perhaps implicitly the goal was to bring down the government. But it could be argued that the country's cultural institutions were destroyed as surrogates for the government or state. The biblioclasm that occurred in Albania in the 1990s, attacks by extremists on cultural institutions that represented a despised establishment, may best be characterized as the generalized outburst of a group so profoundly disillusioned and lacking in alternate visions that nihilistic violence seemed the only means of asserting power and control.

The social implosion of Albania was echoed a decade later when Iraqi mobs rampaged in Baghdad in 2003 after the city fell to the Americans. A commentator on National Public Radio pointed out that "looting art and antiquities for profit is part of modern war in the Middle East," and certainly the looting and burning of cultural artifacts was not without precedent in Iraq ("Art World Works" 2003). Iraqi troops had all but picked Kuwait clean during the Gulf War; looting and burning had been the prime means by which the Shiites were ethnically cleansed after their uprising. Thus Saddam had promoted the notion that cultural destruction was acceptable. He has even been accused of fostering a contempt for culture and a gap between people and culture in which an indifference to books played an important part (Mite 2004). Saad Iskander, postinvasion director-general of the national library and archives, later lamented years of neglect at the hand of Saddam's regime: the Ba'thist minister of culture hated the National Library and called it a "cemetery of books" (Mite 2004). Because of attitudes and economic problems, Iraq's university libraries had purchased almost no books since 1990 (USAID 2003).

In Baghdad and throughout Iraq, Saddam's security state kept a lid on the misery that had escalated since the United Nations had initiated post–Gulf War sanctions. Poverty, food shortages, and high infant mortality rates, especially among the Shiite poor, were common. As in Romania, all that had held the country together was a dictator with fearsome powers. For non-Sunni Iraqis who had suffered under Saddam, including the two million Shiites who lived in squalor in the slums of Saddam City, the American invasion and fall of his regime spelled opportunity. In one sense, they were unlikely biblioclasts; being poorly educated, they were unable to appreciate the damage they were doing to their country (McGeough 2003). They were, however, eager for action after decades of oppression, and they swarmed through government buildings, hospitals, and private businesses, stealing everything from bathtubs to ambulances. The looting and vandalism that accompanied it brought more damage to Iraq's civilian infrastructure and economy than had three weeks of American bombing (Chandrasekaran 2003). Once the mobs realized that the American troops were not going to protect cultural institutions, these too became fair game.

Journalist Andrew Lawler (2003, 583) provided this timeline: On April 9, Baghdad fell. On April 10, "thousands of men, women and children, many of them armed with rifles, pistols, axes, knives and clubs, as well as pieces of metal torn from wrecked cars," burst into the grounds of the National Museum

(Burns 2003a, A1) and looted the administrative areas. On April 11, the plundering continued in galleries and storerooms, and on April 12, Iraqis secured the museum and the media arrived. Not until April 16 did the Americans secure the museum. Journalist John Burns (2003b) described Iraqis storming out of the National Museum complex as carrying antiquities in handcarts, bicycles, boxes, and pockets. Left behind were smashed glass cases, shattered ceramics and statues, and torn books. Their burnt-out torches made of rags soaked in gasoline littered the hallways and started some fires. Storerooms and workshops were destroyed, along with archeological records and photographs. It was discovered later that the most important items had been secreted away by the curators, but cavernous storerooms with thousands of unclassified pieces were ransacked, and 10,000 pieces have not been recovered. Unfortunately, no records exist for much of the looted material: some had been excavated in the last decade and not yet processed, and thousands of cuneiform tablets had never been read or translated. "The whole world opens up as a document is deciphered. If it's never read, it's a loss to our collective past," said Gary Vikan, director of Baltimore's Walters Art Museum, in response to Iraqi losses (Holmes and Randerson 2003, 8). The world was stunned as scholars and art enthusiasts contemplated the fate of the remnants of 5,000 years of civilizations: the Sumerians, Akkadians, Assyrians, Persians, Greeks, Parthians, Jews, Sassanians, and Arabs.

All of Baghdad's libraries suffered to varying degrees. The losses would have been even more devastating without preinvasion staff interventions and community involvement. During that week of unfettered pillaging, the National Library was burned twice by fires. It had housed one million books and millions of documents—everything from early Islamic texts that had survived the Mongol sacking of Baghdad in the thirteenth century to modern Iraqi newspapers and periodicals. The National Archives on the second floor, which contained royal court records and documents from the earliest Islamic periods to contemporary times, sustained severe damage (Lemonick at al. 2003). Some losses were prevented when, soon after the fall of Baghdad, a library employee alerted a local Muslim clergyman to the danger; he had manuscripts, books, and randomly selected archives transported to a mosque for safekeeping. The staff at the National Library welded shut a door and saved several floors, but a major section of the front of the building was burnt severely and the infrastructure lost. Books fared better in the fires than archives. UNESCO and outside observers later noted that incendiary materials were used to start the fires, causing some to believe that the destruction was deliberately organized to focus on the archival collections (Deeb, Albin, and Haley 2003). In 2004, Dr. Saad Eskander, new Director of the National Library, stated that Saddam, with the Americans approaching, had ordered employees to burn compromising documents related to his party (Stringer 2004). Although locals looted the archives for quick money, the majority of documents were purged by Saddam's people. Fortunately, some of the rare and important documents had been moved to the Board of Tourism building in the previous months; these survived the looting of Baghdad but were heavily damaged from flooding that resulted from the invasion. According to preliminary UNESCO reports, perhaps 30 percent of the collection was lost.

At the Awqaf Library, the oldest public manuscript collection in Iraq, thousands of manuscripts were packed into metal trunks and moved to secure places. In the chaos, however, 32 trunks were moved back to the library. A ministry driver who was a primary eyewitness to the building's demise described "highly organized and intentional" looting and burning: Arab males in civilian clothes drove up to the library in various vehicles, filmed the removal of 22 trunks, and then used a yellow substance (probably phosphorus) to burn the entire library in less than 15 minutes. The staff members thought the men were Kuwaitis, reasoning that "Iraqis might have stolen the MSS [manuscripts] for personal profit, but they would never have burnt them" (Al-Tikriti 2003). An estimated 600 to 700 manuscripts were lost in the flames. UNESCO estimated that about 40 percent of Awqaf's manuscripts and 90 percent of its printed books were lost (Arnoult 2003). The Saddam House of Manuscripts was another key collection; it contained 50,000 manuscripts with 7,000 gathered from all over the country for an extensive microfilming and digitalization project. Four months before the conflict, manuscripts were taken to one shelter, microfilms to a second, and CD-ROMs to a third (Al-Tikriti 2003). The air-raid shelters had four sets of doors, and looters repeatedly tried to force the doors. People in the neighborhood stood guard, chased away looters, and burned their vehicles.

Anecdotal evidence exists that students, teachers, and neighbors tried to save schools and academic libraries while government buildings burned across the city. A journalist interviewed one student who had intervened when the Baghdad University Islamic Studies building was attacked and set on fire. As Ammar Yaser, a 21-year-old geography major, ran into the building, he saw that the looters were not only looting office equipment but smashing glass cases in the school's museum. The "[l]ooters had ripped off the head off of a stuffed tiger, tore the wings off stuffed birds, even smashed a jar containing a human fetus and left it on the tile floor" (Schofield 2003). When they began heading upstairs, where 20,000 volumes were stored, Yaser confronted the looters, effectively fending them off and guarding the collection for four days until help came.

Institutions without such defenders were openly preyed upon. The Iraqi House of Wisdom, a center for research in the arts and humanities and a repository for Ottoman documents, royal archives, and contemporary documents, was looted and burned. It housed an auditorium, music hall, printing press, computer lab, and libraries of both Western and Middle Eastern publications. Waves of looters made off with an Ottoman costume exhibit and stripped the facilities of everything portable, then stripped the libraries and publication departments of their books (Al-Tikriti 2003). A small manuscript collection (which included a ninth-century Koran) was lost. Many of the books and computers appeared soon after for sale in a nearby square. After an American tank crashed through the front gate of the Iraqi Academy of Science (an independent research facility) and its crew removed the academy's flag and left, looters swarmed in and stripped the building of everything, including electrical fixtures. What makes this incident notable is that some of its books were *not* looted, and the facility itself was *not* burned. The staff attributes this to a lesser degree of organization than that which characterized attacks on other facilities (Al-Tikriti 2003). Even so, 2,000 manuscripts and 58,000 published works went missing, an estimated loss of 80 percent of the collection.

As the anarchy abated, a clearer picture of cultural losses began to emerge. Three major reports appeared in the first year. One, by a UNESCO team led by Inspector General of Libraries Jean-Marie Arnoult, provided many of the figures given above. Another was issued by Nabil Al-Tikriti from the University of Chicago, who visited Iraq from May 25–31, 2003. USAID reported on a libraries and facilities assessment conducted in December 2003. By putting the reports together, a picture emerges of attacks not only in Baghdad, but on manuscripts, archives, and libraries, throughout Iraq. The reports estimated damage and gave the general fate of each institution, indicating whether mobs contented themselves with looting the books and infrastructure or whether they went on to destroy the facility itself. There was a hodgepodge of information available. Although the University of Baghdad Central Library was neither looted nor burned, the Baghdad Medical College Library was looted and lost 8,000 of its most important books. The Baghdad University College of Arts, the only graduate humanities library in the country, was stripped of furnishings, and its entire collection of 175,000 volumes and manuscripts was burned (USAID 2003). The Mustansiriyya University Main Library was looted. Mosul Museum was looted and destroyed, while the Mosul Central University Library lost 30 percent of its books to vandalism and looting but was not burnt (Al-Tikriti 2003). Basra University Library sustained losses of 75 percent. Basra's Islamic Library was looted but not destroyed. The Central Library of Basra was both looted and destroyed, but a librarian saved 30,000 of her books and periodicals—70 percent of the collection—by secretly hiding them in the homes and restaurants of her friends.

Al-Tikriti, UNESCO, and USAID helped to quantify losses, but it is qualitative reports that advance our understanding of motivation, the primary concern of this book. This kind of information came mainly from journalists who spent the postinvasion period taking "the most pathetic of tours" through devastated institutions (Martin 2003). Their interviews with heartbroken curators, caretakers, and ordinary Iraqis often conveyed eyewitness accounts of the pillaging and provided clues as to the motivation of the mob and Iraqi interpretations of their actions. An ineffectual watchman at the looted national theater explained later: "They do these things without thinking because they hate the government. They had guns. What could I do?" ("Ashes to Ashes" 2003). Baha Abdul Rakhman, guard at the shattered Saddam Center of the Arts, said the shouting crowd arrived with axes and iron bars and declared that because there was no government, they could do what they liked and everything belonged to them (Martin 2003). These accounts seem to indicate that the looters took responsibility for their actions. Some Iraqi interviewees made comments that, on the other hand, projected blame onto outsiders and focused on organized greed as the primary impetus. They claimed that the looting was planned and led by U.S.-influenced Kuwaitis or other non-Iraqis bent on stripping the city of everything of value; the fires were set to conceal their robberies. Others felt that the United States had allowed it to happen because it reinforced the U.S. position that the Iraqi people were desperate to be free of Saddam's oppression (Burns 2003a, A1). Even Iraqis skeptical of conspiracy theories were alienated and embittered at the failure of the American troops to stop the looting. Many saw the Americans as the new Mongols, remembering the last time, when Genghis Khan's grandson burnt the city in the thirteenth century, and, according to legend, the Tigris River ran red with blood, then black from the ink of books. It was easier to assign blame to outside forces than to confront the destruction as the opportunistic vandalism of the Iraqi people, committed in play, malice, and vindictiveness. Unlike Albania, Iraq was a nation that prided itself on its literary and cultural heritage. The notion that its people would so quickly resort to antihumanistic nihilism and anarchy was hard to bear.

For Westerners, unfamiliar with Iraqi culture and society under Saddam, the crowds' behavior was inexplicable. We lament the destruction of libraries as the collateral violence of combat, but we can comprehend it on some level. Given the exigencies of war, it is akin to natural disaster. Determination of motives proceeds quite naturally from analysis of destruction based on ethnic conflict (as in India and Sri Lanka), on the vicissitudes of civil war (as in Nigeria), on ideological premises (as in Pol Pot's Cambodia), and on symbolic and revolutionary impulses (as in the purging of Ceauşescu's works in Romania). But it takes a leap of imagination to comprehend the engine of internal cultural devastation as fueled not by ideology or the pursuit of tactical advantage but by anarchy, opportunism, and generalized hatred. To the world audience, the mobs in Iraq seemed a bizarre group of people who had suddenly turned on their own culture. Were Albania's story more widely known, events in Iraq might not have seemed so anomalous to the world. In both Albania and Iraq, the weakened grip of an authoritarian and oppressive regime allowed alienated and impoverished groups to rampage in a process somewhat like the build-up of pressure underground that causes a volcanic eruption. Natural metaphors have also been used to suggest the regressive aspect of this kind of violence: animalistic, a context of survival of the fittest. Civil rampage can be a product of mental and emotional numbness, which may emerge during war with destructive and opportunistic mindsets. But as we saw in pogroms in India, the pillage in Iraq (and Albania) can also be understood as a choice: through vandalism, rampaging Iraqis were protesting against everything that had oppressed them. They were in the grips of nihilism, and this gave their vandalism a definite social orientation, even while it displayed strong affective and cognitive elements.

The book and library destruction that occurred in Romania is evidence that rampage is a choice, though one mediated by cultural inclination. Although brutalized for years by a dictator who imposed austerity through terror, Romanians still had strong literary and cultural predispositions. They saw themselves as responsible actors, not as helpless victims. They had ideological notions that posed books as key to a more just civil society and believed that progress and access to books was personally and socially empowering. They channeled their hatred into hopeful revolutionary zeal rather than impetuous vandalism, and their biblioclasm was contained, symbolic, and iconoclastic. They burned books authored by Ceauşescu and his wife as a sort of emotional exorcism and expected that credible new leaders would emerge and initiate intellectual freedom. In contrast, in Albania, the iconoclastic destruction of Hoxha's works was subsumed in recurrent episodes of rampage that demonstrated disillusionment with the leadership and ideology in general and brutish abandonment of ideas of a cultural commons. In Albania and Iraq in 2003, dangerous renegades were spawned by a regime that had schooled the population in collective values at the expense of individual rights and free will, while promoting militarism and violence and modeling greed and the abuse of power. Both regimes discouraged people from reading books and participating in a civil society. By their corruption, leaders soured their populations on using ideas and reason as a path to social reform. After shaking off totalitarian controls, the population had few leaders who could supply vision and integrity and counter disillusionment, foster hope, and provide a vision that accorded cultural institutions and artifacts a socially important role. Not for them, the heady pleasures of dismantling institutions so as to build anew; instead, they became nihilists, who believed that nothing matters very much, passive about pursuing reform and assertive about seeking advantage. This is a definite step on the path to affective and cognitive forms of vandalism. In the end, for many, vandalism may have boiled down to the numb opportunism usually seen in war. In Baghdad, an Associated Press correspondent watched a bearded 41-year-old man going through old bound newspapers and tearing out pages with illustrations that appealed to him: "I came yesterday to see the chaos, and when I saw it, I decided to take what I could" (Hanley 2003).

REFERENCES

Akinsha, Konstantin, and Kozlov, Grigorii. 1995. *Beautiful Loot: The Soviet Plunder of Europe's Art Treasures*. New York: Random House.

"Albanian President Visits Agricultural University." 1997. *Albanian Telegraphic Agency News*, September 9, 1997. http://www.telpress.it/ata/1997%5Csep_97%5Chadarch09.htm.

Al-Tikriti, Nabil. 2003. *Iraq Manuscript Collections, Archives, and Libraries*. Situation Report. Oriental Institute, University of Chicago. http://www-oi.uchicago.edu/OI/IRAQ?docs/nat.html. June 8, 2003.

Anafulu, Joseph C. 1971. "An African Experience: The Role of a Specialized Library in a War Situation." *Special Libraries* 62 (1):32–40.

"Armed Bands Cause Terror in Sarande." 1997. *Albanian Telegraphic Agency News*, March 2, 1997. http://www.telpress.it/ata/1997%5Cmars_97%5Chdarch02.htm.

Arnoult, Jean-Marie. 2003. *Assessment of Iraqi Cultural Heritage: Libraries and Archives.* UNESCO Contract (926 00 00 526A) Report. http://www.Ifla.org/VI/4/admin/iraq2207.pdf. June 27–July 6, 2003.

"Art World Works to Recover Looted Iraq Antiquities." 2003. *National Public Radio, Morning Edition*, April 16, 2003.

"Ashes to Ashes, Books to Dust." *Los Angeles Times*, April 19, 2003. http://www.theage.com.au/cgi-bin/common/popupPrint Articles.pl?path = /articles/2003/04/18.

Burns, C. Delisle. 1933. "Militarism." In *Encyclopedia of the Social Sciences*, Vol. 10, eds. Edwin R. A. Seligman and Alvin Johnson. New York: Macmillan, 446–451.

Burns, John L. 2003a. "Baghdad Residents Begin a Long Climb to an Ordered City." *New York Times*, 14 April, p. A1.

Burns, John. L. 2003b. "Looters Make Off with Treasures of Iraqi Museum." *Honolulu Star-Bulletin*, 13 April, p. A1.

Carlton, Eric. 1990. *War and Ideology.* Savage, Md.: Barnes and Noble Books.

Chamberlain, Russell. 1983. *Loot: The Heritage of Plunder.* New York: Facts on File.

Chandrasekaran, Rajiv. 2003. "Iraqi Curator Appalled by Looting: Priceless Antiquities Protected from War but Lost to Vandals." *Honolulu Advertiser*, April 13, p. A5.

Codrescu, Andrei. 1991. *The Hole in the Flag: A Romanian Exile's Story of Return and Revolution.* New York: William Morrow.

Cohen, Stanley. 1973. "Property Destruction: Motives and Meanings." In *Vandalism*, ed. Colin Ward. London: Architectural Press, 23–53.

Conquest, Robert. 1970. *The Nation Killers: The Soviet Deportation of Nationalities.* New York: Macmillan.

Davis, Donald G. Jr., and Cheng Huanwen. 1997. "The Destruction of a Great Library: China's Loss Belongs to the World." *American Libraries* 28 (9):60–62.

De St. Jorre, John. 1972. *The Brother's War: Biafra and Nigeria.* Boston: Houghton Mifflin.

Deeb, Mary-Jane, Michael Albin, and Alan Haley. 2003. *The Library of Congress and the Cultural Property Office of the U.S. Department of State Mission to Baghdad.* Report on the National Library and the House of Manuscripts. http://www.oi.uchicago.edu/OI/IRAQ/mela/LCIraqReport. October 27–November 3, 2003.

Enu, Cosmas E. 1970. "The Effects of the Nigerian Civil War on the Library Services in the Former Eastern Region." *Libri* 20 (3):206–217.

Fedoruk, Alexander. 1997. In *The Spoils of War: World War II and Its Aftermath: The Loss, Reappearance, and Recovery of Cultural Property*, ed. Elizabeth Simpson. New York: Harry N. Abrams, 72–76.

Fisk, Robert. 2002. "Something Evil Has Visited Kuwait City." In *The Saddam Hussein Reader: Selections from Leading Writers on Iraq*, ed. Turi Munthe. New York: Thunder's Mouth Press, 288–291.

Flood, John L. 2002. "Varieties of Vandalism." *Common Knowledge* 8 (2):366–386.

Galloway, George, and Bob Wylie. 1991. *Downfall: The Ceausescus and the Romanian Revolution.* London: Futura.

Greenfield, Jeanette. 1995. *The Return of Cultural Treasures.* Second Edition. New York: Cambridge University Press.

Grimsted, Patricia Kennedy. 2001. *Trophies of War and Empire: The Archival Heritage of Ukraine, World War II, and the International Politics of Restitution.* Cambridge, Mass.: Harvard University Press.

Hanley, Charles J. 2003. "Looters Ransack Iraq's National Library." *Yahoo!News.* http://www.story.new.yahoo.com/news?tmpl = story2&cid = 540&e = 1&u = /ap/20030415/ap-on-r. April 15, 2003.

Hobsbawm, Eric. 1993. "The New Threat to History." *New York Review of Books* 40 (21):62–64.

Holmes, Bob, and James Randerson. 2003. "Humble Clay Tablets Are Greatest Loss to Science." *New Scientist* 178 (2394):8.

Honan, William H. 1997. "Journalist on the Case." In *The Spoils of War: World War II and Its Aftermath: The Loss, Reappearance, and Recovery of Cultural Property,* ed. Elizabeth Simpson. New York: Harry N. Abrams, 153–155.

Human Rights Watch. 1998. "Albania: Human Rights Developments." Report. http://www.hrw.org/worldreport/Helsinki-01.

Kaye, Lawrence M. 1997. "Laws in Force at the Dawn of World War II: International Conventions and National Laws. " In *The Spoils of War: World War II and Its Aftermath: The Loss, Reappearance, and Recovery of Cultural Property,* ed. Elizabeth Simpson. New York: Harry N. Abrams, 100–105.

Kline, Thomas R. 1997. "Legal Issues Relating to the Recovery of the Quedlinburg Treasures." In *The Spoils of War: World War II and Its Aftermath: The Loss, Reappearance, and Recovery of Cultural Property,* ed. Elizabeth Simpson. New York: Harry N. Abrams, 156–158.

Knuth, Rebecca. 2003. *Libricide: The Regime-Sponsored Destruction of Books and Libraries in the Twentieth Century.* Westport, Conn.: Praeger.

Korte, Willi. 1997. "Search for the Treasures." In *The Spoils of War: World War II and Its Aftermath: The Loss, Reappearance, and Recovery of Cultural Property,* ed. Elizabeth Simpson. New York: Harry N. Abrams, 150–152.

Lang, Kurt. 1968. "Military." In *International Encyclopedia of the Social Sciences,* Vol. 10, ed. David L. Sills. New York: Macmillan Company and Free Press, 305–312.

Lani, Remzi. 1997. "Albania: May 1997 Report." http://www.balkansnet.org/albania1. html. May 22, 1997.

Lawler, Andrew. 2003. "Mayhem in Mesopotamia" *Science* 301 (5633):582–88.

Lemonick, Michael D., Andrea Dorfman, Aparisim Ghosh, Adam Smith, Grant Rosenberg, and Elaine Shannon. 2003. "Lost to the Ages." *Time Europe* 161 (17):34–37.

"Librarians Rally in Bucharest to Protect Romanian Libraries." 1990. *American Libraries* 21 (3):180.

Malcolm, Noel. 1992. " Property Is Still Theft." *Spectator* 268 (8542):11–12.

Maldis, Adam. 1997. "The Tragic Fate of Belarusan Museum and Library Collections during the Second World War." In *The Spoils of War: World War II and Its Aftermath: The Loss, Reappearance, and Recovery of Cultural Property,* ed. Elizabeth Simpson. New York: Harry N. Abrams, 77–80.

Martin, Susan Taylor. 2003. "Baghdad Museum Now Image of Destruction." *St. Petersburg Times,* April 25, 2003. http://www.sptimes.com/2003/04/25/news_pf/columns/Baghdad_museum_now_im.shtml/.

McGeough, Paul. 2003. "Rich Past Stripped as Future in Tatters." *Sydney Morning Herald.* April 14, 2003. http://www.smh.com.au/articles/2003/04/13/1050172478179.html.

Melson, Robert F. 1996. "The Armenian Genocide as Precursor and Prototype of Twentieth-Century Genocide." In *Is the Holocaust Unique?*, ed. Alan S. Rosenbaum. Boulder, Colo.: Westview Press, 87–99.

Middle East Watch. 1992. *Endless Torment: The 1991 Uprising in Iraq and Its Aftermath.* New York: Human Rights Watch.

Mite, Valentinas. 2004. "Iraq: Years of Ba'athist Rule Leave Legacy of Indifference to Books." *Radio Free Europe/Radio Liberty.* http://www.rferl.org/featuresarticleprint/2004/07/a8439cf9–3d9e-48b5–9bd0–4aadf53f767a. July 12, 2004.

Nwafor, B. U. 1971. "Recorded Knowledge: A War Casualty." *Library Journal* 96 (1):42–45.

Okpa-Iroha, N. 1971. "Reconstruction of Devastated Library Services in War Affected Areas of Nigeria." *Library Association Record* 73 (6):108–109.

Oluwakuyide, Akinola. 1972. "Nigerian Libraries after the War." *Wilson Library Bulletin* 46 (10):881–882, 947.

O'Toole, James. 1993. "The Symbolic Significance of Archives." *American Archivist* 56 (2):234–255.

Radway, Laurence I. 1968. "Militarism." In *International Encyclopedia of the Social Sciences*, Vol. 10, ed. David L. Sills. New York: Macmillan Company and Free Press, 300–305.

"Romanian Libraries after the Revolution." 1990. *Library Journal* 115 (13):881–882, 947.

Schofield, Matthew. 2003. "Damage Would Have Been Worse, If Not for Ardent Volunteers." *San Jose Mercury News*, April 26, 2003. http://www.bayarea.com/mld/mercurynews/news/special_packages/iraq/5722653.htm

Sopova, Jasmina. 1997. "Albania's Threatened Heritage." *UNESCO Courier* 50 (718):79.

Stringer, Ian. 2004. Posted Notes from a Speech by Dr. Saad Eskander, Director of the Iraq National Library, at the Internet Librarian International 2004 Conference. iliglist@yahoogroups.com. November 9, 2004.

UNESCO (Memory of the World Program). 1996. *Lost Memory: Libraries and Archives Destroyed in the Twentieth Century.* Paris: UNESCO.

"Unrest Spreads in Albania Despite PM's Removal." 1997. *Albanian Telegraphic Agency News*, March 2, 1997. http://www.hri.org/news/balkans/ata/1997/97–03–02.ata.html.

USAID. 2003. *Libraries and Facilities Assessment: Baghdad Visit 17–22 December, 2003.* USAID-Iraq HEAD Report. http://www.stonybrook.edu/usaidhead/04–01A.htm. December 17–22, 2003.

Vickers, Miranda, and James Pettifer. 1997. *Albania: From Anarchy to a Balkan Identity.* New York: New York University Press.

CHAPTER 10

Errors of Omission and Cultural Destruction in Iraq, 2003

> Every nationalist is capable of the most flagrant dishonesty, but he is also—since he is conscious of serving something bigger than himself—unshakeably certain of being in the right.
> —George Orwell, "Notes on Nationalism"

In the last 60 years, political protestors have destroyed scholarly institutes in Germany and the Netherlands. Hindus have attacked Muslim books in India, and Muslim militants have shredded the written works of Kashmir's Hindus. The Sinhalese in Sri Lanka burned the distinguished Tamil library; Saddam's forces obliterated Shiite libraries in Iraq; and the Taliban destroyed Afghanistan's secular and Persian works. Economic and social breakdown in Albania in the 1990s and a power vacuum in Iraq in 2003 led to looting and vandalism by disillusioned and frustrated crowds retaliating against oppressive establishments. The logic of total war resulted in the obliteration of cities and their libraries in World War II. In previous chapters, we have visited the French Revolution as an antecedent to the Nazis' racist destruction of Jewish and Polish texts and other egregious cases of libricide, and we have moved forward in time, employing a sociological lens to consider modern book destruction that falls within the realm of vandalism. In each case, the havoc-wreaker is extremism, the greatest modern threat to preservation of the written record. Time and again, destruction has been committed by extremists on the grounds that books and libraries are repositories of antithetical doctrines and tools of establishments that they despise. Driving this destruction was grievance of one kind or another, often empowered by righteousness. The transformation of ideas into ideology, and subsequently into political objectives, created a blueprint for action. Repeatedly, this action took the form of systemic campaigns to eradicate texts that denied the extremists' truth and institutions that supported alternate systems of power and social influence. To extremists, culture is an entity requiring guidance and, when necessary, purification in the name of orthodoxy and a greater good. The social violence involved in purification was justified by the promise of a triumphant good and the enactment of its potential to transform so-called sick societies.

Ethnic and political rivalry, civil unrest, and war between nations are conditions that fan the flames of extremism and permit leaders to further rationalize acts of cultural destruction. In localized conflicts, small collections of books can fall prey to protestors seeking symbolic targets. The danger is especially acute during widespread civil conflict. Typically, law enforcement breaks down, riots occur, and mobs act out their frustration on public institutions. Full-scale war creates combat conditions in which the survival of books and libraries becomes problematic; total war, of course, leads to widespread cultural devastation, whether through collateral losses or programs of ethnic cleansing and colonization for which war serves as a cover. Few belief systems in the twentieth century were impervious to the seductive powers of extreme ideas. More than once, aggressive rogue states set into play parallel militaristic and nationalistic, even racist, mindsets that also drew the leadership of their opponents into extremism. In the fog of war, fears concerning cultural survival caused even democratic leaders to adopt policies that compromised their humanistic foundation. When leaders are confronted by the perceived exigencies of modern war, military thinking drifts toward militarism, and this often results in the commissioned and collateral destruction of books and libraries (libricide and strategic bombing), but also destruction by default—errors of omission. It was errors of omission by the U.S. administration that made possible the Iraqi people's looting and destruction of their own books and libraries in 2003.

In Chapter 9, I characterized the majority of Iraqi looters and vandals as being in the grip of anarchy, opportunism, and revolutionary iconoclasm. I focused on the actions and possible motivations of the perpetrators, the rabble as biblioclasts. But there is more to the picture of what happened after the fall of Baghdad. In the pattern of rationalization that is particular to extremists, the American government justified its attack on Iraq on the basis of self-defense and used military action to assuage the fear and sense of violation caused by the September 11, 2001, attacks on New York's World Trade Center and the Pentagon. The campaign was presented first as a defensive, preemptive strike against a dangerous foe who possessed weapons of mass destruction and harbored terrorists; and, second, as a way of bringing democracy to the beleaguered Iraqi people. These formulations made the campaign palatable to many Americans who may otherwise have objected to the unprovoked invasion of another nation. Posing the United States as "at war" justified the urgency of militaristic mandates and allowed "softer" considerations, such as social and moral responsibility, to be set aside.

During the period leading up to the American invasion of Iraq, prominent coalitions of experts foresaw and publicly warned of the danger of cultural devastation. On March 26, 2003, 10 institutions and 130 scholars and heritage managers from all over the world signed the Archaeological Institute of America's "Open Declaration on Cultural Heritage at Risk in Iraq" ("Editorial" 2003, 222). It was an attempt to pressure the U.S. government and its allies to proactively protect Iraq's cultural legacy in the event of war. The statement urged all governments to recognize that fragile cultural heritage is inevitably damaged by warfare and to respect and protect cultural sites. It pointed out the value of Iraq's cultural heritage both to the Iraqi people and the world. This was but one of many warnings. The International Council of Museums warned of the possibility of pillage and cited the looting of 7 out of 12 of Iraq's regional museums in civilian disorders at the end of the Gulf War. The statement of the International Committee of the Blue Shield, which represents nongovernmental organizations in the fields of archives, libraries, monuments and sites, and museums, urged combatants to protect Iraq's cultural resources and fend off losses to the historical record. The Blue Shield organization, charged with the protection of cultural sites (a mission parallel to that of the Red Cross but directed at protecting cultural, not medical, sites), advised adherence to the 1954 Hague Convention for the Protection of Cultural Property in the Event of Armed Conflict. The Society of American Archivists and Association of Canadian Archivists issued statements asking that the protection of documentary history be a priority, so as to safeguard the rights and freedom of Iraqi citizens. Two weeks before the fall of Baghdad, the Pentagon office charged with rebuilding Iraq, the Office of Reconstruction and Humanitarian Assistance, sent a five-page memo to senior commanders at the Coalition Forces Land Component (Martin 2003; Lawler 2003). This memo urged them to protect the Iraqi National Museum (second on the list) and 15 other sites from looting. The State Department's Bureau of Near Eastern Affairs was putting together a group to protect cultural sites once Iraq was secured. "But it was too late. The war's progress overtook the State Department's efforts" (Witt 2003).

Despite all the warnings, the administration of George W. Bush and his military leadership made no plans for protection of cultural heritage immediately following the collapse of Saddam's government. With the fall of Baghdad on April 9, mobs swarmed into public institutions and looted, smashed, and burned with abandon for five days. Shocked journalists reported from Iraq on the chaos and losses, which in the first few days seemed of horrific proportions. Lawlessness reigned throughout the country as throngs of Iraqis sacked offices, businesses, hospitals, and cultural institutions and made away with "everything from porcelain bathtubs and police uniforms to forklifts and ambulances" (Chandrasekaran 2003). In Mosul, despite the fact that the mosques pleaded for an end to anarchy, citizens set fire to the government printing office and ransacked the Mosul University Library and its ancient manuscript collection. After the city fell, as the troops rolled in, residents shouted at them: "Why are you so late?" (Espo 2003). The anarchy in Baghdad resulted in devastating losses as Iraq's prestigious national collections were decimated. Iraqi librarians, curators, and staff noted that, although there were insufficient troops to control the entire city, the American troops capably defended those facilities that they had been ordered to protect: the Ministry of Oil, Palestine Hotel, Sheraton Hotel, the airport, the Republic Palace, and other locations deemed strategic. Iraqi Academy of Science staff members reported that when an American tank crashed through the institution's front gate and its crew removed the Iraqi flag at the entrance and then left, it was seen as essentially an invitation to looters (Al-Tikriti 2003). When they were asked to protect the National Library, U.S. soldiers informed the librarians that "our orders do not extend to protecting this facility" and that "we are soldiers, not policemen" (Al-Tikriti 2003). Frantic officials begged Jay Garner, the lieutenant general in charge of setting up an interim government, to prevent more looting: "The battle of Baghdad was so easy for you. Why is this so hard?" (Kniffel 2003, 40). According to an April 11 Associated Press article, command center officials in Qatar said that they had expected a release of pent-up anger at a regime that had brutalized and repressed the population for decades (Jelinek 2003). Commanders also said that the U.S. forces did not intend to crack down on looting in Iraq because doing so might alienate the Iraqi people they were trying to win over (Hess 2003).

Their reticence seemed to have the opposite effect. The cultural losses struck a deep chord with educated Iraqis to whom the country's history and intellectual traditions were important. These Iraqis held the troops directly responsible for the losses, and the U.S. administration lost ground in its attempts to win their hearts and minds. "This is not a liberation; this is a humiliation," Iraqi archeologist Raid Abdul Ridhar Muhammad told a journalist, "If a civilization is looted, its history ends. Please tell this to President Bush" (Griffiths 2003). Although many Iraqis expressed relief at the overthrow of their despotic leader, others felt the cure was worse than the disease. Gailan Ramiz, a Princeton-educated professor at Baghdad University, sought out reporters to make his statement: "I believe the United States has committed an act of irresponsibility with few parallels in history, with [allowing] the looting of the National Museum, the National Library and so many of the ministries. People are saying that the U.S. wanted this—that it allowed all this to happen because it wanted the symbolism of ordinary Iraqis attacking every last token of Saddam Hussein's power" (Burns 2003, A1). This claim, that there was a deliberate motive for the troops' refusal to protect Iraqi cultural institutions, was supported by journalists' reports that in Basra, British officers who allowed the looting of Ba'ath party buildings, which housed important administrative documents, stated that this was a way to demonstrate to the Iraqi people that the party had lost control of the city (Human Rights Watch 2003). Numerous interviews with Iraqis indicated that American troops were being condemned in the tribunal of popular opinion in Iraq. On April 14, a journalist spoke with a group of Iraqi professionals who had volunteered to help get utilities back up in Baghdad (McGeough 2003).

Engineer Abbas Reta commented: "I've seen nothing new [in terms of the promised democracy and relief from Saddam's police state] since Saddam's fall. All that we have seen is looting. The Americans are responsible. One round from their guns and all the looting would have stopped." Another engineer agreed: "[T]hey are letting thieves take everything from the Iraqi people." During the course of the interview, as another tank went by, ignoring the looting that was going on, Fouad Abdulla Ahmed bitterly observed: "The army of America is like Genghis Khan. America is not good and Saddam is not good. My people refused Saddam, and they will refuse the Americans" (McGeough 2003).

The first media reports to reach the United States reported unrestrained and ongoing looting of Iraq's national collections. For example, the entire collection of the National Museum, 170,000 precious artifacts of world history, including the earliest examples of writing, were reported as having been carried off or smashed. The National Archives and National Library were reported as twice victimized, first by looters and then by arsonists. Reporters wrote that they watched helplessly as Iraqi looters came back for more books and artifacts, and some criticized the administration for lack of planning. According to one, "The U.S.-led forces invaded Iraq at a time of America's choosing, but they arrived in Baghdad with insufficient boots on the ground to impose law and order in a city where pent-up anger and frustration [were] always going to erupt; or to protect the fabric of this society and the ancient ones that predate it" (McGeough 2003).

In the United States, appalled scholars wrote e-mails, signed petitions, and made appearances on television and radio programs. They stressed the importance to world culture of Iraq's heritage. An American Library Association (2003) statement lamented the losses: "Cultural heritage is as important as oil. Libraries are a cornerstone of democracy and are vital resources in the re-establishment of a civil society." On April 11, as the looting in Baghdad raged without check, UNESCO Director-General Koichiro Matsuura exhorted U.S. authorities to protect Iraq's sites and cultural institutions. Matsuura cited UNESCO's recent experience in other war-torn situations, which had shown that "culture can play a key role in consolidating the peace process, restoring national unity and building hope for the future" (UNESCO 2003). Globally, scholars, librarians, archivists, and heritage managers listed the treasures that were presumed lost and mourned the loss of the tools with which societies study the past and fashion their future (Mehegan 2003). It was not easy to articulate exactly what had been lost. Eminent book historian Robert Darnton (2003, B01) pointed out: "libraries and archives, museums and excavations, scraps of paper and shards of pottery provide all we can consult in order to reconstruct the worlds we have lost. The loss of a library or a museum can mean the loss of contact with a vital strain of humanity." It is only by studying the actual words and possessions of our ancestors that we can learn what they considered important and how they organized their lives (Holmes and Randerson 2003). The recovery of individual tablets from a decimated collection is never a full recovery of meaning; their dispersal has often stripped them of their provenance and disrupted their substantiation via context, the day-to-day life of citizens of an ancient civilization (Waldbaum 2003). Without recorded knowledge tied to a specific place and group, a complex society cannot perform the constant reassessment crucial for the task of "knowing who you are by knowing who you were. That kind of knowledge must be continuously reworked. Destroy the possibility of replenishing it, and you can strangle a civilisation" (Darnton 2003, B1). All these attempts to pinpoint the real ramifications of the losses pointed to one clear premise. The loss of records and archives would hinder the development of a new civil society for Iraq and would hold back the nation's progress in joining the international community.

Voices of the press and concerned individuals became strident as the U.S. government refused to address the looting of cultural objects. It seemed incongruous to critics that the military had time to topple statues and chip away at a disrespectful mural of former President George Bush on the floor of the Al Rashid Hotel, yet claimed to have insufficient resources to save the national collections (Manier 2003). Dominance, rather than leadership and stewardship, seemed the primary concern of the troops and their leaders. On April 16, in the highly charged aftermath of the fall of Baghdad, the Boston-based American Schools of Oriental Research compared the museum looting to the sack of Constantinople, the burning of the Library at Alexandria, and the ravages of the conquistadors (Lawler 2003). In an April 20 *New York Times* article, Maureen Dodd described U.S. leaders as "swaggering like Goths as Iraq's cultural heritage goes up in flames" (Garrett 2003, 52). Although perhaps hyperbolic, such comments rightly pointed out a tone of conquest on the part of the Americans, which may have something to do with the humiliation Iraqis describe feeling about the looting. Studies of rape in war have shown that war can create a psychological backdrop for expression of preexisting ideas of contempt (Miranda 2005). There is an aspect of cultural destruction that emotionally is like the humiliation and vulnerability a rape victim feels at being physically conquered. It causes us to ask whether the egregious behavior of military guards at Abu Grabi was another example of contempt. Did the cultural devastation that was permitted in Iraq have anything to do with preexisting attitudes among American leaders toward Iraqis and Iraqi culture? What part did the cultural destruction play in demonstrating American might and superiority, and did the pillage, in some measure, contribute to a disrespect for Iraqis among U.S. troops?

UNESCO, the cultural arm of the United Nations, and other national and international groups were involved in some quick responses to the devastation—responses that were in sharp contrast to those of Bush officials, who brushed off the cultural destruction as insignificant. When experts met at UNESCO headquarters in Paris on April 17 to discuss the losses, they publicly denounced the destruction and looting and rhetorically invoked the Hague Convention. Plans were made to deploy curators and conservators to help repair what was left of Iraq's cultural heritage. The International

Council on Archives, the International Federation of Library Associations and Institutions, and the International Councils of Museums each issued statements calling for the protection of Iraqi culture. Human Rights Watch urged the preservation of government records to ensure property rights, to counter claims that could trigger ethnic violence, and to use in future trials of Saddam's officials for crimes against the Iraqi people (Human Rights Watch 2003). These calls for action received little response.

The international community and the Iraqi people were not alone in condemning the American leadership for failing to address the civil breakdown that had been predicted to be the result of deposing Saddam's regime. Some within the Bush administration quit and went public with their disgust. On April 14, Martin E. Sullivan (2003, 15), Chairman of the President's Advisory Committee on Cultural Property (normally charged with export violations), resigned in symbolic protest over the "wanton and preventable destruction" of culture in Iraq. Sullivan (2003, 15) explained: "While our military forces have displayed extraordinary precision and restraint in deploying arms— and apparently in securing the Oil Ministry and oil fields—they have been nothing short of impotent in failing to attend to the protection of [Iraq's] cultural heritage."

American officials struggled in responding to questions about security policies and priorities, such as whether or not the looting had been expected and whether there had been a plan to deal with postinvasion security problems. They contradicted themselves repeatedly, no doubt because there was no clear way to shift responsibility and satisfactorily address criticism. If they said that they had anticipated looting, then their failure to curtail it was revealed to be a tactical choice. If they claimed the looting was unexpected, then, in light of all the warnings, the administration opened itself up to accusations of criminal negligence. Secretary of Defense Donald Rumsfeld rebutted the suggestion that the Americans did not have a plan to deal with civil disturbance ("Donald Rumsfeld" 2003), yet no plan for restoring order was put forward. During the days of heavy looting (April 9–15), it seemed as if Pentagon officials were simply waiting for the looting to die on its own (Sandalow 2003). Richard Myers, Chair of the Joint Chiefs of Staff, stated that protection for cultural institutions had been a consideration, but it was assigned less importance than ongoing combat operations. He pointed out that at the same time the museums were being looted, American soldiers were being wounded and dying. The military's priority was, of course, "to finish the combat task" (Lemonick et al. 2003). Officers said they stuck to the war plan, securing oil wells and infrastructure ahead of the main advance, and upon arriving in Baghdad, they immediately secured the oil ministry (Craig 2003). As a *San Francisco Chronicle* editorial pointed out, a "regrettable, if unintended" message was sent to Iraqis and all Arabs, already skeptical of the Americans' motives: protecting civilians, hospitals, and cultural centers was apparently not a priority (Ryan 2003). Individual officers and troops on the ground repeatedly stated that they did not see policing as an appropriate role for the troops, an indicator that cultural awareness in war theory was still primarily rhetorical and that the military was trained for traditional warfare rather than for total war and new types of military interventions.

In the five days after the fall of Baghdad, the world press published commentaries charging crimes against history and humanity. Images of Iraqis looting banks, libraries, and hospitals were broadcast around the clock, and the International Red Cross warned of a humanitarian crisis. During the same time, Rumsfeld went on record as saying that looting was "unfortunate"; that "bad things happen in life, and people do loot" (Craig 2003). Rumsfeld redirected criticism to the media for overstating what was isolated looting and exaggerating the extent of the damage. He complained that the media's focus on anarchy detracted from the fact that the country was being liberated. Freedom, after all, is "untidy," and "free people are free to make mistakes and commit crimes and do bad things" (Ryan 2003). Rumsfeld's refusal to acknowledge the extent of the losses and his lack of empathy for the Iraqi people was troubling to many, as was his apparent lack of awareness of any global loss and violation of the world as a community. American social commentator Molly Ivins (2003, A13) found his comments "embarrassing":

Does no one in this administration have any manners?. . . . When something even more horrible happens in the course of war . . . what we say is: "What a terrible thing. We're so sorry that happened. Even though it was not our fault, we—like all civilized people—regret and mourn the irreplaceable loss to the history of civilization." That's all we have to say. It is not necessary to become defensive and react as though the looting were some attack on one's professional competence, and it is certainly not necessary to become sarcastic and try to belittle the loss.

Rumsfeld's defensiveness and rigidity reflected poorly on the values of an administration seeking acceptance as liberators and crusaders against tyranny. The administration celebrated media images of Iraqis toppling statues of Saddam and embracing coalition troops, because these images seemed to reinforce the "rightness" of its war. In its eyes, the images demonstrate that the invasion was about achieving freedom for oppressed Iraqis and that America was a friend to the Arab people and would help them to create a better society. Pictures of looting had a much darker message: the anarchy indicated that a significant number of Iraqis were not buying into the notion of "freedom" and better times to come. They were seizing the moment. Rumsfeld's refusal to seriously address the issue of looting was a choice that might have been tied in with the U.S. leadership's need to be perceived as conducting a legitimate war: images of looting contradicted Iraqis' identification with the U.S. leadership's projections. By denying the importance of the looting, Rumsfeld was defending notions of Iraqi support for the war. And it may be that the looting simply was not perceived as affecting American interests. Rumsfeld's comments to the press made transparent a value system in which his nation's interests were accorded absolute primacy: this focus on reasons of state, so common in wartime, was an indicator of high levels of militarism and nationalism. When asked at an April 15 news briefing, just after looting had peaked, if lessons had already been learned from the war, Rumsfeld said the Defense Department could improve and become more efficient "so that it best serves the American people and our values and our principles" ("Donald Rumsfeld" 2003). It is a clear statement that war was perceived by America's leaders as an instrument of self-interest, not the ideals of freedom they claimed.

It was apparent that Rumsfeld was accurately portraying a prevalent conservative diminishment of the importance of Iraq's cultural losses and portrayal of the media as hysterical. On April 11, in a tense news conference during a period when the looting dominated the news, Rumsfeld dismissed the media by calling them "Henny Pennies," a reference to a children's tale in which the main character runs around, declaring that the sky is falling. In a Fox News recap of this press conference, conservative commentators focused not on Rumsfeld's comments, but on the questions about looting to which he was responding. These questions, they said, lacked historical perspective and were the product of some sort of media meltdown. The looting was described as merely a sideshow that distracted from the triumph of "the most amazing military success in human history" (Hume et al. 2003). As reports appeared in May and June that, in fact, many of the most valuable articles and manuscripts had been saved by curators and volunteers, conservative commentators began to joke about the looting and characterize the uproar as an "example of academic exaggeration, media gullibility, and Iraqi mendacity" (Lawler 2003). On May 9, 2003, while 10,000 catalogued objects from the National Museum were listed as missing (most are still missing as of 2005) and experts were busy evaluating the condition of shattered institutions, Rumsfeld went on record as denying the looting altogether and claiming victim status for the military. Criticism of the military for failing to stop the looting of antiquities, he said, would have been a "bum rap," even if the items had been looted. He did concede that the loss of irreplaceable antiquities from the National Museum would have been a "terrible thing" if it had happened (Agence France Presse 2003). There was an effort to pose the pillage as a "non-event." John Podhertz in the *New York Post* "reported" that the original count of 170,000 objects lost had plummeted to a figure that could be counted on "two hands and two feet" (Lawler 2003). Margaret Beckett, the British Minister of Rural Affairs, announced on June 29 that the looting of the National Museum was now considered to be "a pack of lies," and that things thought to be stolen had actually been stored away before the war began (Carver 2003, 442). Denial of the magnitude of losses was tied in with a defensive attitude toward any criticism of the invasion. As mentioned above, the looting raised too many questions about America's rationale for war and the invasion's legitimacy.

On June 13, a *Washington Post* editorial entitled "Hoaxes, Hype and Humiliation" accused the media, Western and Arab alike, of parroting false numbers provided by Iraqi officials in order to make the United States look bad, even criminal (Lawler 2003). In the article, conservative journalists characterized the liberal media as supposedly desperate to highlight the dark side of the liberation of Iraq, and thus willing to suspend skepticism about the scale of looting and indulge in "deeply satisfying antiwar preening" (Krauthammer 2003, A29). Charles Krauthammer, the author of the piece, saw lamentations about the cultural rape of Baghdad as narcissistic snobbery that hypocritically gave greater importance to the destruction of a museum (which he claimed did not even happen) than to the toppling of Saddam's sadistic regime and the liberation of 25 million people. Krauthammer (2003, A29) condemned criticism of the looting as an expression of the "cheapest instincts of the antiwar left." He said that the left, which had done everything it could to prevent the war, had been "shamed" by the jubilation of Iraqis upon their liberation and had therefore used criticism of looting as a ploy to change the subject and taint the victory. Overall, conservatives deflected criticism of the invasion by charging American dissenters with being unsupportive of the troops and unpatriotic; foreign criticism was dismissed as the product of anti-Americanism. This approach was one often taken by extremists in the past.

Bush officials assumed no moral responsibility for the cultural losses that had occurred. By accusing academics and the media of hysterical overreaction and dismissing the furor over looting as a "convenient liberal tool to criticise the war" (Lawler 2003), the government and its supporters redirected public attention away from critics' claims that the Bush administration had been guilty, at the very least, of criminal neglect. In an April 15 article in the *Chicago Tribune*, journalist Phillip Kennicut (2003, C1) pondered the possibility of "a darker side of American pragmatism":

When Rumsfeld accused the press of being Henny-Pennys he was taking a pragmatic view of war and its consequences. Others might call it the omelet theory of war: Some eggs get broken—get over it. Pragmatism looks to the hard details of the matter, not to high-minded abstractions. At its best, it keeps the mind focused on the real and tangible facts of the world. At its worst, it becomes a philosophy scornful of higher ideals.

Inasmuch as they would acknowledge any destruction at all to culture, conservatives laid moral responsibility squarely on the Iraqis (Pipes 2003). Frenzied cultural theft and self-destruction is rare, they claimed, citing as a single precedent the Iraqi action in Kuwait in 1990–1991. Conservative media figures, no doubt influenced by what had happened in Kuwait, explained the pillage as a "possibly unique Iraqi penchant for cultural self-hatred" and the "excesses of a country singularly prone to violence against itself" (Pipes 2003, 20). Pentagon officials evaded the issues of critiques of the war plan, problematic actions by individual American soldiers, and the reasons behind the lack of U.N. involvement. Further, they brushed aside concerns about the United States' failure, as an occupying power, to assume responsibility for civic order (Vanden Heuvel 2003). Rationales that the looting was inevitable, relatively insignificant, and the unique product of a specific national character exempted the Department of Defense from acknowledging the necessity for revamping Pentagon policies on providing security during power vacuums and preserving cultural heritage sites during war.

An important question has been posed: "How did a coalition of such over-whelming might, and so confident of its own morality, allow such a thing to happen?" ("Editorial" 2003, 221). The very act of waging war (and that is how the United States framed its campaign in Iraq) carries with it a suspension of business-as-usual. The Americans may have expected the devastation to be accepted as the normal byproduct of war. After all, war is understood to be institutionalized competition, organized violence deliberately undertaken to protect and promote national interests (Carlton 2001). The sheer might of the U.S.-led coalition that attacked Iraq was never in question. And, in fact, there is little disagreement that the combat part of the campaign was conducted with professionalism and savvy. However, an overemphasis on the means (strategy, technology, manpower and firepower) seems to have resulted in an underem-phasis on the postconquest goal of a liberated, democratic Iraq. Militarism within the leadership overtook the humanistic values, freedom and democracy, upon which the legitimacy of Operation Iraqi Freedom nominally rested.

As we have seen repeatedly throughout the book, the subtext of extrem-ists in action, including rogue governments that wage war in the name of ideology, is a web of entitlement, grievance, and self-defense. As George Orwell (1968, 363) observed, "Nationalism is power hunger tempered by self-deception." The end result, in modern wars, is the expedient targeting of *all* material resources of the enemy with the ultimate goal of dominance and victory. An application of this principle is that the military, although not directly targeting cultural institutions (as in Iraq), may nevertheless permit their destruction because they do not perceive civil policing and preservation to be part of their mission. In this respect, the U.S. government was overlook-ing the lesson of World War II, which demonstrated the tendency of total war to invest even democracies in extreme mindsets (nationalism and militarism) that impair leaders' ability to recognize the reality and consequences of war. However, this is not the only lesson we should come away with. The other lesson is that extremism, when fed by humiliation, defensiveness, and a vested righteousness, and when backed by military capability, can set the stage for devastating human and cultural losses.

Extremists are inclined toward viewing their group as chronically belea-guered. They believe that they must be ready to engage in life-or-death strug-gles over the survival of their ideas and way of life. Attacks ultimately validate their fears and solidify the defensive mindset. The September 11 terrorist attack on America, itself the product of extremists, triggered defensive and emotional responses of massive proportions that were shaped by the Bush administration and media frenzy. Heightened security procedures were put in place; threat levels were posted on an almost daily basis; and global terror-ism dominated the news. The media and administration's perception that the nation was at war began with the nation's shock at the attack, but was fed by a siege mentality that showed evidence of being fed by political extremism. The Homeland Security measures (the quasimilitarization and reorganization of agencies into a central core), the monitoring and publicizing of threat levels, and wartime rhetoric set in motion a fight-or-flight response and conditioned the general public to see repression and organized violence as a solution to the threat. Afghanistan was subject to invasion because it harbored terrorists. Afghani "prisoners of war" were incarcerated in prison camps where they were not subject to the rule of U.S. law or accorded Geneva Convention rights. U.S. righteousness and totality of commitment was evident in the fact that beyond token attempts to enlist the United Nations' support, the United States was willing to proceed unilaterally in Iraq.

Whether or not the administration was forthright and honest (with itself), it became clear as the campaign progressed that military action was serving the purposes of reasserting American might and redressing the helplessness that was experienced by Americans after the September 11 attacks. Technological determinism also may have crept into the thinking. Because it was technologically possible to bring down Saddam, this alone posed a temptation not unlike that which propelled the Allies to extremes with their perfection of urban bombing. Like the airpower doctrine that promised timely surrender as a response to massive bombing raids, new techniques of "shock and awe" (speed and force) promised quick decapitation of Iraq's power structure and collapse of resistance.

After the fact, it is readily apparent that the United States was proceeding with rigidity of thought, a lack of humility, an unwillingness to seriously engage other nations in the process of dealing with Iraq, and a penchant for aggression. An analyst for the RAND study on the conduct of the war (Bensahel 2005) concluded that planning during the 12 months preceding engagement focused on the combat phase and gave little attention to postcombat security or reconstruction planning. Because of this, there were not enough troops on the ground to provide security and prevent looting (and they were neither trained for nor charged with that mission). Rumsfeld expected that the Americans would be greeted as liberators, and the Iraqi bureaucracy would basically remain in place but with a new orientation toward democracy, with reconstruction managed by a minimum number of troops (Bensahel 2005). The failure to provide postcombat security mechanisms turned out to be the Achilles heel in the campaign and allowed the looting to occur. The loss of cultural treasures distracted from the success of combat tactics and brought negative responses from the Iraqi people and the global public. The loss of infrastructure impaired subsequent reconstruction efforts, and the looting of arms dumps set the stage for ongoing violence.

Before and during the invasion, the Bush administration, with the active participation of the conservative media and the relatively passive acquiescence of other commentators, was able to shut out internal and international dissent. Extremist mindsets could then surface, exist unquestioned, and be put into action. Bush officials and media supporters appealed to latent undercurrents of xenophobic and populist prejudice in order to ostracize those who would not go along with ideological agendas. Intense patriotism was the order of the day. The irrationality that accompanies chauvinism was evident when, after France questioned American motivation and legitimacy, suggestions were made in the United States to rename "French fries" and boycott French imports. Academics, pundits, a critical media, and government officials who warned of the possible pitfalls of deposing an authoritarian regime without planning for ensuing civil disorder were largely ignored. Scholars and curators who warned of possible cultural disaster were dismissed as effete, hysterical, and out of touch with wartime realities. Xenophobia, anti-intellectualism, antihumanism, and antiliberalism are, of course, manifestations of nationalism and militarism, clear signposts on the road to extremism. As militarism gained momentum in America, a sense of urgency around the need for "defensive" measures came into play and "non-essential" considerations were more easily brushed aside. Concerns about ethical considerations, peace, internationalism, pluralism, and respect for the preservation of culture and heritage were seen as detrimental to the war effort against terrorism. Once combat began in Iraq, dissenters were ostracized and their concerns reduced to the single unacceptable issue of "not supporting the troops."

Various explanations can be posed for U.S. failure to anticipate civil disorder and protect Iraq's cultural institutions. It seems feasible that the cultural devastation may have been a function of simple negligence on the part of an administration mesmerized by jingoist fervor and oddly naive about cultural destruction. An additional explanation, involving the primacy of militaristic mindsets, is that there was a "cynical disregard for the inventories of 'soft' culture—the arts, literature, history—in favor of the accoutrements of 'hard' culture, namely those measurable, material things like wealth, consumption, military and commercial power and assets" (Garrett 2003, 52). Certainly, it is the hard inventories that count in militaristic mindsets. Other explanations for the U.S. government's negligence involve dominance issues: allowing looting served the purpose of exposing the degradation of the Iraqi people who were obviously (as the thinking may have gone) in dire need of democracy and Western influence. Allowing Iraqis to turn on public institutions was a means of demonstrating to the world that the Iraqi people rejected every vestige of Saddam's rule, thus their anarchy was a form of revolution, and the past was to be torn down as part of a new beginning.

Political conservatives, ironically, have a constellation of values that are susceptible to extremes: a propensity for authoritarianism, a "sensitivity" to threat, a stress on the importance of the military and patriotism, nationalism, and concern for national security. These values were amplified for American conservatives in the wake of the September 11 attacks, which confirmed their deepest fears: a deadly enemy that sought nothing less than the annihilation of the American way of life. With conservatives in power, the general public's feelings of vulnerability and beleaguerment, inevitable products of the attack, were given outlet in intensified identification with the nation and patriotism, hatred for the enemy, and xenophobic posturing against countries that would not fall in with U.S. plans to invade Iraq. The climate became what, in less extreme times, would have been seen as dangerously right-wing. In an extreme climate, an expanded security system, censorship and surveillance (as in the Patriot Act), and a heightened emphasis on military options seemed rational to many Americans (Hoffman and Bozo 2004).

The violence of war requires "a justificatory moral framework": soldiers must fight for something, and the effort must have the support of the people (Carlton 2001, 49). The Bush administration justified the war first as a matter of survival and then on a premise of "messianic idealism" (Hoffman and Bozo 2004, 67). The Iraqi people had to be saved from tyranny and steered toward democracy. Powerful neoconservatives such as Donald Rumsfeld and vice-president Dick Cheney advanced the view that "might confers right" and that democracy is an obvious good. It was a universalized democracy, stripped of humanistic values such as tolerance. Bush, Rumsfeld, Cheney, and like-minded individuals seemed determined to bring the entire world under the hegemony of a democracy enforced by the United States. Their reasoning appealed to certain strains of Enlightenment thought that pose injustice as requiring action, and also to a strand of Western discourse (with links to the mindsets of eighteenth-century colonialism) that holds war as legitimate when waged by a civilized nation against an uncivilized one (Moses 2005). Bush and his officials employed the same mechanism as twentieth-century extremist regimes that they would not dream of comparing themselves with. They capitalized on turbulent sociopolitical conditions, fanned the flame of national identity, encouraged polarization and grievance, moved the belief system (in this case, democracy) toward ideocracy, and rationalized the use of power to advance toward utopia.

It is chilling to admit this about my own country.

When leaders pose charismatic ideas as a solution to current woe and channel their population's impotence and victimhood into hatred of other groups, the destruction of those groups' books and libraries becomes an expedient measure and a morally acceptable means of promoting the proposed agenda. The failure of the United States to provide security for Iraq's institutions was not outright libricide. However, the absence of intent to destroy culture coupled with an acceptance of the necessity of extreme violence are markedly similar to the Allies' collateral destruction of cultural objects in World War II, which was the result of employing total-war tactics. And in both cases, the clash of civilizations enabled those in the grip of battle to forge ahead without compunction. In both cases, powerful armed forces were directed by leaders whose militaristic mindsets and moral certainty blinded them to the human and societal consequences of their attacks. The Bush administration's use of morality–a humanistic and Christian morality, in fact—as justification for war was followed by a rapid slip in norms. Extreme ideas naturally bring in their wake the urge to extend their influence. The imperative of orthodoxy involves the numbing of critical faculties and silencing of dissent. Bush believes that morality and power should be vested in the same people, and he has worked hard to undermine the separation of church and state at home. This kind of moral and political fusion results in looking upon those in opposition as recalcitrant and ignorant or immoral. Bush's administration has doggedly chosen to ignore criticism and to deplore dissent. It is one of the great ironies of American history that the roots of American Christianity lie with those who claimed dissent as a right and rejected orthodoxy. By seeking to export a narrowed form of democracy by force, Bush was resurrecting orthodoxy, dismantling the pluralist scaffolding of a truly democratic state, and defeating the principles that his religious and political predecessors worked so hard to uphold.

Accompanying modern military aggression is an investment in ideas that, when posed as under threat, are transformed from belief into a militant ideology. The Allies' war was against fascism and for the preservation of freedom. They defined freedom, of course, in terms of democratic beliefs, and based it on a value for autonomy and free choice. The Nazis and the Japanese Imperialists were claiming freedom also: the freedom to act out their ethnocentric and imperialistic agendas and overwhelm their enemies. Modern wars have often been clashes over the right to pursue mandates and act on beliefs. Strategic issues aside, in 2003, American nationalists believed they were bringing the gift of emancipation to the Iraqi people. They were caught up in the momentum of demonstrating their military capabilities and mesmerized by a morality that was conveniently divested of ethical mandates that might otherwise have tied their hands tactically. "American-style democracy prizes freedom above all other values," observed news analyst Jennifer de Poyen (2003). "But other democracies— Canada, Germany, France, Britain—also weigh in the balance fraternity and equality, seminal democratic notions that presuppose communal rights and the value of a common culture." As we saw in the case of World War II, even a truly defensive war (i.e., one that history subsequently decrees as just) compromises democracy and plunges its defenders into situational extremism. If we can learn from the past, then strategic bombing and total war are sober warnings of the necessity of monitoring technological zeal, militaristic logic, and the rationalization of violence by feelings of moral rightness, especially when nationalism is providing impetus for aggression.

When perpetrators directly target books and libraries as possessions or symbols of the enemy and when emotions make the vandalism playful, malicious, or vindictive, biblioclasm is primarily linked to affective and cognitive rewards. In cases of destruction that are distanced or collateral in nature, biblioclasm is usually tactical and ideological and linked to social motivations. In these cases, the perpetrators are simply deployed to accomplish ends. The passionate opportunism and anarchism of Iraqi mobs existed side by side with the cool-headed militaristic logic of an American leadership taking its creed of democracy to ideological extremes. In this case, American troops did not perpetrate cultural vandalism, but by failing to protect Iraq's culture, they laid their nation open to accusations of barbarism and imperialism.

The case of Iraq in 2003 illuminates the others in this book in an enlightening way. In the grips of nationalism, it was easy for the Americans to justify aggression and shirk responsibility for cultural destruction by denying their involvement in the looting. Their myopia in the heat of defense concerns and war had parallels in World War II, when wartime exigencies led to cultural destruction even by those who would never deliberately target books and libraries. Nationalism can take the form of a benign patriotism that may be ennobling for individuals who muster personal resources in dedication to something larger than themselves. But nationalism has an extreme side and is often the core value that intensifies the process by which reactions to extreme circumstances lead to the ratcheting up of belief systems, embrace of totalistic thinking, and, ultimately, attacks on others in the name of self-defense or moral mandates. American nationalism created the conditions for biblioclasm in Iraq. Nationalism is, of course, not the only passion driving political and social violence: there is also racism, secular religions such as Communism, and religious fundamentalism as has been so thoroughly demonstrated by the Nazis, Japanese Imperialists, Sri Lanka Sinhalese, Pol Pot's Communists, and the Taliban. All of these regimes felt beleaguered, thwarted, and defensive like the United States felt after September 11. All of these regimes seized their opportunity to use power for ideological purposes, just as the Bush administration did. One can only hope that there is not another phase in which the Americans pull out, Iraq dissolves into civil war, and fundamentalists seize power and purify Iraqi society along the lines of the Taliban's deconstruction of Afghanistan. The stage is certainly set for this to happen.

Groups that deliberately destroy books and libraries, such as the protestors and militants in Amsterdam, India, and Kashmir, are those on the periphery. Their attacks on cultural institutions and artifacts are protests against marginalization, a state they find particularly frustrating if they perceive themselves as possessing "superior" beliefs or innate racial or ethnic superiority. These are extremists who seek to influence the form of society at a local level and, if unchecked, may proceed to seize control of the central belief system of their country. Extremists who succeed in taking over the government nevertheless retain the mindset that they are peripheral and deprived of what they are entitled to possess. They create a new center and periphery situation, by seeing themselves as marginalized in terms of the global community. Attempts may be made to extend their sphere of influence and hegemony by attacking other nations. Their deliberate attacks on books and libraries are merciless and committed, rationalized by mandates that require them to overturn despised humanistic values and ethics. More insidiously, the same dynamics of extremism may result in collateral destruction that is no less devastating despite lack of intentionality. In Chapter 1, I introduced the idea that there exists a sociological construct of communication that is useful for looking at biblioclasm as well as vandalism. I think the case has been made that there is wisdom in attending to localized vandalism as a message of disaffection that signals potentially dangerous levels of social conflict. Biblioclasm can be viewed as a particular form of message that sounds a warning rattle at the local level and a death knell at national and international levels.

If we recognize that extremism poses a grave threat not only to books and libraries but to freedom itself, then the irony of modern notions of freedom becomes evident. Freedom is the very thing that allows extreme ideas to flourish. The ideals of freedom from traditional authority and the efficacy of using reason to fashion action and further social justice, which we proudly inherited from the Enlightenment, have given birth to public moralists and secular crusaders (Wokler 2000, 163). These ideals also laid the foundation for liberal democracy and human rights and, by extension, the possibility of tolerance and global peace. But as the French Revolution demonstrated, the dismantling of an autocratic establishment opens up a public space of randomness where, with religion and traditional morality displaced, anything at all is possible—a ripe environment for anarchy or the capture of the state by extremists (Katznelson 2003, 82). Enlightenment notions of freedom can be channeled toward individual entitlement or, quite the opposite—it can shut off the free flow of ideas and shift responsibility away from autonomous, thinking individuals and toward the state. By becoming totalitarian, it became possible for the nation-state to also become the enemy of the people—certainly those "fractious" people who resisted its absolute authority and orthodoxy (Wokler 2000, 176, 178). Those who hijacked the Enlightenment's potential for empowering individual freedom had to dismantle the liberal premises to which it had given birth, including the distinction between the state and civil society. The masses had to be organized "on the basis of total, often unthinking, loyalty to national identities, causes, and regimes" (Katznelson 2003, 110). The intellectual freedom and pluralism manifest in liberal notions of libraries were, of course, counterproductive to ideological orthodoxy and imposed homogeneity.

The vast majority of books destroyed in the last century were lost because of ideas and the extremism they engendered: ideas that rationalized internal violence and controlled the choice of wartime tactics, but also ideas that defined group and national entitlement, determined the path of civilization, and even sought to clarify the nature of truth itself. Modernity's displacement of certainty at the start of the twentieth century left civilization in a position of promise and peril. With the moral certainty of religious truths and divine hierarchies renounced, and with social turbulence calling the promises of the Enlightenment into question, many turned to religious fundamentalism or to the parallel certainty of secular dogma transformed into ideological truth. In each case, the door opened to totalitarianism, total war, and genocide. The freedom that comes with modernity has a price. When one abandons or relinquishes certainty, the pursuit of meaning is much harder work; it requires tolerance of other perspectives on truth, an appreciation for nuances, and a belief in the innate goodness of humankind. Enlightenment notions of liberal democracy, nurtured by eighteenth-century revolutions, provided a viable substitute for absolute truth and kept the potential for human progress alive, which of course is why extremists posed it is as an arch-inimical force and so often destroyed its haven, the library.

Enlightenment thinkers introduced the notion that unbounded freedom provided conditions in which human intelligence could be directed toward shaping just institutions and fostering social transformation. New ideals and human intelligence, they believed, could light the way to a better future. From the historical perspective of our time, the destruction of books in recent history can be seen to stem from the fanatic implementation of this notion. With the totalistic imposition of one doctrine, the mandate for initiating change in the name of ideas is immediately foreclosed and yet, paradoxically, remains in place insofar as it justifies intolerance and aggression. Identification with an exclusivist group metamorphoses into rejection of other groups and beliefs, and this rejection can take the form of direct attacks on enemies' cultural institutions and artifacts or negligence in according importance to cultural preservation in times of war. When extremists gain power, their sense of mission and the scale of their attacks inflate commensurate with their power. We have seen more than once that a single rogue group can ultimately threaten world peace and the whole of civilization. The illumination wielded by extremists is like a laser that ultimately sears and burns.

Countering rogue forces requires the existence of people who seek sustainable progress, adhere to freedom and intellect as tempered by empathy and tolerance, and strive for an inclusive world community. Internationalism makes most sense when it acknowledges that there are ethical boundaries to freedom and that might does not make right. Of course, its potential for sustaining peace, stable intergroup and state relationships, and tolerance is one of the reasons that extremists, who claim unilateral aggression as a right, constitute internationalism as a toxic force.

As we move into a new century, we continue, through international law, to institutionalize liberal humanistic ideals of tolerance and pluralism and notions that the freedom of any group must be bounded by respect for the freedom of others. This is a nuance, not a contradiction to freedom. The last century demonstrated the danger that universalized ideals may bring intolerance and imposed hegemony in their wake. A continuing challenge for the international community is adhering to an ethical, pluralistic, and human-rights-oriented path, and steering clear of the road to orthodoxy, in which the collective good is conflated with the agenda of ideologues. There will continue to be challenges from those who overtly justify the destruction of lives and culture during war and civil conflict, and from those who engage without thought in tactics that allow for devastation to occur. Ironically, both groups are responding to many of the same impulses. We may be on the brink of a shift in consciousness of parallel magnitude to that set in motion by Enlightenment thinkers. Just as societies rejected slavery in the nineteenth century, political violence involving cultural destruction may soon become internalized as a taboo. With significant progress in this direction, further losses may be averted. Danger lurks in failing to address the disaffection of modern biblioclasts and the powerful messages of angst they send through library destruction. Protecting civilization from the machinations of extremists will require better methods of addressing social injustice and the toxic forces it puts into play. With a renewed commitment to the Enlightenment notion that progress is possible and can benefit all, we may be able to shape more inclusive communities and institutions and, ultimately, a society whose "center" is more responsive to its periphery

REFERENCES

Agence France Presse. 2003. "Rumsfeld Says Criticism over Iraq Museum Looting a Bum Rap." *Agence France Presse*, 9 May.

Al-Tikriti, Nabil. 2003. *Iraq Manuscript Collections, Archives, and Libraries*. Situation Report. Oriental Institute, University of Chicago. http://www-oi.uchicago. edu/OI/IRAQ?docs/nat.html. June 8, 2003.

American Library Association. 2003. Press Release: "ALA Joins International Community in Assisting Iraq National Library" (April 23, 2003).

Bensahel, Nora. 2005. "The Day after Saddam: U.S. Planning for Postwar Iraq." Paper Presented at the Annual Meeting of the International Studies Association, Honolulu, Hawaii, March 1–5, 2005.

Burns, John F. 2003. "Baghdad Residents Begin a Long Climb to an Ordered City." *New York Times*, 14 April, p. A1.

Carlton, Eric. 2001. *Militarism: Rule without Law*. Burlington, Vt.: Ashgate.

Carver, Martin. 2003. "Editorial." *Antiquity* 77 (297):441–444.

Chandrasekaran, Rajiv. 2003. "Iraqi Curator Appalled by Looting: Priceless Antiquities Protected from War but Lost to Vandals." *Honolulu Advertiser*, 13 April, p. A5.

Craig, Bruce. 2003. "Situation Iraq—Amid Ruins, Heritage Community Acts with One Voice." *National Coalition for History (NCH) Washington Update* [9(16)], April 17. http://www.h-net.org/~nch/.

Darnton, Robert. 2003. "Burn a Country's Past and You Torch Its Future." *Washington Post*, 20 April, p. B1.

De Poyen, Jennifer. 2003. "Looting of Iraqi Museum Was a Blow to All Peoples." *Copley News Service*, 22 April.

"Donald Rumsfeld and Richard Myers Hold Regular Defense Department Briefing." 2003. FDCH Political Transcripts. *FDCHeMedia*, 15 April.

"Editorial." 2003. *Antiquity* 77 (296):221.

Espo, David. 2003. "U.S. Military Expands Control over Iraq." *Associated Press Online*, April 11, 2003. http://www.micro189.lib3.hawaii.edu:2138/universe.

Garrett, Jeffrey. 2003. "On My Mind." *American Libraries* 34 (6):52.

Griffiths, Jay. 2003. "No Time Like the Present." *Ecologist* 33 (6):12–13.

Hess, Pamela. 2003. "Rumsfeld: Looting Is Transition to Freedom." *United Press International*, 11 April.

Hoffman, Stanley, with Frédéric Bozo. 2004. *Gulliver Unbound: America's Imperial Temptation and the War in Iraq*. New York: Rowman and Littlefield.

Holmes, Bob, and James Randerson. 2003. "Humble Clay Tablets Are Greatest Loss to Science." *New Scientist* 178 (2394): 8.

Human Rights Watch. 2003. "Iraq: Protect Government Archives from Looting." News release, April 10, 2003. www.hrw.org/press/2003/04/Iraq041003.

Hume, Brit, Mort Kondracke, Fred Barnes, and Mara Liasson. 2003. "All-Stars Discuss Looting in Iraq." Special Report. *Fox News*, 11 April.

Ivins, Molly. 2003. "Prize for Bad Behavior Has Long List of Contenders." *Honolulu Star Bulletin*, 22 April, p. A13.

Jelinek, Pauline. 2003. "Pentagon Defends against Criticism about Looting, Lawlessness in Iraq." Associated Press. *Washington Dateline*, 1 April.

Katznelson, Ira. 2003. *Desolation and Enlightenment: Political Knowledge after Total War, Totalitarianism, and the Holocaust.* New York: Columbia University Press.

Kennicut, Phillip. 2003. "Images of War: In Broken Baghdad, Photo Negatives." *Chicago Tribune*, 15 April, p. C1.

Kniffel, Leonard. 2003. "Through Devastating, Iraq Library Losses May Be Less Than Feared." *American Libraries* 34 (6):40–41.

Krauthammer, Charles. 2003. "Hoaxes, Hype and Humiliation." *Washington Post*, 13 June, p. A29.

Lawler, Andrew. 2003. "Mayhem in Mesopotamia." *Science* 301 (5633):582–88

Lemonick, Michael D., Andrea Dorfman, Aparisim Ghosh, Adam Smith, Grant Rosenberg, Elaine Shannon. 2003. "Lost to the Ages." *Time Europe* 161 (17):34–37.

Manier, Jeremy. 2003. "U. of C. Pleads for Iraq Artifacts." *Chicago Tribune*, 15 April, sec. 1, p. 6.

Martin, Paul. 2003. "Troops Were Told to Guard Treasures." *Washington Times*, April 20. http://dynamic.washtimes.com/twt-print.cfm?ArticleID=20030420-48494890.

McGeough, Paul. 2003. "Rich Past Stripped as Future in Tatters." Sydney Morning Herald, April 14.www.smh.com.au/articles/2003/04/13/1050172478179.html.

Mehegan, David. 2003. *Daily Globe*, April 21, 2003. http://www.boston.com/dailyglobe2/111/living/Reconstruction-time-againP.shtml.

Miranda, Alison. 2005. "Wartime Sexual Violence: Questions of Masculinity?" Paper Presented at the Annual Meeting of the International Studies Association, Honolulu, Hawaii, March 1–5, 2005.

Moses, Jeremy. 2005. "Humanitarianism and International Law: The 'Standard of Civilization' in Contemporary International Relations." Paper Presented at the Annual Meeting of the International Studies Association, Honolulu, Hawaii, March 1–5, 2005.

Orwell, George. 1968. "Notes on Nationalism." [Originally published in *Polemic* 1, October 1945]. In *As I Please 1943–1945*, eds. Sonia Orwell and Ian Angus. Boston: Nonpareil Books, 361–380.

Pipes, Daniel. 2003. "Blame Iraqis for the Pillage." *Human Events* 59 (14):20.

Ryan, Joan. 2003. "Why No Tank at the Doors?" *San Francisco Chronicle*, 15 April, p. A19.

Sandalow, Marc. 2003. "Rumsfeld Calls Looting an 'Untidiness.'" *San Francisco Chronicle*, 12 April, p. A10.

Sullivan, Martin E. 2003. "Letter of Resignation as Chairman of the Eleven Member President's Advisory Committee on Cultural Property." *Washington Report on Middle East Affairs* 22 (5):14–15.

UNESCO. 2003. "UNESCO to Make a Preliminary Assessment of the State of Iraq's Cultural Heritage." ARCHIVES@LISTSERV.MUOHIO.EDU, April 16, 2003.

Vanden Heuvel, William J. 2003. "A Job for UNESCO." *New York Times*, 17 April, p. A25.

Waldbaum, Jane C. 2003. "Iraq's Plundered Past." *Archaeology* 56 (4):6.
Witt, Louise. 2003. "The End of Civilization." http://www.salon.com/news/feature/2003/04/17/antiuities/index_np.html. April 17, 2003.
Wokler, Robert. 2000. "The Enlightenment, the Nation-state and the Primal Patricide of Modernity." In *The Enlightenment and Modernity*, eds. Norman Geras and Robert Wokler. New York: St. Martin's Press, 161–183.

Index

About the Author

REBECCA KNUTH is Chair of the Library and Information Science Program at the University of Hawaii, where she is also Associate Professor. She is the author of *Libricide: The Regime-Sponsored Destruction of Books and Libraries in the Twentieth Century* (Praeger, 2003).